The CME Vulnerability

The Impact of Negative Oil
Futures Trading

The CME Vulnerability

The Impact of Negative Oil Futures Trading

editor

George Xianzhi Yuan

Sun Yat-sen University, China & Soochow University, China &
Shanghai Lixin University of Accounting and Finance, China

NEW JERSEY · LONDON · SINGAPORE · BEIJING · SHANGHAI · HONG KONG · TAIPEI · CHENNAI · TOKYO

Published by

World Scientific Publishing Co. Pte. Ltd.

5 Toh Tuck Link, Singapore 596224

USA office: 27 Warren Street, Suite 401-402, Hackensack, NJ 07601

UK office: 57 Shelton Street, Covent Garden, London WC2H 9HE

Library of Congress Cataloging-in-Publication Data

Names: Yuan, George Xian-Zhi, 1965– editor.

Title: The CME vulnerability : the impact of negative oil futures trading /
    editor, George Xianzhi Yuan, Sun Yat-sen University, China & Soochow University, China &
    Shanghai Lixin University of Accounting and Finance, China.

Description: Hackensack, New Jersey : World Scientific, [2021] |
    Includes bibliographical references and index.

Identifiers: LCCN 2020038649 (print) | LCCN 2020038650 (ebook) |
    ISBN 9789811223198 (hardcover) | ISBN 9789811223204 (ebook for institutions) |
    ISBN 9789811223211 (ebook for individuals)

Subjects: LCSH: Chicago Mercantile Exchange--Rules and practice. | Petroleum industry and
    trade--United States--Finance. | Petroleum products--Prices--United States. |
    Commodity futures--United States.

Classification: LCC HG6047.P47 C58 2021 (print) | LCC HG6047.P47 (ebook) |
    DDC 332.64/422820973--dc23

LC record available at https://lccn.loc.gov/2020038649

LC ebook record available at https://lccn.loc.gov/2020038650

British Library Cataloguing-in-Publication Data

A catalogue record for this book is available from the British Library.

For any available supplementary material, please visit
https://www.worldscientific.com/worldscibooks/10.1142/11908#t=suppl

Desk Editors: Aanand Jayaraman/Lai Ann

Typeset by Stallion Press
Email: enquiries@stallionpress.com

Printed in Singapore

Preface — The Fundamental Challenge Caused by CME's Negative Trading Price for WTI Oil Future

George Yuan

George_Yuan99@yahoo.com

Abstract

In 2020, the global lockdowns caused by the COVID-19, or coronavirus, pandemic resulted in a sharp drop in demand for crude oil. This impact was so severe that on April 8, 2020, a proposal to update the Chicago Mercantile Exchange Holdings Inc. (CME) trading rule to permit negative prices was applied to CME's WTI oil futures contracts; this led to a novel phenomenon in which the closing clearing price of WTI oil May future was -37.63/barrel based on fewer than 400 contracts' trading volume in the last three minutes, reflecting less than 0.2% of the total trading contracts volume on April 20, 2020. This occurrence of negative closing clearing price for CME's WTI oil futures trading cannot just be simply explained by the principle of supply and demand; instead, it highlights vulnerabilities caused by CME's allowance of negative price trading (based on its trading platform), a decision which brings potential and fundamental challenges to the global financial system.

This event challenges not just our basic concepts of "value" and trading "price" of commodities and goods that have underlined our understanding of general equilibrium theory established by generations of scholars since Adam Smith in 1776 but also has wider implications on our fundamental framework when it comes to value and labor in the organization, activity, and behavior of civilizations and individual liberties.

The scope of this book is limited to covering some key impacts of the negative oil futures derivatives' trading between April 20 and 21, 2020. This book focuses on exploring the issues, challenges, and possible impacts on global financial markets due to the negative clearing prices of WTI oil futures contracts and related problems from different perspectives. Topics covered include the responsibilities and liabilities of CME; critique of the fundamental theory of economics and the modern understanding of value and labor; challenges to the global financial systems and businesses; and introduction to new methods of application.

Keywords: Best Practice, CME vulnerability, COVID-19, the principle of supply and demand, negative trading price, rule changing, value and pricing, behavior of civilizations and individual liberties, general equilibrium theory, negative asset pricing, negative oil prices, risk management, blockchain option model

The Background

Beginning in early 2020, the outbreak of the COVID-19 coronavirus pandemic caused global lockdowns; as a consequence, the demand for crude oil dropped sharply. On April 8, 2020, Chicago Mercantile Exchange (CME) Holdings Inc.'s proposed changing (or saying loosely, updating) of the trading rule to allow negative price due to CME was applied to CME's WTI oil future contracts. On April 20, 2020, for the first time, the closing clearing price of WTI oil May future contracts was $-37.63/barrel, based on less than 400 contracts' trading volume in the last three minutes, a figure less than 0.2% of the total trading contracts volume for that day.

What's Wrong with CME?

Since April 20, 2020, it has become "impossible to believe" that the occurrence of negative closing clearing price for CME's WTI Oil future trading truly happened, and to represent the basic fundamental supply and demand for the economy and business as usual of crude oil trading markets in both domestic and international markets as claimed by CME Group Chairman and CEO Terry Duffy [1] caused by the slowdown of the economy globally due to the spread of COVID-19 since December 2019. But despite the fact that the COVID-19 outbreak has continued to impact economies since April 2020, we have yet to see negative oil clearing prices again since April 21, 2020 as of today, July 21, 2020, the time of writing this chapter. The absence of negative clearing prices in trading activity for WTI since April 20, 2020, is definitely against the claim "[the] futures market worked to perfection" made by Duffy [1] on April 22, 2020. While there are numerous questions to address on this situation, our primary concerns are identifying the following:

(1) What is the fundamental reason and cause for the occurrence of CME's negative trading price of WTI crude oil May/2020 futures contract [2]?
(2) What were the weaknesses in CME's pushing for a speedy timeline from announcing it would allow negative trading prices to its implementation in the trading system in April 2020 [3]?
(3) As a leading global exchange, why did CME not follow "best practice" in its business model conduct in April 2020?
(4) And more...

The Fundamental Challenge by CME's Allowing Negative Trading Prices to Human Civilization

We would also like to emphasize that CME's action to allow negative pricing in exchanges not only fundamentally challenges the global financial system, but it also challenges basic concepts of "value" and trading "price" for commodities (in general, for all trading goods made of labor/work) under the framework of general equilibrium theory in economics since the concept of the invisible hand was established by Adam Smith in 1776 for market economies [4].

Within the history of human development, the idea of Smith's "invisible hand" proposed in *Wealth of Nations* has been fundamental to formalizing today's market economy in terms of positive values (never below zero), also known as equilibrium prices under a general framework of equilibrium theory [4].These concepts have been further developed by a number of Nobel prize winners in Economics including Samuelson [6], Arrow and Debreu [7], Nash [8], and many others. Today, a fundamental assumption of economic theory is that the trading price should never be negative in any situation as this is how we conduct valuation for any assets in financial markets for business trading activities (see [10]).

Despite this, on April 8, 2020, CME Group released an advisory note #20-152 [2] announcing that CME Clearing recognized the possibility of negatives in certain energy options contracts and would address the "switch to Bachelier options pricing model" (instead of the Black–Scholes model) on April 21, 2020 [9]. The given reasoning behind negative strikes and negative prices for the underlying commodities was the outbreak of the COVID-19 pandemic in many countries worldwide.

On April 21, 2020, the closing price of WTI oil May/2020 futures contract (with the delivery month of May 2020) closed at $-37.63/$ barrel — the first time a price traded at below-zero in the history of mankind. This is significant as the negative strike and underlying prices not only disrupt the framework of equilibrium economic theory in competitive economies since the last century, but they also put almost all financial institutions not able to deal with risk measurement for financial assets/instruments in negative values, which would lead in the crush of risk managements for financial markets [11] as the negative price allowed by the exchange for any asset is against the basic value of human labors' work capital. In other words, negative values after an asset is produced by human labor violates human beings' activities and work (as tied to labor) and questions our understanding of the basic fair values of human rights by devaluation of production [5].

When CME allowed negative pricing in April 2020, it was equivalent to allowing the possibility of denying the value of human work. This violates our understanding of basic principles of human rights in terms of tying value to labor contribution [5].

The occurrence of negative pricing as practiced by CME is a challenge to human civilization and should be avoided.

In conclusion, the goal of this book is to focus on CME's negative clearing prices on WTI crude oil futures contracts and explore its issues, challenges, and possible impacts on global financial markets. We will examine: (1) CME's possible vulnerabilities by not following best practices and allowing negative oil futures trading pricing; (2) why oil prices plunged and settled negative only on April 20, 2020; and (3) how we meet the challenge of negative pricing and management in practice, introducing alternative solutions to modeling options with underlying negative strike and/or asset prices, even by considering using blockchain as a tool in pricing options for a physical settlement of commodity futures. In particular, the contents of this book are divided into three parts, as follows:

Part I: The CME Vulnerability: The Best Practice and the Impact of Negative Oil Futures Trading Price

1. The Overview of WTI Crude Oil Futures' Epic Fall, by Chern Lu.
2. The Better Way for CME's Execution: Based on the Perspective of Industry's Best Practice, by Rongbing Huang and George Yuan.
3. Impact of Negative Oil Price on Risk Measuring, by James Zhan.
4. Three Legal Reflections on the "Crude Oil Treasure" Incident: Starting with the CME Rule Change, by Duoqi Xu, Peiran Wang, and Yicheng Wang.

Part II: Why Oil Prices Plunged and Settled Negative

5. Why Oil Prices Plunged and Settled Negative: A Game-Theoretical Perspective, by Chenghu Ma and Xianzhen Wang.
6. Tanker Shipping and Negative Oil Prices: More Than Just the Freight Rates, by Cong Sui and Mo Yang.
7. Option Pricing with Shifted Lognormal Model for Negative Oil Prices, by Henry Yang.
8. The Paradox of Negative Oil Prices, by Bin Zhu.

Part III: To Meet the Challenge with Negative Price and Management in Practice

9. The Challenges of Negative Oil Future Price Posed to Risk Managers and Quants, by Michael Peng.
10. Negative Asset Pricing and Moral Hazard, by Weiping Li.
11. The Bachelier Model: Option Pricing with Negative Strike and Asset Price, by You Zhang and Stanley Meng.

12. Blockchain-based Options for Physical Settlement of Commodity Futures, by Yali Chang, Jianwu Lin, and Chengying He.

We would like to bring readers' attention to the following two things, which indeed indicate the importance of this book's publication for topics covered and discussed!

The first, as of August 13, 2020, CME made the following new announcement: "Further to Clearing Advisory 20-171 dated April 21, 2020, CME Clearing will revert its options pricing and valuation methodology, currently based on the Bachelier model, effective for trade date on Monday, August 31, 2020. Products will transition from Bachelier back to Whaley or Black 76, depending on the products." (of 62 kinds of options, see [13] for more details)

This action means that CME now only allows the positive price of underlying, so they (CME) moved back to positive (prices) after allowing negative prices on April 13, 2020 for underlying. This was another bad behavior as they only allowed a transition time of 17 days (including weekends).

The second, we would also like to mention that as of August 4, 2020, Bloomberg Business Week (see [14] for more details) reported that a small group of traders (called Vega Capital London Ltd.) in London made a fortune on oil's unprecedented plunge into negative territory (related to CME's movement by allowing negative prices in April 2020). They are now being scrutinized by regulators. Currently, the United States Commodity Futures Trading Commission, the United Kingdom's Financial Conduct Authority, and CME Group Inc., owner of the Nymex exchange where the trading took place, are examining whether Vega's actions may have breached rules on trading around settlement periods and contributed to the oil price's precipitous fall, according to people with knowledge of the probes. Let's see what would come out soon.

Before the end of this Foreword, of course, I would like to thank all contributors for their hard work on this special book, which was published within such a short time. On behalf of all authors, our thanks also go to Ms. Rebecca Fu, the leader of this project's team in World Scientific (located in Singapore) and affiliated units.

Finally, we do wish that this book would bring useful insights for people and the community with new challenges raised from the perspective of the practice of the financial industry, risk management associated with the valuation issues, the way to follow the best practice in professional ways, the fundamental concepts from economics, and history of human being's civilization, in particular to learn how to respect the value of human being's labor. This is fundamental for the progress of our civilization!

References

[1] CME Group Chairman and CEO Terry Duffy said "The futures market worked to perfection" in an interview regarding the negative prices, see CNBC, April 22, 2020, https://www.cnbc.com/2020/04/22/cme-boss-says-his-exchange-is-not-for-retail-investors-and-its-no-secret-futures-can-go-negative.html , last visited May 1, 2020.

[2] CME Clearing, CME Clearing Plan to Address the Potential of a Negative Underlying in Certain Energy Options Contracts, April 8, 2020, https://www.cmegroup.com/notices/clearing/2020/04/Chadv20-152.html#pageNumber=1, last visited May 5, 2020.

[3] See CME Clearing, Testing Opportunities in CME's "New Release" Environment for Negative Prices and Strikes for Certain NYMEX Energy Contracts, April 15, 2020,

[4] A. Smith. An inquiry into the Nature and Cause of the Wealth of Nations (1776). Reprint, edited by E. Cannan Chicago: University of Chicago Press, 1976.

[5] The Mission of International Labour Organization (ILO) (available from https://www.ilo.org/global/lang--en/index.htm).

[6] P. A. Samuelson, (1947). *Foundation of Economic Analysis*, Harvard University.

[7] K. J. Arrow and G. Debreu, (1954). Existence of an equilibrium for a competitive economy. *Econometrica*, 22 265–290.

[8] J. Nash, (1950). Equilibrium pints in N-Person Games. *Proceedings of the National Academy of Sciences*, 36 48–49.

[9] The CME Advisory Notice: Switch to Bachelier options pricing model & allow Negative Strike, April 21, 2020(available from https://www.cmegroup.com/content/dam/cmegroup/notices/clearing/2020/04/Chadv20-171.pdf).

[10] John Hull, (2015). Options, futures, and other derivatives (9th Edition) 9th Edition. Pearson Education, Inc.

[11] Basel IV FRTB SBA may need to amend Commodity delta definition and Risk Weight definition & calibration because current settings are under positive price assumption; give second thought on the representativeness of stress period selection for different asset classes

(2008–2009 financial crisis vs 2020 COVID-19 crisis) (available from https://www.bis.org/bcbs/publ/d457.pdf).

[12]   C. H. Ma and X. Wang, (2020). Why oil prices plunged and settled negative: A Game-Theoretical Perspective, the chapters in this book.

[13]   CME Clearing: Transition Back to Whaley and Black 76 Options Pricing Methodology — Effective Trade Date August 31, 2020, August 13, 2020, https://www.cmegroup.com/notices/clearing/2020/08/Chadv20-320.html.

[14]   L. Vaugham, K. Chellel, and B. Bain. London Traders Hit $500 Million Jackpot When Oil Went Negative. Bloomberg Business week. August 4, 2020, https://www.bloomberg.com/news/articles/2020-08-04/oil-s-plunge-below-zero-was-500-million-jackpot-for-a-few-london-traders.

About the Editor

George Xianzhi Yuan is Chair Professor of Sun Yat-sen University School of Business, and Shanghai Lixin University of Accounting and Finance, China. He is the Editor in Chief of *International Journal of Financial Engineering*, and holds memberships on a number of editorial boards for several academic journals.

Dr. Yuan has a Bachelor's degree, a Master's degree, and a PhD in mathematics from Sichuan University (Chengdu, China), University of Toronto (Toronto, Canada), and Dalhousie University (Halifax, Canada).

Dr. Yuan currently focuses on the study of financial industries by applying big data approach from the perspective of finance technology.

Dr. Yuan has rich working experience in academic institutes and financial and technology sectors, financial engineering, financial mathematics, and related big data disciplines from theory to industry practice. He has published more than 150 academic papers and two monographs.

About the Contributors

Bin Zhu is the Deputy General Manager of Nanhua Futures, and concurrently serves as the Director of Nanhua Futures Research Institute, Chairman of China Futures Analysts Club, member of the Research and Development Committee of China Futures Association, and member of the Academic Committee of Futures and Options Research Center of Dalian Commodity Exchange. Zhu joined the futures industry in 1993 and has more than 20 years of experience. He has served as the manager of the marketing department and the investment department. He has a profound understanding of the operation of the futures market. Since 1998, he began to focus on the analysis and research of futures. Zhu himself specializes in the research of commodities and financial derivatives, and has a deep understanding and has conducted research on the macro economy and commodity market. The Futures Research Institute led by Zhu has been rated as the best Futures Research Institute by *Securities Times* and *Futures Daily* for many years. Email: gann888@nawaa.com.

Chenghu Ma is Professor of Finance at the School of Management, Fudan University, China. He graduated from the University of Toronto in 1992 with a PhD in Economics, after earning Master's of Science in Control Theory from Shandong University. He has taught at McGill University (1992–1999), the University of Essex (1999–2006), and Xiamen University (2006–2009). He was a visiting professor at Kyoto University (2009) and visiting senior fellow at the National University of Singapore (2014).

His research interests include asset pricing theory, sequential portfolio choice, financial risk measurement and management, options and financial derivative, modeling term structure of interest rates, decision theory, game theory, and theory of incomplete contract. He has published more than 30 articles in academic journals and book chapters, and is the author of *Advanced Asset Pricing Theory* published by Imperial College Press in 2011.

He has been serving as an Associate Editor for *Advances in Decision Science*, *Annals of Financial Economics*, and *Journal of Risk and Financial Management*. He was also a Guest Editor for the *Journal of Mathematical Economics*. Email: machenghu@fudan.edu.cn.

Chengying He received his Bachelor's, Master's, and Doctor's degrees from the Department of Accounting, Southwestern University of Finance and Economics; School of Economics, Zhejiang University; and School of Economics, Xiamen University, respectively. He worked in the School of Economics of Zhejiang University, Shenzhen State-owned Assets Management Office, Shenzhen Investment Management Company, United Securities, and Guosen Securities. He is a visiting scholar at Wharton School of University of Pennsylvania and School of Mathematics of Oxford University. He has published more than 300 papers in *China's Social Science, Economic Research, Management World*, and other SCI (Science Citation Index) and EI journals. He has won many awards from the China Securities Regulatory Commission, Securities Association of China, and Shenzhen Stock Exchange. Email: 2098533681@qq.com.

Chern Lu, Applied Math PhD of Courant Institute of Mathematical Sciences, New York University, CFA FRM PRM. Adjunct Professor of the University of Hong Kong, SPACE ICB. Dr. Lu has over 14 years of Wall Street quantitative trading, portfolio management, and risk management experience, and has developed proprietary Falex intraday trading strategy to trade for several well-known Wall Street investment banks. After the 2008 financial crisis, he returned to Asia to work for two global consulting firms: PwC and Deloitte, and was in charge of market risk, asset liability management, counterparty credit risk management consulting services and led the consulting team to help implement Basel II/I risk management system for a variety of international clients. One of his projects for a large Southeast Asian bank won the prestigious Asia Risk Consultant Award of the year

2013 sponsored by *Asian Risk* magazine. In 2013, Dr. Lu was invited to be one of three overseas trading risk management experts to help guide Everbright securities resolve its shocking exchange-traded fund (ETF) arbitrage trading incident. In 2014, Dr. Lu led Deloitte risk management due diligence task team to successfully complete 2014's largest merger and acquisition (M&A) deal between China's COFCO and Noble's Agriculture Business. Later, he became the Chief Risk Officer of the hedge fund company of the almighty Chinese insurance conglomerate Ping An Group. Dr. Lu helped lead the trading firm to win 4th place in the 2015 PE star contest with an AUM (assets under management) of 11 billion. Currently, he is working in a fintech company to develop innovative asset management solutions augmented by artificial intelligence driven risk management tools. Email: luchern@yahoo.com.

Cong Sui received his PhD degree from Dalian University of Technology. He is currently Professor of finance at School of Maritime Economics and Management, and the Vice Director of Collaborative Innovation Center for Transport Studies at Dalian Maritime University. His current research interests include mispricing, option price, shipping finance, risk contagion, and systemic risk. Email: suicong2004@163.com.

Duoqi Xu is Professor of Fudan University Law School and Affiliated Professor of Shanghai Advanced Institute of Finance (SAIF), Shanghai Jiao Tong University. Professor Xu is the executive council member of the China Law Association on Science and Technology and the executive council member of the China Law Association on Tax and Fiscal Law. Her research has focused on fintech law, cybersecurity, tax and fiscal law, etc. Professor Xu has published over 80 papers in SSCI (Social Science Citation Index) and CSSCI (Chinese Social Science Citation Index) journals. She has presided over two National Social Science Fund Projects and more than 10 provincial and ministerial level and international cooperation projects. Professor Xu has visited and taught at Harvard University, New York University, Duke University, University of New South Wales, National Taiwan University and other universities. Email: xuduoqi@fudan.edu.cn.

Henry Yang, CPA, MBA, has an MBA (Master of Business Administration) from Cornell University, a Master's in Professional

Accounting, and a Bachelor's of Business Administration from the University of Texas at Austin. He was previously a consultant at Ernst & Young in Houston. Email: py87@cornell.edu.

James Zhan is a senior risk quant and leader with over 18 years of experience in market and credit risk modeling and system development with a top-tier Canadian bank to meet internal and regulatory capital requirements, including Basel I, II, and III. More recently, his focus has been on design and implementation of the FRTB (Fundamental Review of Trading Book) — the latest market risk framework. He holds a PhD in Mathematics from University of Toronto. Email: yi.zhan@bmo.com; zyjames@yahoo.com.

Jianwu Lin received dual Bachelor's degrees in Engineering and Economics and a Master's degree in Engineering from Tsinghua University as well as a PhD and dual Master's degrees from the University of Pennsylvania. Dr. Lin is a Finance Professor in Tsinghua Shenzhen International Graduate School. His research interests include Financial Technology, Financial Engineering, Meta learning, Machine Learning, Behavioral Finance, Quantitative Investment and Financial Risk Management, Internet Finance and Supply Chain Finance. He is the Chairman of special sessions for financial big data and track of intelligent finance in several IEEE conferences.

Lingtong Meng (Stanley) is an option quantitative trader at Derivatives China Capital. He earned his undergraduate degree in Financial Mathematics and Statistics from the Universality of Sydney and holds an MSc (Master of Science) in Mathematics and Finance from Imperial College London. His thesis focused on modeling high-frequency implied volatility surface dynamics together with Dr. Antoine Jacquier and Deutsche Bank AG, London. He subsequently joined the firm and worked as a quantitative trader on EMEA flow equity derivatives e-trading desk and later a front-office FIC quantitative researcher on EMEA inflation and bond ETF (exchange-traded fund) desk. His primary research interests lie in high-frequency volatility modeling, market microstructure, orderbook dynamics, and practical machine learning in finance. Email: menglingtong@derivatives-china.com.

Michael Peng, PhD, Senior Director of Risk Practice at Boston Consulting Group, specializes in the area of credit and counterparty risk management and model implementation. Dr. Peng has more than 20 years of Wall Street and academic experiences, which include Directorship at Bank of America/Merrill Lynch Structure Product Group (Hong Kong), Directorship at Fitchrating, and Senior Manager at KPMG. Dr. Peng is a frequent contributor to *Asian Financial Times*, where he writes about global financial issues. He is also an overseas advisor and Adjunct Professor at People's University Financial Engineering School/SuZhou campus. Email: mkpeng2007@gmail.com.

Mo Yang received his PhD degree in Statistics from the Australian National University. He is currently Assistant Professor and Deputy Dean of the Department of Insurance and Actuarial Science at School of Finance of Dongbei University of Finance and Economics. Dr. Yang's research interests include statistical inference, Bayesian analysis, and econometrics. Email: mo.yang@hotmail.com.

Rongbing Huang is the Associate Director in Deloitte China, providing professional consulting services in risk advisory for the financial services industry. He specializes in market risk management consulting, credit risk management consulting, Basel compliance consulting, IFRS 9 implementation consulting, trading system validation, model development, and validation. He has consulting service experience at various financial institutions. He graduated from Huazhong University of Science and Technology in 2010 with a PhD in Management. Email: ronghuang@deloitte.com.cn.

Peiran Wang is a Research Assistant at Financial Law Research Center, Fudan University. He graduated from China University of Political Science and Law with the honor of Beijing Outstanding Graduate. He has visited and studied at Chuo University. Email: peiranw@yahoo.com.

Weiping Li, Tenure Professor and Watson Faculty Fellow at Oklahoma State University, Editor-in Chief of *Journal of Finance and Data Science* (2015–2020), and Dean of the Institute of Finance and Big Data at Southwest Jiaotong University. Research focus on dynamic asset pricing, optimal portfolio in asset allocation, and corporate finance, fixed income, and credit risk. Email: w.li@okstate.edu.

Xianzhen Wang is a PhD candidate in Finance at Fudan University and is doing research on asset pricing and corporate finance. After receiving a Master's degree in Econometrics at Xiamen University, Wang worked as a securities analyst in securities companies for five years since 2009, and then as a co-founder of a hedge-fund firm since 2014. Wang has a solid understanding of how financial markets work and the behavior of asset prices, and a rich experience in securities research and investment, including fixed-income, equities, and derivatives. Email: xzwang19@fudan.edu.cn.

Yali Chang has a Ph.D. in Finance and is a Lecturer at the Business School of Guangxi University. She was previously a Visiting Scholar at the Department of Finance of University of Illinois at Urbana-Champaign (2015–2016). Her research areas are the application of blockchain in finance, financial system structure, and the macroeconomic and financial supporting system of China-ASEAN (Association of Southeast Asian Nations) investment and trading. She has presided over four research projects, including one national-level research project and two provincial and ministerial-level research projects. She has also published 10 articles in domestic journals including *Economic Research Journal* and the *Journal of Quantitative & Technical Economics*. Email: changyali197@126.com.

Yicheng Wang is currently a Juris Master Candidate at Fudan University Law School. He has earned his Master of Laws from Washington University in St. Louis School of Law. Email: wangyicheng@wustl.edu.

You Zhang (Joey) Chairman/CIO of Derivatives China Capital. Bachelor of Finance and Executive Master of Business Administration (EMBA) of PBC School of Finance (PBCSF) from Tsinghua University. In charge of volatility trading at Goldman Sachs (Asia); oversaw the firm's APAC equity derivatives trading business; managed a book with over $2 billion balance sheet and delivered 10 years of consistent returns. Counseled Shenzhen Stock Exchange and China Financial Futures Exchange on options products. Email: zy@derivatives-china.com

Contents

PART I

The CME Vulnerability: The Best Practice and the Impact of Negative Oil Futures Trading Price

Chapter 1

The Overview of WTI Crude Oil Futures' Epic Fall*

Chern Lu

Chief Economist of Mushroom Digital Technology Co. Ltd
Distinguished Professor of Harvard Business Psychology BPSY
Adjunct Associate Professor of Hong Kong University SPACE ICB
luchern@yahoo.com

Executive Summary

In this chapter, I would like to zoom in from the gloomy global economy fettered by the savaging COVID-19 pandemic to delve into the debacle of West Texas Intermediate (WTI) crude oil futures; endeavor to put all these mind-boggling market events into a rigorous and robust financial pricing and trading framework; rationalize the unthinkable with a goal to untangle the mess; and demystify the puzzle of how WTI crude futures contract settled below the sentimental zero point for the very first time since the establishment of the ancient commodity trading exchange, the Chicago Board of Trade (CBOT), in 1848, which was deemed to be utterly unimaginable and improbable, before the Black-swan-infested inauspicious 2020.

The highly infectious COVID-19 has brought literally all economic activities to a complete standstill, disrupted people's normal

---

*The views expressed in this paper are those of the author and do not represent the views of the affiliated institutions.

lives, and inflicted a heavy toll upon individuals and corporations, to the extent of raising questions about their fundamental survival.

The lockdowns and social distancing taking place globally, as the sole panacea for combating this cunningly mutable virus, threw the staggering geopolitics-plagued world economy out of balance with an unprecedented tapering from both demand and supply sides. The stalemate economy is shrinking at an alarming rate without any foreseeable near-term remedies.

One of the worst hit areas is the crude oil market, due to the failure to reach an agreement to cut oil production among OPEC (Organization of the Petroleum Exporting Countries) member countries. Crude oil's still burgeoning supplies contrasted with scarcity of the crude storage spaces, jointly smashed the WTI crude futures' May contract settlement price, leaving it deeply submerged in the sea of negative numbers.

Inspected through the lens of macro and microeconomics, the obnoxious negative WTI crude futures settlement price was the offspring of four major events: the Chicago Mercantile Exchange's (CME) astonishing introduction of negative price compliant crude futures trading system; the feeble global crude demands; the overcapacity of crude oil storage in Cushing, Oklahoma; and last but not the least, the fact that WTI crude oil futures contract only allows for physical delivery.

All of these events, individually seeming not so harmful, joined forces to form a formidable crushing power at a highly sensitive historic moment to deliver the deadly blow.

In this chapter, I will discuss CME's hasty adoption of the negative crude oil futures pricing scheme and its substantial damaging consequences to the whole crude industry and a kaleidoscopic spectrum of investment products linked to crude futures, and assess whether it should have been rolled out in a more precautious manner, at least, augmented by some risk mitigating procedures such as fixing a negative price bottom threshold to serve as the risk limit for edgy investors, an installation of negative price circuit-breaker, or a much wider settlement price calculation window in face of mounting trading liquidity pressure.

I would like to present indisputable evidences from the tick-by-tick WTI crude trading data to refute the CME Chairman's declaration that "Everything is going perfectly" as it was a blatantly misleading statement, to say the least.

As the world's leading commodity trading hub, CME is obligated to step up to shoulder the bounden responsibilities, not to sidestep and shun away from its primary duty of maintaining an orderly and smoothly operating trading exchange in the best interest of its stakeholders and all market participants, regardless of whether they are institutional or retail investors. Fairness, integrity, and transparency should be raised to the highest priority.

CME did not seem to comprehend the crucial fact that the whole modern futures trading risk management fortress is built upon a seemingly firm ground, and beneath that unshaken surface lies the simple but ultimately critical axiom that all exchange-traded instruments are priced above zero, for without it the fortress would become a castle in the sky and just crumble and tumble.

CME's trading-market-oriented crude oil pricing dogma has its own merits and fanfares, but it irrevocably opened a potentially ruinous crack on the floor, which could be morphing to a yawning crevasse to engulf our treasured financial palace.

This crude futures crisis shouldn't be brushed aside and wasted. Instead, it should be cherished as a rarely available opportunity to self-check our complicated and interconnected financial system and fix the issues exposed by this negative price debacle.

Borrowing the classical pricing theories from modern finance and economics, I will closely scrutinize both fundamental and psychological or sentiment components of the crude futures' negative price with due consideration of the unnerving trading environment.

I will adopt Shleifer and Summers' "noise traders" approach and Nassim Nicholas Taleb's famous "minority rule" analyzing methodologies to analytically and empirically examine how the passive trade-at-settlement (TAS) orders, traders' over-strung sentiments, and convoluted trading dynamics behind the scenes helped formulate the far-reaching negative settlement "fair" price for WTI crude oil futures.

Last but not the least, powered by the explosive growth of trendy index funds and exchange-traded funds (ETFs), the raging passive investment legion has dethroned the classical active investment tribe, taking the rein of the global financial market to reshape the ecosystem of the financial world since the 1980s.

In particular, crude oil ETFs, championed by the colossal giant, the United States Oil Fund (USO), with their mighty investment capital power under the belt, have exerted a profound impact on WTI crude futures market. I will drill down to uncover their linkages beneath the surface, and decipher the role played by crude oil ETFs in this momentously epochal crude oil rout.

Keywords: Negative price, crude oil futures, asset pricing theory, trading liquidity, null value, Black swan, macroeconomic, trading risk control, risk management, Yuan You Bao, trading-at-settlement, VWAP, physical settlement, backwardation, contango, market sentiment

1.1 Introduction

I used to be a mathematician many years ago, cranking upon ordinary differential equations, proving the theorems for integrable Hamiltonian systems, calculating asymptotic solutions for nonlinear partial differential equations, and putting on a wild thinking cap to imagine what would it be like in the high dimension Hilbert spaces.

Mathematics has been dubbed the most robust and rigorous branch of science, serving as the solid foundation for the whole sprawling science edifice, buttressing and propping up the whole skyscraper with its seamless logical reasoning powers.

Mathematics itself is constructed upon the bedrock of axioms and paradigms, which act as the faiths and creeds to motivate the devoted math-loving folks like me to plough forward earnestly and avidly.

After my over 20 years of enthusiastic tangling with mathematics, I can solemnly and categorically proclaim that mathematics has many attractive features such as aesthetics, elegance, and whimsical charming powers, but one thing it definitely lacks is the sentiments and dispositions possessed by emotional humankind, in particular, capriciousness, which is really hard to predict and control.

People, regardless of race, ethnicity, religion, or domicile, share some common preferences: they all love positive numbers, despise the negative ones, embrace the plus, and shun away from the minus side. This is the unanimous favorite out of people's minds spontaneously; our brains have been pre-programmed and fine-tuned to predispose us towards the positive side, naturally without any explicit explanations, or perhaps none may be needed.

In the aromatic garden of mathematics wonderland, one can spot all kinds of numbers in blossom: positive, negative, real, complex, rational, irrational, etc. But mathematicians are more fair-minded; the seemingly bothersome negative number never constitutes a blasphemy and the more elusive and unfathomable imaginative number is never frowned upon. For these curiously searching souls, the untiring chase for the innate structural symmetry and hidden dualities would deliver the most pleasures and delights.

Zero value, or alias naught, null, and nil, originated from 2nd millennium BC, from the Babylonian era, simply as a placeholder. Around the 4th or 5th century AD, ancient China and India helped develop the idea of void or nothingness, establishing its unique footing in the numeric number system.

The Italian mathematician Fibonacci (c. 1170–1250), who grew up in North Africa, is credited with introducing the decimal system to Europe.

For negative numbers, they first appeared in the ancient Chinese book "Nine Chapters on the Mathematical Art", which in its present form dates from the period of the Chinese Han Dynasty (202 BC–AD 220), but may well contain much older materials.

Around the 7th century AD, ancient Indian mathematician Brahmagupta described the use of negative numbers as debts or liabilities.

But if one enters the insanely crazy financial trading world, one can immediately sense that the landscape is vastly different there: quick-tempered uncouth traders are dealing with either tangible commodity assets or virtual financial instruments; inside the grand pompous trading exchange, the flashy fleeting ticker-tapes measure the vibrant pulse of modern economic civilization with one distinctive contrast — the pricing marks are all uniformly above zero. The reason? Survival bias — people only chase and trade the highly desired items that have "value" (let's leave the ordeal of nailing down the precise definition of "value" to those erudite loquacious economists). If something is out of vogue (no value), people just simply dump it and walk away, not bothering to chase it into the annoying negative domain, which would force our brains to function and operate in a reverse manner, that is surely a wearisome and arduous task!

The null value completely shuts the door to the other unexplored dark world, leaving us to revel and indulge in the safe haven. Human beings, with that resounding assurance, proceed to build an increasingly complex and interconnected financial system and start the monetary flow churning.

There is indeed one category of assets that is marked out by negative signs. They are the assets that have been sold short (in trading floor's succinct lingo, shorted) on market, which by definition means that the financial assets are not owned by the short seller, but borrowed by them to sell on the market with an adamant belief that the asset's price will be falling precipitously so that the short seller would buy it back (cover) to reap in decent profits from the marked price differences.

The shorted assets are booked on the liability side of trading desk's balance sheets. Hence, traders treat them with an invisible negative sign in their astute minds!

Items on the liability side are mostly on the "slow" valuation track powered by a plethora of intriguing accounting rules, such as commercial loans, etc., but for the shorted securities, the regulatory authority decided to adopt the cruel trading world's mark-to-market (MTM) rule for the sole purpose of reflecting their true economic values in a timely manner, which narrows, if not eliminates, the shortfall between benign classical accounting conventions and brutal financial trading markets' rituals.

However, this steadfastly held belief of positive price was smashed and shattered miserably on the tumultuous trading day of April 20, the expiration date for the West Texas Intermediate (WTI) crude oil futures May contract traded in the New York Mercantile Exchange (NYMEX).

Without too much fanfare, the crude futures price fell unprecedentedly below the sentimental zero point, nosediving and tumbling toward $-37.63 with an ominous negative sign; the negative crude settlement price shocked the world, shaking investors' undoubted faith, making the impossible and improbable a hard-to-believe reality, a bitter fruit that investors had no choice but to swallow down.

The fossil fuel that helped build human's modern world, so prized to be known as "black gold", was now not an asset but an annoying liability. This was saddening and pathetic.

If history is the sole fortune-teller or harbinger of the near future, then we look at the not-too-far-away history of the tumultuous period of 2008 financial crisis, which might throw a dim light on what has been going on recently, and chart the course going forward.

In the 2008 global financial tsunami, the world economy suffered from a massive oil demand destruction, which brought about the epic contango in the crude oil futures term structure.

The crude oil contango manifests the market situation where the future oil prices are much higher than the current spot prices. The astute market players will charter the tankers to ship and store the cheap spot crude and sell the futures to be delivered at a later time in order to profit nicely from the upward-sloping curves of crude futures term structure.

So, we could draw some useful lessons from the historical crude market's rewinding, with only one caveat: the past won't necessarily teach us all the tricks to solve today's dilemma.

As exclaimed by the overtly defiant author of "The Black Swan", Nassim Nicholas Taleb, in his thought-provoking voluminous magnum opus *Incerto*: it is not what one knows to be imperatively important, it is what one doesn't know that will mark the sand line of life or death.

Black swans descend from the fourth quadrant of human cognition realm: unknown unknowns. They are not living in our normal perceptive world as demonstrated by the epochal collapse of WTI crude oil futures.

The chapter is organized as follows: in Section 1.2, after a brief discussion of the seemingly mundane importance of non-negative price, I will conduct a thorough review of the full development of the mind-bending crude futures' negative price rout, focusing upon the pivotal role played by the trading exchange giant, the Chicago Mercantile Exchange, analyzing its pledged responsibilities and liabilities.

Several suggestions would be made to improve and strengthen the beleaguered financial trading system. The ultimate goal is to avoid, by all means, the re-occurrence of insidious negative crude prices by discovering the loopholes and fixing the broken pipeline as soon as possible.

In Section 1.3, I will discuss the contagious COVID-19 pandemic and its overwhelming impact on the global economy, in particular on the crude oil market. I will go over some basic and important facts about WTI and Brent crude oil futures trading, as well as the well-known crude futures term structure and its economic implications, which constitute the main driving forces for both pricing and trading of crude futures.

In Section 1.4, I will engage in a macro analysis of the global economy to close in on the key targets of WTI crude futures' trading micro-structure through the utilization of a variety of powerful analysis tools: analytical versus empirical and fundamental versus psychological sentiment to figure out the possible causes of the WTI crude futures' epic fall.

In Section 1.5, I will touch upon the global sweeping trend of passive investment and the explosive assets under management (AUM) growth of crude oil exchange-traded funds (ETFs) (such as the United States Oil Fund (USO)), which have exerted a huge influence and pressure on the WTI crude market. I will also elaborate upon USO's trade-at-settlement (TAS) order placements and its grave consequences, as well as the significance of its monthly position rolling.

In the last section, we make a few closing remarks to conclude the whole chapter.

1.2   CME's Designated Roles, Responsibilities, and Liabilities

Looking retrospectively, it is unequivocally clear that the global gargantuan futures trading powerhouse, CME, pulled the trigger, firing the very first alerting shot to stir up the panic-stricken trading crowds for the upcoming crude storm.

In April, CME caught everyone off guard by making the astonishing announcement of testing opportunities in CME's "New Release" environment for negative prices and strikes for certain NYMEX energy contracts.

In the message, it stated, "Recent market events have raised the possibility that certain NYMEX energy futures contracts could trade at negative or zero trade prices or be settled at negative or zero values, and that options on these futures contracts could be listed with negative or zero strike prices. Were this to occur, all of CME's trading and clearing systems would continue to function normally. Support for zero or negative futures and/or strike prices is standard throughout CME systems. All file and message formats support such prices, and we have a variety of products which have long behaved in this manner, for example NYMEX BY (WTI-Brent Bullet) futures contracts and NYMEX BV options on those futures contracts." [2]

Clearing Advisory 20–152 was published on April 8, 2020, and detailed the process, considerations, and timing by which CME would transition from the Whaley option pricing model to the Bachelier option pricing model for margining and settlements for particular groups of products.

CME's impromptu actions sent out a strong alarming message to the whole shaky and volatile crude market, but unfortunately, it was totally ignored by many investors, in particular the edgy retail investor clan, who were left to fight to the last ditch for their hard-earned trading capital.

"It might not have been pretty to some but the crude-oil market worked as it should have on Monday," according to Terrence Duffy, CEO of CME Group. Nobody should have been "under the perception that it can't go below zero", said the head of the world's largest exchange platform by market capitalization.

Duffy said on CNBC's "Closing Bell" that it was no surprise that the May contracts for the United States (US) crude benchmark WTI traded in negative territory in the final days before expiration. "We worked with the government regulators two weeks prior to making our announcement that we were going to allow negative price trading," Duffy said. "So, this was no secret that this was coming at us. We have to do things to allow the market to go to a price that is reflecting the **fundamentals** of the product. *The futures market worked to perfection.*" [9]

This aftermath response from the highest-ranking officer of CME was apathetic, aloof, and disappointing, to say the least. He pointed a big finger to crude market's jitters and churnings, shirking CME's due responsibilities, shrugging off the complaints. This is the same good old trick wielded by the maestro Alan Greenspan to dodge the pouring complaints for his laissez-fair free market approach, which sowed the seeds for the devastating 2008 financial crisis that wreaked havoc on the global economy. Sounds a bit familiar?

Now, he is more like Greenspan's sounding board, reciprocating the master's clichés, the keyword collection stays the same: "I don't know", "market behaviors", "unanticipated", etc.

The CME boss singled out a lack of follow-through on oil purchase promised by the US government as the key reason for the crude trading liquidity crunch, which left the market with no big buyers to step in as the savior of those despondent speculating traders during the critical rollover period for WTI crude May contracts.

CME's CEO also mentioned that USO, the largest crude oil ETF behemoth, was out of the May futures contracts on Monday, and it was just a few speculators and commercials with open positions. He said open interest in May WTI crude contract on Monday was 130,000 hands and 154,000 traded Monday, with 80% of the traded prices above zero.

Well, to be fair, the market's churning and roiling shouldn't be dismissed or underestimated. But, CME, as the most prestigious trading exchange in the world, serving as the last ditch to uphold the market's integrity, fend off trading risks, and protect investors, shouldn't refrain from doing what it fiduciarily ought to do on behalf of the whole futures market.

CME ought to engage in deploying more trading risk control procedures such as negative price risk limits or negative price circuit breakers to mitigate and contain potential damages that cannot be anticipated beforehand since nobody has the prior experience or knowledge. This is the perfect black swan set-up of unknown unknowns. But, one thing we are categorically sure about is that we do not know!

Continental Resources Inc. founder Harold Hamm has filed a complaint with CME and written a letter to the Commodity Futures Trading Commission (CFTC) asking for a probe into "potential market manipulation, failed systems or computer programming failures".

"The sanctity and trust in the oil and all commodity futures markets are at issue as the system failed miserably and an immediate investigation is requested and, we submit, is required," Hamm said in the letter in which he detailed the unusual activity.

CFTC has confirmed to look at these unusual market disruptions closely, and will take due actions if deemed necessary.

CME clarified on April 15 that negative prices were theoretically possible, even though they had never happened in crude oil trading. "Support for zero or negative futures ... is standard throughout CME systems," CME Group announced.

Counting from April 15, when CME started twisting its futures trading and clearing systems, all together five days, including the weekend to April 20, against the backdrop of the coronavirus-triggered lockdowns and so many thorny futures trading system issues need to be worked out, is not a sufficient amount of time reserved for this unprecedented daunting task.

For example, two traders using the Connecticut-based Interactive Brokers (IB) trading platform thought they have bought the WTI crude oil futures at a record low (positive) price, without realizing, actually, at that time on April 20, the WTI crude contracts have plunged into the negative area because the IB software could not display the abnormal negative crude futures' prices at real time. IB has committed to making up for the clients' boggling trading loss of over 100 million dollars, paying the hefty price for this failed costly experiment.

CME's dogmatic refutation about the possibility of zero or negative prices sounds hackneyed and a bit trite. At the turn of the last century, when French mathematician, the dubbed forefather of modern mathematical finance, Louis Bachelier, brought in Brownian Motion and Stochastic Processes to unravel the puzzle of the financial market's random-walk-like behaviors, zero and negative prices were permissible and treated on equal footing with positive ones in his ground-breaking derivative pricing models.

However, his pioneering work later faded into oblivion, quickly disappearing from the human's cognitive world. Modern investors and financial professionals are rarely aware of his research ideas, and never take zero or negative prices as a viable option for traded financial products.

Now, after so many years, the rewinding nostalgic rhetoric sounds out of touch with reality by lambasting people not to treat the subjective probability as a tangible objective probability. With a swirl of the magic wand, CME tried to resuscitate and resurrect the obsolete zero or negative prices from their dusty grave.

Is this the rationality assumption in the classical economics doctrines?

If this sacred cognitive axiom of positive price is in jeopardy and gets compromised, then the whole grand trading exchange castle will be ramshackle, on the brink of collapse. Well, the operational trading rules could be replaced or switched swiftly, but not the fundamental creeds and axioms, otherwise, investors will be led into an unknown world and have to start everything from scratch.

After the apocalypse of the 2008 financial crisis, the global risk management framework has been overhauled, the regulatory landscape has been reshuffled, and trading exchanges have been assigned with more critically important duties to safeguard modern capitalism and maintain the financial market's stability and orderly operations. They undoubtedly constitute the last line of defense in the fierce trading world without any excuses whatsoever.

A regulated futures trading exchange is different from a luck-seeking boisterous casino, in that the exchange doesn't simply open the door, usher in avid investors, then step aside to count the money. It needs to fulfill its obligations of maintaining an orderly, fair, and trustworthy trading environment, and implementing a plethora of trading regulations, rules, and risk measures to curb excessive speculations, not to let loose humans' greedy temperament to overpower the fundamental bottom line, which will turn a thoughtful and calculated investment into a reckless heady gamble. Behind the scenes, the zero price acts silently as the dutiful righteous law-enforcer to keep the unruly desires in check.

But, after the WTI crude price drifted into the negative muddy waters, the table has been turned upside down. WTI crude futures trading literally morphed into a gambling game overtaken by emotions.

In the tortuous progression and development of the modern financial market, people have paid a hefty price to learn the hard lessons that absolute free market capitalism, laissez-faire will unavoidably and inevitably lead to financial disasters, catastrophes, and unrests; financial regulations, oversight, and monitoring are the must-haves to contain potential damages wrought by human being's unquenchable greed and fears.

In the last 2–3 decades, a comprehensive and interconnected financial risk management framework has been established, increasingly complicated and convoluted risk models have been deployed, and new-fangled risk control procedures have been installed to make capital markets more durable, stable, and resilient.

The sturdy foundation of the modern financial risk management system is a set of axiomatically putative assumptions, which are deeply etched into human beings' cognitive processes. One of the primarily essential hypotheses is that the lowest possible boundary for traded price is the dull zero point, not to mention the enchanted ivory-tower darling of Gaussian Distribution.

The most powerful weapon in trading exchanges' arsenal is the modern financial risk management treasure box bundled with clients' margin accounts' depository safe cushion, which would be adjusted according to the dynamic trading risk exposures swinging with the external trading environment. Combined, they are believed to be able to defeat almost all intruding ferocious enemies.

In today's hustling-bustling, throat-cutting futures trading, with the margin account serving as a sensitive and effective risk barometer, either futures brokerage firms or trading exchanges will earnestly enforce sufficient margin balance as a life-saving apparatus. Margin call is the SOS alarm to alert customers that the trading market risk, for the specific moment, surpasses the margin account's risk absorbing capability, and more capital needs to be pumped in to buffer the adverse poundings. If the client refuses to replenish, then the risk profile will migrate from market risk into counterparty credit risk (CCR), a special type of nasty credit risk.

In general, market risk is much easier to handle compared with credit risk, where human being's intricate inner sentiments and dispositions are more closely involved.

The safest way to make sure the futures trading's risk profile stays within the market risk domain is to mandate customers to provide the full margin, that is, the pledged trading capital should cover the full nominal value of the traded products.

But, wait a moment, here we have subconsciously undertaken the zero-as-the-lowest-boundary axiom to obtain the worst scenario of losing all notional amount of the traded securities, be it futures contracts or other trading instruments. If futures' price would be allowed to go negative, then the above reasoning would be flawed, and the argument would fall apart, crumbling miserably.

Consequently, CME's flagship dynamic margin calculating algorithm SPAN (Standard Portfolio Analysis of Risk) would be taken down from the holy altar due to the same flaw deeply embedded in the framework of the designated risk engine.

A now well-known retail investment product, Yuan You Bao (Crude Oil Treasure) issued by Bank of China, the state-owned almighty financial behemoth, became the most publicized vulnerable victim of CME's abrupt trading axiom swapping experiment.

Yuan You Bao is a pooled trust investment to trade WTI crude's front month futures contracts. Its horrendous losses, estimated to be over 80 million dollars, provide the undisputed evidence to substantiate our claims that CME's seemingly non-ill-intentioned fundamental trading law changes toppled the supporting pillars that carry the weight of the entire futures trading risk management chateau.

Bank of China, acting as the servicer and risk manager for Yuan You Bao's customers, carved out an ingenious master plan to eliminate all involved risks so that the financial powerhouse could reap a decent "risk free" return. The Bank required Yuan You Bao's customers to prepay the entire notional amount of WTI crude futures investment when opening their accounts.

As long as crude futures' prices stay positive, keeping this notional amount of cash as collateral would be safe and sound, completely trouble-free. The preemptive risk control measures seem to seal the deal once and for all.

Again, the whole risk management set-up hinges upon that critical zero price as the bottom-line assumption, and everyone holds an unwavering belief in it. However, as soon as crude prices glided into the negative region, the whole modern financial risk management building collapsed, and almost all existing risk control infrastructures were defunct, like a 21st-century version of the Maginot Line.

CME should have anticipated and evaluated the grave consequences of its engaged actions, and consulted with major stakeholders and relevant trading industry parties before hastily rushing out this far-reaching negative price trading system update, which is deemed dubious and inappropriate, placing investors in a highly disadvantaged situation facing unknown risks.

Duffy evaded the accusations by throwing out the curve ball of proclaiming that CME had informed the regulators about its intended trading system update. But nobody could deny the fact that there is a huge information asymmetry between CME and regulators regarding the complicated bells and whistles of commodity futures trading, not to mention the trade at settlement volume-weighted average price (TAS VWAP) or settlement price determination procedures. The involved intricacies shouldn't be underestimated as biased expectations become the hotbed of fermentation for risks.

Did everyone fully understand the possible devastating implications and ripple effects by removing the supporting board beneath the feet of investors, leaving them to teeter on the brink of a possible abysmal fall to the bottomless blackhole?

Given its prominent and dominant position in the futures trading world, CME is obliged to take a much broader view, a thorough investigation, as well as a well-rounded analysis before taking upon these monumental changes.

According to CME Group and Duffy, the unparalleled jittery trading environment made them pull the trigger of the impromptu changes of the crude futures trading system. The major consideration was that the classical equilibrium balancing point of the crude price wouldn't be attained within the normal positive price range with the savaging COVID-19 pandemic shattering the global economy and crippling demand for crude oil, as well as the huge imbalance of crude futures trading liquidity.

As I have argued in the early part, the ominous negative price tag for crude oil manifests its new categorization as the burdensome liability. Similar to its positive counterpart, the astounding negative WTI crude price is composed of two pieces, the first part is what has been phrased as "the fundamentals" in Duffy's pugnacious statement: "We have to do things to allow the market to go to a price that is reflecting the fundamentals of the product. The futures market worked to perfection." More bluntly, this is related to the crude storage cost or shipping expenses, etc. The second part is the add-on of "negative emotions", that is, how vehemently the frantic speculative traders hated carrying on the WTI crude May contracts, eager to give them up and escape out of the brutal battlefield. Both components will be analyzed more closely in the ensuing sections.

Although, Duffy played ostrich by shunning the cruel reality with a self-claimed assertion that the futures market worked to perfection, privately, NYMEX executives appeared to have been extremely concerned about the size of certain speculative positions. The excess speculation had emerged as a destabilizing force in unsettling crude prices at the worst possible time, which, in turn, had shaken confidence and shattered trust in the crude trading markets.

Before we drill down to the nitty-gritty trading details on April 20, an important trading term needs to be explained first.

Trading at settlement (TAS) order allows investors to buy or sell a futures contract at the settlement price before the markets close. TAS is an order type that allows an investor to execute at a spread to the settlement price at any time during the trading session. One can enter a defined number of tick increments above or below the settlement or marker price as set forth in the current Market Regulation Advisory Notice concerning Rule 524.

Now, pushing the line of the CME argument a bit further, the behind-the-scenes logics of the last three minutes VWAP was to avoid the price manipulation such as "banging the close", because in the normal trading environment, there are sufficient trading liquidities in terms of depth and breadth, CME had strong reasons to believe that nobody could effectively control and manipulate a bulk of the trading volumes in the last three minutes, with which the critical settlement VWAP price would be calculated.

On April 20, frantic sell orders had been pouring in overnight and any trader who connected to the NYMEX platform that morning could see a bloodbath was coming [10].

By 7 a.m. in New York, the price on WTI crude futures for May delivery was already down 28% to $13.07 a barrel.

As the critical settlement period was drawing near, a potential trading liquidity crunch of the WTI crude futures May contract was becoming increasingly likely.

In the afternoon, with trading volumes thin and sellers overpowering buyers, who were few and far between, the liquidity dry-up started encroaching the TAS mechanism at its most needed juncture in face of the relentless pummeling of liquidating sell orders.

The TAS contracts swiftly reached the maximum discount allowed, of 10 cents per barrel, and trading in these contracts were terminated.

CME swiftly lifted the ban to the forbidden zone without re-engineering the necessary facilities to accommodate the upcoming tumultuous trading ambience. The TAS order used to be the close ally for the intra-day crude trading. Now, it turned its cold shoulder to those helpless traders due to the stringent normal trading stipulations.

CME should have considered some suitable upgrades for TAS orders given that so many investors' stakes were linked to this critical number. The swing amplitude limit of TAS orders should be relaxed correspondingly to alleviate the palpable trading liquidity pressure.

The normally sleepy postprandial 20 minutes leading to the settlement period was morphing into an unalloyed chaos, more precisely, a dark moment for black gold.

Table 1.1.   Intra-day prices for May and June WTI crude contracts

Daytime (EST)	May	Jun	Comments
April 17 (Friday) – 14:30	$18.27	$25.03	CME Daily Settlement
April 20 (Monday) – 10:00	$11,69	$23.17	Yuan You Bao halted Trading
April 20 (Monday) – 14:08	$–0.01	$21.79	May WTI price below 0
April 20 (Monday) – 14:30	$–37.63	$20.43	May WTI Settlement Price
April 20 (Monday) – 20:03	$0.01	$21.61	May WTI price above 0
April 21 (Tuesday) – 14:30	$10.01	$11.57	CME Daily Settlement

Source: CME data.

In the minute between 2:08 p.m. and 2:09 p.m., 83 WTI futures contracts, scheduled for May delivery, rapidly changed hands at an epic $0 a barrel. Then in the same minute, crude futures, encountering little resistance, jackknifed lower to trade at -1 cent a barrel. WTI crude futures was put on a roaring rocket to explore the uncharted cosmos of the negative prices.

At 2:29 p.m., one minute before settlement that Monday, a single May crude futures contract traded at the jaw-dropping unimaginable price of $−40.32 a barrel, marking the lowest handle ever witnessed in the most liquid crude oil contracts in the world [11].

Traders who were crude diehards holding on firmly to their May futures contracts were duly rewarded as oil price turned positive again shortly. On the evening of April 20th, one lone crude futures contract ventured back into positive territory, trading at 5 cents a barrel, just before slipping below zero again in the early hours of Tuesday.

All of the vivid flashbacks interspersed with tick-by-tick transactions just revealed one indisputable fact that a tiny amount of trading volumes, even at the lowest permissible end of one contract, could paint the tape in flying colors.

Three minutes, which used to be deemed sufficient to obtain a fair value for the crude settlement price, now looking pale and feeble facing the mounting liquidity imbalance, was highly likely subject to some rogue traders' ill-intentioned manipulative executions.

The crude settlement price calculating period should be lengthened due to the very same consideration of avoidance of price manipulation in face of a dwindling liquidity pool and overwhelming selling pressure, which have made the critical crude settlement price suffer a double whammy.

Michel Marks, the founding father of the NYMEX crude oil futures contract, which was launched on March 30, 1983, said, "Anticipating trading cataclysms and global calamities, like the COVID-19 pandemic, is all part of the job. But that doesn't necessarily make it easy."

"Black swans are hard to anticipate," he said. "The bottom line is to maintain a fair and orderly market."

Marks' aired opinions struck the same chord as ours; CME has all required liabilities and responsibilities to maintain and safeguard a healthy well-functioning and smoothly-operating trading market that assuages investors' anxieties at the critically needed moment.

In Duffy's statement, he stressed that over 80% of trading volume was executed with positive prices, that is categorically correct, but the same statistical information just helps drive home the point that an unfairly small quantity of trading executions orchestrated the season finale of the show, the last three minutes of the negative price climax.

When an atomic bomb gets detonated, immediately after the first wave of blasting comes the second round of shockwave (called second wave) emanating from the centre of the explosion to shatter and crush anything it encounters on its marching path.

The implosion of WTI crude oil futures was the "atomic bomb" in the commodity trading market, after the first blasting wave of negative settlement price, the second destructive wave was on its way to level anything it was connected to.

Many of the market participants caught in the crossfire of negative crude price were not sophisticated investors, but simply members of the retail public who did not understand how crude futures contracts work. They fell the pathetic victims to the CME's trading rule revamping, and became the prey of some insatiable Wall Street predators.

These inexperienced investors, who were still struggling with the COVID-19 pandemic, felt the crushing power of WTI crude negative price's shockwave, not only lost their hard-earned trading principal, but also absurdly owed a hefty amount of negative price overdraft. The pains were just unbearable for them at that difficult time.

After the calamity, a number of economists, executives, and former exchange officials found negative oil prices very disconcerting and unsettling, noting that if physical traders were shying away from the futures market, then the futures trading exchange's primary function of price-discovery would be thrown into jeopardy, its reputation would be tarnished, and trust would be lost, which are the soul and spirit of trading exchanges that originate from the May 17, 1792 Buttonwood Agreement and 1848 Chicago Board of Trade's (CBOT) establishment.

Veteran oil economist Philip Verleger expressed his misgivings, calling for immediate reforms by the US Securities and Exchange Commission, as well as the Commodity Futures Trading Commission, to ensure negative oil futures prices would never happen again.

In a recent market note, he wrote that the negative price swings "represented a failure of the market that, if allowed to repeat, will threaten the global energy industry's entire financial foundation". He added, "The Chicago Mercantile Exchange allowed individual traders or producers to put their precarious financial circumstances ahead of the interests of the industry or consumers."

It is in the best interest of CME and its stakeholders, as well as the whole commodity industry, to take necessary precautions for the purpose of maintaining an orderly functioning trustworthy futures trading exchange.

But have some perspective, notes Marks of NYMEX fame. "There are more important things in life," he says, "than the price of oil in Cushing."

1.3   WTI Crude Oil Futures and the COVID-19 Pandemic

With the unexpected arrival of COVID-19 at the beginning of 2020, the whole world immediately went into a chaotic tailspin. The contagious coronavirus had been sweeping across the continents, moving from Asia to Europe and America.

Given its mighty infectious capabilities, the best protective measure human beings could take to save themselves was to enforce a complete lockdown isolation, shutter the factories, ban social gatherings, and stop people from traveling around. The global economy was contracting at a hard-to-believe pace.

The airline industry and cruise industry, two of the oil consumption behemoths, were floundering and stumbling at the mercy of the invisible and seemingly invincible virus enemy.

The pandemic had reduced the global demand of crude oil from 100 million barrels a day one year ago, to 29 million barrels a day. But OPEC (the Organization of the Petroleum Exporting Countries) only agreed to cut a modicum of oil production by 9.7 million barrels. It doesn't need a mathematician to get the equation right. The previous crude oil supply and demand's equilibrium has been knocked off ferociously, leaving a huge supply of crude roaming on the market like freaky zombies. Everyone was shunning away, there were no buyers at all!

Storage capacity on land had been filled up quickly. Many oil-importing countries had stored large quantities of crude oil, taking advantage of cheap prices that may not last long. Countries including China and the US were considering filling up massive underground storage caverns with crude oil, helping alleviate the pressure on other storage and transport systems.

Some oil producers, hoping to maintain their market shares, had stored their excess oil at sea, paying a hefty amount to keep tankers loaded with tons of overfilled crude to float at sea.

Nobody knows the exact number, but it is believed to be in excess of $100,000 per day for each tanker. According to some estimates, over 140 million barrels of oil are now rocking on the sea. The world consumed, at its heyday, about 90 million barrels of oil a day. That number should now be considerably much lower.

The deepening problem of crude's global supply-demand imbalance has been gradually manifesting and unfolding itself in crude oil price, pushing it lower and lower.

In the world's crude oil market, there are two pivotal camps. First, spot market where transaction deals are all conducted with the real tangible crude oil, so physical shipping and delivery as well as storage are the must-haves. Second, the crude oil futures gang settles the deals in flashy commodity trading exchanges with cash, not commodity. Futures contract is the first generation of the so-called derivatives, which, by any referential definition, means that their valuations and pricings are dependent upon some other underlying simple assets. Futures market was born in the late 1970s and early 1980s, when all existing major asset classes (equity, interest rate (government bond, credit), foreign exchange, and commodity) were experiencing some stomach-churning fluctuations due to a variety of economic, financial, and geopolitical reasons.

In particular, for the crude market, the tipping point of the crisis was the long-lasting feud and duel between the Middle Eastern Arabian countries and the indomitable newly-established Israel, and the OPEC's oil embargo, the 12 OPEC Arabian countries stopped selling crude oil to the United States and other Western countries as a retaliation and revenge for their support of Israel. The oil embargo had sent gas prices through the roof. Between 1973–1974, gasoline prices more than quadrupled, which had wreaked havoc upon developed countries' economy and contributed heavily to the United States' notorious 1980s stagflation.

Futures were created as a means for containing the asset price's adverse future movements. That is, futures contract's price is the underlying asset's designated forward price nailed down currently, although the (physical or cash) settlement will occur in the future to honour the legal contractual binding. This means that futures price is the traded upcoming future spot price at this moment. From its origin, futures are used mainly for risk hedging purposes, not for high-stake speculative gambling games.

While both trading camps are competing against each other, more importantly, they are interacting with, influencing, or being influenced by each other to fulfil futures market's most critical mission: price-discovery.

Crude oil futures market has experienced an impressively meteoric growth, with the lightning speed of electronic trading and information dissemination; in a blinking split-second, the whole world obtains crude oil's latest price quotes, which undoubtedly exerts a profound influence upon the crude oil's spot market transactions.

The world's crude futures market has been dominated by two reigning regimes: the Intercontinental Exchange's (ICE) Brent crude oil and NYMEX's WTI crude oil futures trading. NYMEX's WTI, which stands for West Texas Intermediate, is a light, sweet crude oil blend. "Light" refers to its low density and sulphur content, ideal for conversion to gasoline and diesel fuel. The contract's ticker symbol, CL, refers to "Crude Light". Its contract size is 1,000 barrels, trading hour is marked as "Sunday — Friday 5–4 p.m., with a 60 minutes trading break at 4 p.m. CT."

Brent crude oil is extracted from the North Sea as a high-quality light, sweet oil blend, which describes its low density and low sulphur content. Brent accounts for around two-thirds of global oil pricing, making it unarguably the most trustworthy global crude benchmark.

On CME Group's WTI CL futures' promotion sheets, it is stated that NYMEX WTI futures trading offers a direct exposure to the buoyant oil market, a key advantage over other ways to trade, whether an investor is looking to hedge risks or speculate on where oil prices are heading.

According to NYMEX, the commodity trading exchange owned and operated by CME Group, daily settlement methodology for the front month is stipulated as follows: The front month settles to the volume-weighted average price (VWAP) of all trades in the outright contract that are executed between 14:28:00 and 14:30:00 ET, the settlement period, rounded to the nearest tradable tick. On the day before the front month contract expires, the front and second months settle to the VWAP of the outright CME Globex trades executed between 14:28:00 and 14:30:00 ET, the settlement period, rounded to the nearest tradable tick. The next five months will settle based on the same procedures mentioned above.

We will see later that it was only in this critical settlement period that the unbelievably reckless selling started emerging and pummeling the WTI crude futures market, squeezing the hopeless long side to get them to succumb and pushing them into the negative price quagmire.

Futures contracts are traded by calendar months. An important fact for the front month crude futures price is that it would be converging to the spot price that was prevalent in the April's sparse crude transactions here and there, as the May WTI crude contract drew near to its expiration date; the convergence mechanism poked through the flimsy fragile protective armor of lofty futures contracts, bringing it down to the shaky ground of cruel reality.

On March 9, a monumental day for the US equity market, which was the 11th anniversary of the prolonged raging bullish market, OPEC held an important conference among its members to negotiate the crucial oil production cut deal against the ongoing COVID-19 pandemic, but the two oil-producing conglomerates, Saudi Arabia

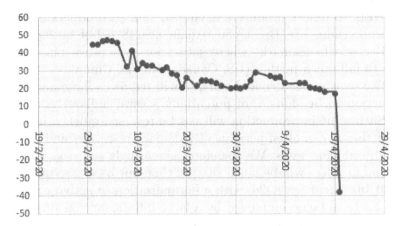

Fig. 1.1. WTI crude oil crash.

and Russia, reached an impasse in the discussion, failing to agree upon the detailed reduction terms.

The fiasco triggered the crude oil's precipitous free-fall and the long-time-not-used US equity market's circuit breaker mechanism.

At the end of March, Golden Sachs' commodities research team, headed by Damien Courvalin, shared some insightful thoughts on the sizzling hot and thorny issue of crude oil storage and the inflationary pressure that was likely to come about as a result. Among the many topics he touched upon, he voiced his grave concerns for a highly possible negative crude price.

"Global isolation measures are leading to an unprecedented collapse in oil demand which we now forecast will fall by 10.5 mb/d in March and by 18.7 mb/d in April (our 2020 YOY demand forecast is now −4.25 mb/d). A demand shock of this magnitude will overwhelm any supply response including any potential core-OPEC output freeze or cut."

"Such a collapse in demand will be an unprecedented shock for the global refining system with margins simply not low enough given the required level of run cuts. Product storage saturation at refineries is therefore set to occur over the next several weeks. At that point, the product surplus will become a crude one and we expect its unprecedented velocity will create similar logistical crude storage constraints. This is the point at which crude prices will fall below cash-costs to reflect producers having to shut-in production. While seaborne crudes like Brent can remain near $20/bbl in 2Q, many inland crude benchmarks where saturation will prove binding are likely to fall much further (US, Canada, Russia, China).

"The scale of the demand collapse will require a large amount of production to be shut-in, of potentially several million barrels per day. Such a hit in production will not be reversed quickly, however, as shutting-in can often permanently damage reservoirs and conventional producing wells. We therefore increasingly see risks that the rebound in prices will be much sharper than our base-case rally back to $40/bbl Brent by 4Q20, with a normalization in activity increasingly likely to be accompanied by a large inflationary oil shock."

The COVID-19 pandemic has greatly debilitated the global economy and sapped the needs of crude oil. The longer it lingers and lurks around, the more severe oil producers' woeful damages will be. Oil is increasingly becoming a stranded asset laden with unbearable carrying costs, while, that is literally a liability!

As time passed, more and more rigs were forced to stop operating, and only a handful were kept operational in order to avoid being compromised. A new balance between supply and demand had to be established at prices that exceed total average cost, that is, holding the ground to stay above zero.

But this didn't bode well for the front month WTI crude oil futures contract. The double whammy dealt by the savaging infectious COVID-19 and failure to reach any meaningful reduction agreements of oil production among OPEC member countries proved to be too onerous for the WTI crude futures market to absorb.

With the paralysis of the economy and crude demand, brimming and overflowing oil storage tanks, in particular, Cushing of Oklahoma, the physical settlement and delivery hub for WTI crude futures, which is not close to either major oil production or consumption areas. What it does have is a lot of physical infrastructures, with a wealth of pipeline connections and a commercial crude storage capacity that is unrivalled. Cushing has 55 million barrels of oil in storage as of the Friday before expiration, about 70% of its full capacity, which is the fullest level in two years.

Diametrically, North Sea Brent crude, widely used as a benchmark in Europe and other markets around the world, is based on trade of physical waterborne cargoes of five different crude grades. While

Brent's nominal storage capacity is lower than WTI at Cushing, it is intrinsically linked to the global market, with the crude making up the Dated Brent benchmark easily deliverable by tankers to refiners in any continents.

The mandatory physical settlement of WTI crude futures dictates that any entity holding open interests into the expiration date has to take physical delivery of the crude contracts, but one of the crucial prerequisites is to locate a stashing tank to hoard the liquid gold foremostly.

Unfortunately, no more empty oil tanks were left in Cushing. This dreadful scenario forced a portion of devoted crude fans, who originally planned to take the laborious physical settlement, to resort to the NYMEX's rambunctious trading floor to unload their held contracts. This group of turncoats aggravated the lopsided imbalance between the long and sell or short side of the May contracts, while futures trading is a zero-sum game, so the potential damages could be easily doubled.

While crude demand was petering out and storage tanks were rapidly filled up, the only surviving buyers of the WTI crude were the entities that were capable of taking physical deliveries like refineries or airline companies.

To bear the brunt of bleak fundamentals of the global economy and overt pessimistic outlooks, the front month WTI crude futures contracts were battered the hardest, since they were set to be expelled from the futures' safe haven to be delivered imminently in the dire backdrop of worldwide lockdowns and the spreading pandemic.

As the spot crude demand deteriorated to its weakest level in recent history, except for those who really wanted to take the physical delivery of fossil fuel, the rest of the trading crowd was more likely to roll their May contracts into the next month contracts or simply closed their positions, which means, a swarm of profit and loss maniacs would have no alternatives but to sell the May, walk away or long the June crude contracts.

These simultaneous selling further hammered down the depressed front month contract's trading marks.

For those WTI crude futures rollers, the spread between the May and June contracts — known as the front month and second month — was now the widest in crude history, which was a phenomenon due to the expiration of the front month contract coupled with the historic plunge in crude prices [1].

Oil prices collapsed on the sunny afternoon, April 20, because oil storage in Cushing, Oklahoma, was pathetically full, which lit the fuse to ignite the dynamite, imploding the WTI crude oil futures.

The May contract plummeted more than 100% to settle at history-making negative $37.63 per barrel, meaning crude producers would be obligated to pay buyers to take the fossil fuels off their hands.

Shortly after 20:00 EST, the contract marvelously bounced back into positive territory and closed at $10.01/bbl the following day, a level much more accurately reflective of physical market economics.

The depressing negative price has never shown up before for an exchange-traded crude contract. If one considers general futures trading's margin account, or option selling's margin account, one could argue that the negative pricing is not a whimsical alien to exchange folks since from time to time, the margin account will be "below zero" with an overdraft, and investors need to send in additional trading funds to move the balance back to our beloved positive territory! Otherwise, for its own safety, profitability, as well as regulatory requirements, the exchange will relentlessly liquidate the trading account to contain the potential damages.

The June WTI contract, which expired on May 19, fell about 18% to settle at $20.43 per barrel. This contract, which had been more actively traded, is a better reflection of the reality in the crude market. The July contract was roughly 11% lower at $26.18 per barrel as time is the best shielded armor to fend off the global oil glut's intrusion at this moment.

The international benchmark, Brent crude, which had already rolled to the June contract, settled 8.9% lower at $25.57 per barrel.

As Nassim Nicholas Taleb used to describe black swan risk, the rarely seen species of nonlinear risks, is coming from the interconnected overcomplexity of a convoluted intertwined system involved with multiple simple and irrelevant factors, which, at the special historical moments, all jump out simultaneously releasing their joined devastatingly crushing firepower to destroy the seemingly sturdy structure of the system, leaving people startled in disbelief.

It is a kind of resonance effect unleashing monstrously destructive power at the least prepared time.

In our focused case, the epic fall of WTI crude oil price is a nonlinear convoluted product of the COVID-19 pandemic, sapping demand of crude oil plagued by stubborn supply, WTI crude futures' idiosyncratic physical delivery mandate, and last but not the least, CME's cursory improvised trading system amendments. All these separate "strings" struck the same jarring chord on April 20, resonating vehemently.

On May 14, the International Energy Agency warned in its closely-watched monthly report that the world crude demand will drop by 21.5 million barrels a day in May, while crude-producing nations and companies will slash output by 12 million barrels a day, a level last seen in 1995. "Domestic economies have suffered a huge shock, many businesses have collapsed and unemployment has jumped to a level not seen since the 1930s," the Paris-based organization said.

1.4   Analyze the Epic Meltdown of WTI Crude Oil Futures from Pricing and Trading Perspectives

The early pricing theory of the futures markets, which goes back to John Keynes [13] [14] and Hicks [12], argued that the natural state of commodity markets is backwardation, and that buying discounted futures must reward speculators' risk capital with consistent profits. Even though the Keynes–Hicks argument was proposed long before energy futures even existed, it was subsequently extended to crude oil.

As the crude futures market was blooming and maturing, the market dominant role, however, was overtaken by financial participants. The new market regime became known as financialization, which reshaped the energy market. The new prevalent normal is the contango structure of futures term structure curve, that is, owning the crude futures will lead to consistently losing money.

Between 2003 and 2006, more and more index investors were classified as financial hedgers rather than speculators. Around that time, investors' ongoing demand for financial hedging started systematically and irreversibly exceeding crude producers' hedging needs.

Even though the words stay the same, the two camps' hedging executions are in contrast to each other. With the crude producers' shorting crude futures versus financial investors' hoarding crude futures, the wind has changed its direction, that development would inevitably influence the crude futures market, causing the net hedging exposure to change from negative to positive. Crude futures contract had gradually morphed from the hedging instrument for producers' inventory to a protection gear against geopolitical risks and spiking inflation on behalf of the financial investment army. Not surprisingly, the pricing and trading of crude oil futures have continuously evolved with the change of the market regimes, accentuated by the investment ambience and investor's sentiment.

In 1.4.1, I will start with some fundamentals of crude futures market, then proceed to adopt several analytical and empirical methods to analyze the chaotic trading melee of the crude meltdown in order to crack the riddle of negative oil prices.

1.4.1 *Fundamentals of WTI crude oil futures' pricing and trading*

In modern derivative pricing frameworks, riskless arbitrage and the substitute portfolio, which could be traded without major constraints, lay the solid foundation for its later buoyant developments. The ideas of replication and long/short arbitrage help determine the optimal theoretical pricing in an elegant manner.

However, the fundamental assets, such as stock, bond, foreign exchange, and crude oil's fair value pricing, don't enjoy the same advantages to obtain a down-to-the-earth solution due to the lack of comparable counterparts.

Instead, fundamental analysis, technical analysis, and statistical analysis have been engaged in an earnest effort to pin down a reliable and satisfactory result.

In finance textbooks, in the framework of the modern asset pricing theory, a security's market price is decomposed into two critical parts: one is along the path blazed by Warren Buffet's academic mentor in Columbia University, Benjamin Graham, whose masterpiece "Security Analysis" established the protocol of fundamental analysis of book value and mechanism of discounted cashflow, the milestone and stepping stone for modern finance.

The second part is the sentiment-based psychological price; a valuation derived from human's feelings, the so-called "bubble" emotion part.

In recent years, Behavioral Finance and Behavioral Economics have rapidly gained ground and popularity, and investors have started to understand more about human beings' temperaments, subjective feelings, and their important bearings on the security pricing process.

A variety of psychological experiments have been conducted either in academic labs or in semi-real market environments, they all ended up with the similar results: under drastic market stresses, investors won't make random cognitive mistakes; they will make "consistently predictable" mishaps. That is, investor's behaviors are converging to the universal stressful patterns.

Besides the universal stress mode, the other two most commonly shared biases are over-confident and over-pessimistic patterns, which drive the greed and fear modes of investment sentiment, and the switching of the emotions help formulate the market cycles.

Every security or asset will bring in both potential profits and risks, or damages. Its overall pricing will be a combination of both conflicting forces. A negative price is screaming loudly that the expenses, costs, or risks overpower the collective future expectation of positive cash flows.

For the psychological add-on portion, a weighted average of the whole market sentiment pool towards this security will provide the desired yardstick. While the positive psychological value add-on means that everyone is yearning for it, negative add-on just means that nobody is interested.

To adopt the above pricing framework into our analysis of the negative crude settlement mark, -37.63, we would like to single out four major contributing components for the ease of our ensuing discussion:

- the saggy economic fundamentals and grimmest forecast;
- enormous unease, anxieties, and psychological uncertainties fermented among investors;
- the rapidly rising physical shipping and storage cost; and
- diminishing short-term expected economic profits.

At normal times, the last item is the major driving force of making the precious commodity asset float above the zero line, while the first three factors are kept in check for not being too dragging or uncooperative.

For example, the world economy was previously growing steadily, albeit in a slow, crawling mode, but now it is in a complete shut-down and stalling mode, which leads to the second aspect: people would not have been worrying gravely about the future previously. For the third dimension, under normal circumstances, buoyant crude demand and high turnovers would leave more oil tanks empty, effectively pushing down the storage costs with a moderate expectation of short-term profits.

But, this dismal April, everything was ruined as the crude market was imbued with strongly depressive and despondent sentiments.

While dumbfounded, the oil price's plunging into negative territory didn't functionally mean that oil companies were en masse having to pay people to take away their products. Rather, it meant that financial market players who had created financial instruments to bet on the price of crude oil were having to pay hefty penalties to extricate themselves from deals they no longer wanted to be in and fled in a frenzy by all means.

Eyeballing the obnoxious negative WTI crude settlement price, a flock of investors spelt out a conspiracy theory, suspecting that behind the scenes, there were a bunch of rogue traders who pulled the wool over people's eyes, or to put it categorically, what just happened was nothing but a trading manipulation. Well, there are ample reasons to believe so: the malfeasances of market manipulation have bedeviled commodity markets since the dawn of futures trading and scandals have broken out sporadically. However, so far, nothing filthy has been confirmed yet, that is, a mentality of "no news is good news!"

Among the investors who avidly traded NYMEX WTI crude futures contracts, a broad rule-of-thumb classification is as follows:

Hedgers use WTI crude futures to minimize the damaging impact of potentially adverse price moves on the value of their oil-related assets. This camp includes a broad cross-section of energy companies, such as oil exploration and production companies, refiners, distributors, as well as import/export firms.

Speculators wield the power of WTI crude futures to gamble on their speculative views of the direction of oil prices. This tribe comprises many voracious hedge funds and covetous trading individuals.

Another interesting classification schema comes from Andrei Shleifer and Lawrence Summers' well-known paper "The Noise Trader Approach to Finance" [3]. Summers was the former US Treasury Secretary, former President of Harvard University, and a renowned productive economist.

In their enlightening paper, all enthusiastic market participants belong to two groups: a minority, in the two authors' language, "arbitrageurs", or in more mediocre mundane articulation, "the smart money". They always make rational level-headed decisions about trading and investments and have the upper hand of trading information. Their mission is to effortfully steer the course of traded prices towards the underlying asset's fundamental fair value beacon through their meticulously calculated arbitrage executions.

Their counterparty, as the majority, deemed as the "noise traders" clan, will rely more upon their serendipitous feelings, sentiments, temperaments, likes, and dislikes to make investment decisions, and be subject to more systematic biases and cognitive misconceptions or illusions.

Another indispensable tool we will utilize is market microstructure analysis, which is mainly concerned with the trading price's formation and discovery, transaction cost, timing cost, trading information promulgation and disclosure, etc.

Within this framework, trading prices and trading volumes are the focal points of the study, as well as their underlying evolving intricate dynamics. Each individual's buy or sell orders sent to trading exchanges will create a certain degree of turbulence or disruption, which is categorized as a permanent trading impact or transient trading impact (short-term) based upon the balance of buying/selling trading liquidity status quo.

A permanent trading impact will move the security away from the currently traded price marks, while a transient trading impact just stirs up the volatile undulations around the traded price's extant equilibrium level.

What matters most during this fierce tug of war is the contrasting competing balances between long and sell or short trading volumes and structural layers, in trading liquidity's lingo, liquidity's breadth and depth.

In the next two subsections, I would like to move back to the penultimate day of WTI crude May contract expiry; rewind the half hour feverish and chaotic trading scenes from 2:00 p.m. to 2:30 p.m.; closely scrutinize through the lens of market microstructure analysis, Summers' "noise trader approach" analysis, as well as Taleb's "minority rule" analysis, and, in particular, place laser-focus upon the last three minutes' most intensive hammering and pounding, delving into the minutiae of hectic trading in order to solve the intriguing conundrum, examining and figuring out how and why the WTI crude oil price stumbled into the uncharted negative territory.

I will illustrate and elucidate why, at this unprecedented historical juncture, the "smart money" failed to be the crude-saving superman.

1.4.2 *An analytical and empirical analysis of WTI crude futures price's epic fall*

Among the WTI crude futures traders, whoever wants to take the physical delivery of the oil contract must obtain an official license issued by CME in advance. The remaining investors, without the CME's designated license, were left with no other alternatives but to liquidate their current holdings by the expiration date.

To close their positions for the May contract, investors would have two options: trade either at a market price (TAM: trade at marker) during the normal trading hours on or before April 20, or at the final settlement price (TAS: trade at settlement), which is the volume-weighted average price (VWAP) based on the three minutes tick-by-tick transactions between 2:28 p.m. and 2:30 p.m. ET, on April 20, 2020.

To those who failed to close their positions at TAM by Monday, April 20, and who were willing to take physical deliveries, their contracts would be cleared at the prescribed TAS or at TAM on the final trading day, April 21, 2020.

The bottom-line, though, is that crude prices fell as the global economy was in the wane, demands for crude oil were nowhere to secure, and storage was out of the question. Crude traders needed to clear their deck before the closing bell rang resoundingly.

The overall selling coalition consists of two brigades: the speculative traders with no intention and willingness of handling physical oil, holding the speculative WTI crude futures long positions; or someone who had long positions and was originally planning to take physical delivery, but later realized they could not accomplish the daunting task, as there was nowhere to store the crude oil.

As of April 17, the unrolled WTI crude futures positions remained as high as 100,000 hands; 5–6 times that of previous contracts. So, it is reasonable to guess that the abnormally large open interests indicated a gluttonous accumulation of speculative positions since the real crude demand had been tapering off rapidly as the lockdowns were being enforced for all developed economies.

These speculative positions were undoubtedly owned by the "ambitiously greedy" investors, who were addicted to bottom-fishing. All they wanted was the shining greenbacks, not the fossil fuels.

As the clock was ticking, the expiration time was drawing near, trading liquidity was running off quickly, and speculators owing large bets on May futures contracts became increasingly desperate and despondent to unwind their holdings and square off their contracts before the music stopped.

The open interest on April 20 and April 21 was 13,044 and 2,427 contracts, respectively, and the average open interest for the last 10 days of the WTI May contract was about 50% more than that of last month's contracts, which manifested the overzealous speculative trading sentiments among the hordes of long position holders.

The crude futures volume traded on April 20 was about 150 million barrels, which was not an insignificant amount. But, a chunk of the big pile was in the camp of the passive TAS orders. This portion of trading volume would be carved out of the actively trading volumes as they wouldn't participate in the adrenaline-pumping tug-of-war normal trading hour game.

As seen from the exchange's trading data, about 60% of the trading volume was priced above $10. What that really meant was that desperately-needed trading liquidity was available if speculative bargain-hunting long-side traders innately took risk as their primary consideration, not the profitability before being pushed into the negative price abyss in the afternoon unless they were determined to chill out to take the settlement price as the last resort.

Soon entering into the most critical 30 minutes settlement period between 2:00 p.m. to 2:30 p.m., WTI crude oil futures price penetrated below the sentimental zero line at 2:08 p.m., roving into the negative price zone for the first time in the whole financial market history, never looking back. The all-time negative climax $-40.32 was attained at about 2:29 p.m., one minute before the closure of settlement period. Remarkably, the total trading volume with negative prices is merely 4,778 contracts, not a significant amount, while for the whole trading day of April 20, the trading volume associated with negative prices is 18,887 hands, versus the whole trading volume 150,000 hands.

Note that a very small portion of trading volumes, less than 1%, has helped cook up the WTI crude futures' settlement price, tormenting the WTI crude futures buyers mercilessly.

In the last subsection of this section, I would like to adopt Taleb's "minority rule" to decrypt the puzzle.

One interesting observation is that when WTI crude futures price teased the zero line, the short-sellers, who were normally the crude producers, shorting crude oil futures to curtail the crude price's downside risks, did not swarm in to cover the short positions promptly. Instead, they just shunned away, waiting patiently, watched the crude price piercing into the deep negative area, reaping in the unexpected windfalls, then covering the short positions and pocketing the originally shorted crude price plus something (the negative part of the crude futures price), per barrel.

From the psychological perspective, trading and public auction bear a close resemblance, in that the on-the-spot heady atmosphere would inevitably dictate and take control of an individual's mood and mentality, sabotaging one's logical reasoning capabilities, which explains why the final settled prices for the majority of auctioned arts or crafts are way higher than the estimated fundamental fair values as a thick layer of emotion premium has been smeared upon the antiquities. The same story for the trading market under stress, too much emotion is at stake.

The zero price bears a tremendous sentimental and economic importance to human beings, and it has been deeply and firmly seared into everyone's sacred religion-like belief framework, untouchable and unarguable. It is the holy watershed to separate our normal perceptive world and another unfathomable world. Watching the

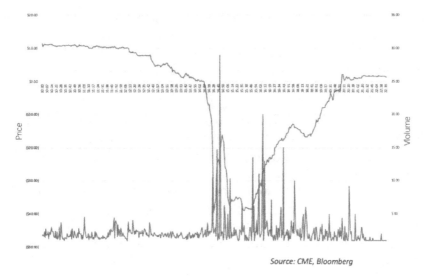

Source: CME, Bloomberg

Fig. 1.2. WTI crude futures trading price and volume.

crude futures price inching towards zero, those speculative traders endured enormous amount of emotional pressure.

It was literally a trading run as speculators were stampeding and rushing for the exit, simultaneously joined by investors who failed to secure the physical delivery for whatever reasons. They were vehemently vying for the trickling liquidity for their lifelines to survive this centennial trading squeeze.

Using our fundamental versus sentiment price framework, the depressive sentiments were so overwhelming that they just totally overpowered the fundamental side and exuberant irrationality started burgeoning. The eerily annoying negative price for the WTI crude futures contract was merely a market stress barometer for the nasty "crude oil run", a distorted fire-sale price, not a reliably authoritative dollar mark for fossil fuel any more.

The June WTI futures contract closed on April 20 at a positive $20 per barrel and had a volume of about 1 billion barrels of oil that day, much more than that of the May contract. So, for WTI, that was a more representative price from the classical financial pricing perspective.

To make this awful situation worse, there were multiple single sell orders issued from the passive investment index funds that couldn't participate in the physical delivery, and must be completed in the last two days, resulting in a natural multi-order overcrowding.

Since the accurate and detailed data about WTI crude traders' profile is not handily available, all ensuing discussions are put forward on a reasonable and justifiable basis which will constitute the founding axioms or basic assumptions for my analysis.

In an effort to improve the ivory-tower-flavored *Efficient Market Hypothesis* (*EMH*), Shleifer and Summers proposed the "Noise Trader Approach" as a much more realistic means to peek into the dynamics of capital markets.

The security's price would be driven by fundamentals (public information, such as news, announcements, etc.) and investors' sentiments. Both are closely correlated. If investors make their investment decisions solely based upon fundamentals, they are said to be "rational" without a tiny bit of personal preferences and emotions involved.

Noise traders are subject to a variety of cognitive biases such as overconfidence, herd behavior, survival bias, representativeness, heuristic, etc. So, the collective demand from their side could erroneously deviate from the authentic fundamental asset value due to their overreacting tendencies.

The role of an arbitrageur is to poke the bubble before it swells too big, correct their misconceptions, and pull the asset's price back to where the fundamental value should stay by conducting riskless or limited risk arbitrage trading.

In a normal market setup, both groups offset each other to reach a perfect stable equilibrium until new market information arrives to nudge trading markets towards the next balancing point.

But when arbitrageurs are under tremendous pressure, presented with only limited opportunities, their countering forces weaken and peter out quickly. The crowd of noise traders takes the helm, leading the course, and their (homogeneous) demands will overwhelmingly drive asset pricing processes. Fundamentals will succumb to sentiments and emotions, bubbles start building up.

In Shleifer and Summers' paper, they mentioned "implication of positive feedback trading" schema, where arbitrageurs, instead of betting against heady noise traders, will jump upon the same bandwagon with noise traders, riding with their overshooting zeal and unfounded complacency to beat them and profit. The world-famous macro arbitrageur George Soros was quoted as saying, "The key to success was not to counter the irrational wave of enthusiasm about conglomerates, but rather to ride this wave for a while and sell out much later."

If we adopt the above method to check out the April 20 crude tumbling, most of the game players in the fleeing crowd, put into Shleifer and Summers' proposed trading market landscape, belong to the "noise trader" category. By definition, they are much easier under the influence of emotions, sentiments, and temperaments.

And to accommodate the draconian WTI crude trading ambience, a more appropriate name should be "the implication of negative feedback trading", where the speculative noise traders and a portion of physical delivery apostates were so determined to liquidate their futures contracts and get away from the cumbersome and costly physical settlement.

They were willing to wholeheartedly push down the crude futures' nominal value into negative territory as far as the urgently sought-after trading liquidity would be emerging, with one caveat that the negative price was not worse than the physical storage and shipping costs. They wouldn't hesitate to grab the next lower bid, breathing a sigh of relief.

As I mentioned in the earlier section, the trading volume below the zero price was very limited, and the few dangling bids were all from short sellers covering trades. Short sellers were not that enthusiastic, knowing that the long side was desperately seeking any available trading liquidities.

In the last half of the century, asset pricing theory started from the landmark capital asset pricing model (CAPM) setup, evolved into the more flexible and powerful Kenneth Arrow and Gérard Debreu's complete equilibrium economy model, which still inherits a lot of optimal logical reasoning that is not fully attested by real markets. The no-arbitrage-pricing framework stepped into the limelight, which relaxed those unrealistic stringent assumptions materially, with more attached emphasis and focus upon existing market's trading activities, became prevalent.

From the early days of commodity futures trading, the business of storing provided the much-needed bridge connecting the present and future allocation of resources. The way this is done in practice is via the "carry trade". The pivotal link between the spot and future price is the financing cost and storage cost and more elusive "convenience yield", which measures the perceptive premium of holding the physical during a special period of time to avoid the so-called "short squeeze" [15].

Here, to fathom the twists and turns behind crude futures' negative price formulation, we are more prone to taking the no-arbitrage-pricing thread with the fierce head-to-head competition between snapping up the plunging traded crude price versus taking the heavy toll from crude's storage and shipping side if still available.

Some might argue that storage and shipping cost shouldn't be mingled with the orthodox putative asset pricing, but an obvious counterargument will be the well-known formula for gold's futures' price, which has the explicit storage cost as part of the pricing considerations.

So, my point is that, for this centennial black swan moment, the negative crude price won't reduce our glorious sacred asset pricing edifice to ashes and ruining everything. Instead, it just puts a tiny dint or a scratch on the shining glassy front door. Some kind of maintenance work will be engaged to fix the issue, then all will resume to operate with normal rituals.

Zero price, meaning for free, used to be everyone's favorite pick, but, at this critical juncture, it lost its magical attracting power faced with the unprecedented economic and social lockdowns, a cascading oversupply of crude oil, and a disheartening gloomy outlook.

The aforementioned futures market's short squeeze has occurred quite a few times in history, but this time the wind changed its blowing direction as what unfolded on April 20 was categorically a "long squeeze."

Short-sellers were fully aware that the trading liquidity was drying up like water in a desert. Given the exposed TAS orders parking upon the transparent open-book, from the market's microstructure analysis perspective, it was an open secret that the short side could easily nudge the jittery shaky market with a minimal amount of trading capital and order volumes, but profit hugely. That is an utterly anti-fragile game, according to Nassim Nicholas Taleb, the famed black swan thinker.

Short-sellers could only start the new positions above the zero price, not below, since it is operationally impossible to short at a negative price, which would induce a slew of counterintuitive baffling conundrums for trading executions.

From that point, it must be true that all the selling under the water was initiated by speculative traders and their allies who were urgently escaping, not from baneful short-sellers.

To be unequivocally clear, at normal times, to short a security near zero price is a highly dangerous, self-destructing move, if not suicidal, since zero price has been the faithfully supporting cornerstone from the inception of the financial market. This has been deeply instilled into every trader's mindset, and to challenge it will be sacrilegious.

But, not at this juncture, because from CME April 15's innuendo regarding the negative price compliant trading system update, the last palpable obstacle was completely removed, and Pandora's box was wide open. Only the subjective sentimental barrier was still lurking around, waiting to be smashed and shattered, so people could get unshackled, free from the century-old restraints.

If one trader initiates a short position near zero price, assuming that the short seller is holding the physical crude, then, at most, what he would suffer is the storage and shipping expenses, ignoring the tiny modicum of shorting proceeds. Then the risk profile for this tempting trade is self-evidently worth trying.

To be fair, the trader did not know for sure the crude futures would plunge to the unforeseeable $−40 level, but the undeniable advantage is that the cost of trial error stays small, while potential profits are irresistibly attractive, a perfect anti-fragile set-up.

With the above hypothetical synthesis, it sounds very plausible that the vicious selling got started from the speculator tribe. When the crude futures price closed in on the zero landmark, watching and sensing the fatigue and hesitation of the speculators' unloading, short sellers just stepped in to lend a "graceful helping" hand to dispel the WTI crude futures price out of positive zone to wade into the negative quagmires.

This hammered the last nail into the coffin, completely unrooting the lingering illusion of zero price support. The shattering of upheld beliefs rekindled the momentum of selling in a fast and furious manner.

As soon as the symbolic zero price was violated, the negative vicious cycle moved into a self-accelerating, self-reinforcing mode. Noise traders gained the upper hand over arbitrageurs, and sellers' unwavering determination and over-pessimistic sentiments permeated the crude trading market. Arbitrageurs sensed the palpable tensions and despairs, clearly receiving the profound negative feedback of the frenetic selling from the speculators, just as elucidated by George Soros: arbitrageurs wouldn't fight against this surging tsunami, they would prefer to join the liquidating army to ride the negative tidal wave charging downside. Now, three different teams marched in the same direction.

1.4.3 Nassim Nicholas Taleb's minority rule applied to WTI crude futures trading

In this subsection, I would like to adopt one new-fangled approach "minority rule", which is borrowed from Nassim Nicholas Taleb's book *Skin in the Game: Hidden Asymmetries in Daily Life* to illustrate the WTI crude futures trading rout.

In the book, Taleb presented a unique perspective: the most intolerant wins, while the stubborn minority dominates and prevails.

In the whole ensemble, a minutely small portion, say, 3–4% of the whole population, makes their preferences prevalent among the whole group. The evidences abound: scientific discoveries, development of technology, society's advancement, progression of democracy, and food selection all demonstrate the validity of its truthfulness.

In the trading world, the market is really dominated by a minority of strongly opinionated intolerant investors, in the sense that they either like or dislike the security ardently compared with other average investors with much calm temperaments and apathetic attitudes.

According to Taleb's theory, it is the small group of emotional advocators or haters who move the security's price, blazing the path and charting the course, with the majority of mediocre crowds following their footsteps.

Modern accounting rules mandate that for any securities traded on markets, the mark-to-market closing price will be used as the security's universal fair value. That is, whoever has traded the security, in Taleb's lingo, the investor has skin in the game, placing themselves into the trading pit; facing the possible adverse impacts, risks and losses; and at the same time earning the power and right to determine the final price.

Despite the camp of active trading investors being outnumbered easily by the hesitant onlooker side, this stubborn minority really coerces the more compliant compromising majority to follow their lead and commands.

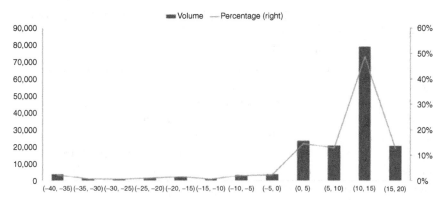

Fig. 1.3. Distribution of WTI crude futures trading volume associated with price.

Actually, if someone doesn't execute any trade for one business day, it is tantamount to placing a passive TAS order for the security and obtaining the auctioned closing print, instead of the last three minutes' VWAP. They literally forfeit an option of participating in the game to nail down the mark-to-market closing price. Doers have successfully enforced their wills on the non-doers.

To facilitate our detailed analysis, the April 20's trading price and volume data have been plotted into a distribution chart with the corresponding trading volume displayed at each discernible price level, as seen from Figure 1.3. The association between the two factors unearths some interesting facts and connections.

On the raucous trading floor, there is one well-known saying among the defiant brutal-force traders: do not care about what one says, only care about what one does. The implication is that if trading data are available, the hidden motivations, innate thoughts, or emotions could be figured out from the trading data analysis, a fascinating game of purpose guessing!

The WTI crude oil futures' price volume distribution diagram sends out the strongest signal that nobody could afford to ignore. From the chart, over 80% of trading volume occurred in the positive price zone, which corroborates Duffy's claim. More than 50% falls into the $10 and $15 price bracket, only about 10% of trading occurred in the negative price zone, and less than 1% of the total trading volume was executed near the bottom below $−35. Nevertheless, only this tiny minority of crude futures trades set the flabbergasting negative mark for the WTI futures settlement price.

A large quantity of TAS orders piled upon the NYMEX's open-book, which left their fates to be decided or manipulated by the active trading minority. The formerly-advocated conveniences and transparency of TAS now morphed into vulnerability and potential risks.

Henceforth, a handful of desperate selling traders, unquestionably a minority of the WTI crude trading party, with their back-to-the-wall desperation, dashed out to launch the fierce selling campaign, pushing the crude futures' price lower and lower. The TAS crowd, the silent subordinate majority, escaped the life-or-death battlefield, yielding the control to the intolerant minority.

Another observation, is that the WTI crude trading price and volume chart looks quite similar to a typical Pareto Power Law distribution curve with the long tail extended on the left-hand side, with the tip of that (traded price between $-40 to $-35) pinning down the critical TAS.

As emphasized by Taleb, Pareto Power Law stands in stark contrast with the more popular but misleading Gaussian Distribution, as the statistics mean does not provide a meaningful and useful indicative value for the whole distribution, with a predominating majority of the collection staying below the "representative" mean, and a tiny minority huddling at the highly compressed tailing part of the distribution, remotely putting everything at the clan's disposal. Minority overpowers the massive majority.

1.5   Passive Investment ETF and WTI Crude Oil Futures

The popularity of passive index funds is underpinned by the philosophy that if one couldn't beat the market index, then one is better off just embracing it and staying on the same side of the market.

Dictated and propelled by the Efficient Market Hypothesis (EMH), the passive investment and ETF industry exploded and burgeoned into a full-fledged almighty behemoth, flexing muscles at the debilitating active management industry.

2020 is deemed to be a milestone year for passive investment, since it is the first time in the whole financial history that passive

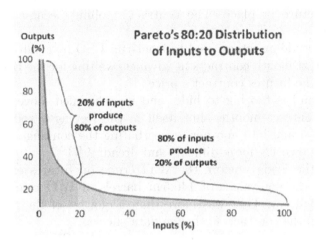

Fig. 1.4.   Pareto Power Law distribution.

investment has dethroned active investment and ETF will catch up with passive index funds by the AUM yardstick.

Given its prominence and strategic importance, crude oil ETF has experienced an explosive growth, seeing its AUM swells furiously. As crude oil prices plummeted in April, USO took it on the chin, and its short-selling interests soared [6].

The seemingly simple and transparent ETF products have attracted a huge crowd to jump on the bandwagon. However, deep beneath the polished surfaces lies the dirty nasty truth of the rolls of futures trading. USO invests in the front month WTI crude futures contract to maintain the needed spot oil price exposure. Of course, the exposure could be going in either direction.

USO used TAS contracts when conducting grand-scale purchases, which ensured that even if contracts were purchased throughout the day, the fund ends up settling at VWAP around the close. Buying TAS contracts is a way of signaling that you are uninformed, which thereby mitigates the price impact of your trades. The issue is, the market can still exploit the other side of the trade.

The most notorious example of such abuse is a manoeuvre known as "banging the close", which the high-frequency trading firm Optiver had been indicted for doing in 2008.

The USO fund's open derivative positions dominate front-month open interest with a loss-inducing super contango crude futures term structure in place. The contract's rolling became evidently gameable.

Other crude investors tried to front-run USO by stealthily piling into the next month contracts in advance, waiting for the rising tides to lift up the futures contract's price.

USO fund is too big to hide, and its scheduled moves between different contract months shot itself in the feet as it rolled out of one position and into another, exacerbating the contango situation, making its own life more difficult and dreadful [7].

As of the Friday before the WTI crude oil futures expiry, the fund held the equivalent of 146.5 m barrels of WTI crude futures for June delivery. That was more than a quarter of the total open interests in the contract, exchange data showed.

To mitigate the potential risk exposures, NYMEX laid out regulation rules imposing "accountability levels" of 10 m barrels equivalent for most US crude futures contracts, above which traders could be ordered to reduce their position to control the inventory risk.

The carnage in the front month WTI crude futures contract shed light on the true colour of those exchange-traded products (ETPs) clad with the veneer of low risk, unparalleled trading convenience, and ample liquidity to gain the exposure to crude oil price movements. The situation was best illustrated by one of Warren Buffet's most famous quotes: "You only find out who is swimming naked when the tide goes out."

USO was the fourth most actively traded ETF in US on Monday morning, April 20, with more than half a billion dollars changing hands before lunchtime in New York, as the WTI crude futures plummeted.

Usually, the TAS market is fairly balanced between sellers and buyers. But the May WTI crude contract was no doubt an exception. Big players had already left the battlefield, completed the position rolling, and TAS was being offered at larger and larger discounts to the settlement price throughout the day.

Increasingly nervous sellers pushed the discount out until it reached its maximum daily limit soon after 14:00 EST and TAS trading was consequently closed by CME. Reaching this limit bumper, set at 10 cents, was unprecedented for TAS, which normally trades at a maximum of 1 or 2 cents above or below the settlement price.

The forced closure of TAS trading signaled a huge liquidity balance gap, which led the few remaining traders to become more agitated, because now long positions could not be liquidated using TAS. They had to resort to the tumultuous open market. 77,076 contracts were executed in TAS before the shut-down.

In contrast, it was a tiny portion of contracts — closer to 10,000 lots, or 10 million barrels of oil, got thrown into the bloodbath of the open market, and again the minority wreaked havoc upon the collective. Taleb's "minority rule" prevailed and powered through.

Before the expiry, the May WTI contract had already made headlines by setting record contango levels as the May/June spread widened to -7/bbl. This reflected the state of the physical market, where storage at Cushing, Oklahoma, the physical delivery hub for the WTI contract, was becoming full.

However, on April 20, the May/June spread got swollen to -60/bbl during the settlement window, before narrowing just a few hours later to around -21/bbl and then expiring the next day at -1.56. All the while physical storage remained virtually unchanged.

The seemingly safe and simple TAS orders have been heavily utilized by passive investment funds to smooth out the crude price's volatility. Given the gargantuan size of those passive index funds and ETFs, they have snatched the lion share of the whole liquidity pie, which aggravated the trading liquidity's fragile situation and made it even worse. TAS trading's shutdown left speculative traders with only one way out: heady reckless selling, and a bloody massacre ensued.

To close the circle, the last three minutes' downtrodden prices interspersed with a tiny amount of trading volume strove to produce the negative settlement price for crude futures. As a returned favor, it would be applied to the heap of TAS orders.

1.6   Conclusion

In this chapter, we adopted both "noise trader approach" and "minority rule" frameworks and methodologies to analyze the possible causes behind the phenomenal debacle of the May WTI crude futures contract; for either positive or negative crude prices, a fundamental plus sentiment analysis approach has been employed in an attempt to crack the secret code of the crude futures' price rout.

Both analytical and empirical methods are utilized to help reconcile the stark contrast between the elegant classical economics pricing theory and jaw-dropping cruel reality.

The troublesome negative oil price, once considered unfeasible, is now a real possibility, and has turned traditional assumptions about risk management in the oil market on their heads, smashing investor's confidence and creating yet more woes for the embattled global oil industry [8].

However, as advocated by the famous Austrian philosopher Karl Popper, any science subjects should be falsifiable on the basis that the new emerging evidence debunks the existing general faithful beliefs, throwing everything we take for granted off track. The falsification process will make the subject or belief become more robust, reliable, and endurable.

For the rarely seen negative crude price fiasco, it will follow in the same vein. As the global market and economy advance, people will be embracing more unthinkable, inconceivable, unfathomable, and unknown unknowns.

Even though the crude prices moved from positive to negative, we shall turn the negative back to the positive, following the line of thinking advocated by Nassim Nicholas Taleb in his book *Antifragile*. The fragility exposed by the crude futures market will be taken as a good opportunity to reassess our highly complex and interconnected financial system to fix the loopholes and strengthen futures market's resilience capabilities, thus gain the power of antifragility.

I would like to use what I wrote on the sleepless night of April 20 while watching the live plunging of WTI crude oil futures as the closing statement of the chapter:

Live longer to see the unforeseen, expect the unexpected, contemplate the unthinkable, rationalize the improbable, contain the intolerable, overpower the invincible, smash the incomprehensible, and last but not the least, have a strong brave heart to embrace this befuddling, uncertain, and insane world.

Your Choices will Make You Who You Are!

References

[1]   E. Huang and P. Stevens, An oil futures contract expiring Tuesday went negative in bizarre move showing a demand collapse, CNBC. Published on April 19, 2020 and updated on April 20, 2020.

[2]   https://www.cmegroup.com/content/dam/cmegroup/notices/clearing/2020/04/Chadv20-160.pdf.

[3]   A. Shleifer and L. H. Summers, The noise trader approach to finance by. *Journal of Economic Perspectives*, 4(2) (Spring): 19–33, 1990.

[4]   A. Powell, Negative Oil: What is behind the Negative Oil Price? April 21, 2020.

[5]   N. Willing, Oil futures explained: Your ultimate guide to WTI and Brent. Capital.com.

[6]   I. Kaminska, Is USO an actively managed fund now? Marketwatch. com, April 28.

[7]   D. Sheppard, Sub-zero oil prices threaten big losses for ETF investors. *Financial Times*, April 21, 2020.

[8]   I. Bouchouev, Negative oil prices put spotlight on investors, Risk.net, April 30, 2020.

[9]   M. DeCambre, The oil 'futures market worked to perfection,' says head of world's largest exchange of crude's historic plunge to $0, Marketwatch.com, April 22, 2020.

[10] An analysis of the 20-minute span that changed the oil market forever, Bloomberg News, April 26, 2020.

[11] L. M. Goodman, Inside the Biggest Oil Meltdown in History on April 20, chaos reigned in oil markets. Here's what happened, May 6, 2020.

[12] J. R. Hicks, *Value and Capital*, Oxford University Press: Oxford, UK, 1939.

[13] J. Keynes, Some aspects of commodity markets. *Manchester Guardian Commercial*, 1923.

[14] J. A. Keynes, *Treatise on Money*, Vol. II, Macmillan: London, UK, 1930.

[15] H. R. Stoll, Commodity futures, and spot price determination and hedging in capital market equilibrium. *Journal of Financial and Quantitative Analysis*, 14(4): 873–894 1979. doi: 10.2307/2330460, [Web of Science ®].

Chapter 2

The Better Way for CME's Execution: Based on the Perspective of Industry's Best Practice Rule*

Rongbing Huang[†] and George Yuan[‡,§,¶,||,]**

[†]*Deloitte China, 21F Bund Center, Shanghai 200002, China*
[‡]*Business School, Sun Yat-sen University,*
Guangzhou 510275, China
[§]*Center for Financial Engineering,*
Soochow University, Suzhou 510275, China
[¶]*Shanghai Lixin University of Accounting and Finance,*
Shanghai 201209, China
[||]*Business School, Chengdu University, Chengdu 610106, China*
[**]*george_yuan99@yahoo.com*

Abstract

The event of Chicago Mercantile Exchange's (CME) negative oil clearing price on April 20, 2020, in which commodity futures traded in a negative range, is significant to the financial community worldwide. Through discussions of the so-called "best practice" rule for professional behaviors in practice with a number of examples and standards established by professional organizations, it seems that a better option for CME's execution would have been to first seek feedback from stakeholders internationally within a reasonable transition period before implementing the proposed new trading (or updating) rule that came into effect in the month of April 2020.

Keywords: Best practice, consultation process, transparency, conflicts of interest, transition period

---

*Please note that the views expressed here are those of the authors, and do not represent the affiliated company or universities. The corresponding author is George Yuan.

2.1 The Impact of Negative Oil Clearing Price Event on April 20, 2020

At 2:30 a.m. EDT (Eastern Daylight Time) on April 20, 2020, the price of West Texas Intermediate (WTI) crude oil futures contract delivery on May 1 (denoted by "WTI2005", with the last trading day on April 21, 2020) trading on the Chicago Mercantile Exchange (CME) plunged to a negative value, falling more than 300% at the closing trading time and closing at a settlement price of -37.63/barrel, a first in the history of futures pricing in CME.

The negative price of crude oil futures has brought a huge shock for the market. The crude oil market has never seen a negative oil price before, and the emergence of negative oil prices has refreshed investors' awareness of risks in the futures market. At the same time, the emergence of negative oil prices led to a huge loss for the bulls holding the contract. A typical example that has attracted widespread market attention is that negative oil prices have caused heavy losses to Bank of China's crude oil treasure customers. Bank of China's "Crude Oil Treasure" (commonly referred to as "Yuan You Bao" by most investors) is a type of financial product issued to individual investors based on the WTI's crude oil futures contracts. The event of negative oil price caused Bank of China's WTI crude oil contracts to settle at -37.63/barrel, resulting in a "short position" and huge loss to both the investors and the Bank.

2.2 Key Factors Leading to Negative Oil Price Events

There have been a lot of news and analysis on the factors causing the negative oil price of WTI crude oil futures, which are briefly summarized as follows (see more from Yuan [12]):

- The sharp drop in crude oil demand caused by the economic shutdown due to the global spread of COVID-19, when combined with the inability to halt crude oil production (closing oil wells would cause huge losses), led to a market that over-supplied with an insufficient demand, resulting in negative prices.
- Significant increase in delivery cost: the supply of crude oil exceeded the demand, the storage cost of crude oil was greatly increased due to insufficient storage space, and the logistics cost of

crude oil transportation all led to a significant increase in delivery cost. Traders sold futures contracts to avoid spot delivery, which caused prices to collapse.

- The negative price was caused by the lack of market liquidity at a special time and took advantage of the new rule that was quickly brought into effect by CME in the month of April 2020.
- Possible market manipulation: short sellers took advantage of the special time atmosphere and asymmetrical information of revised trading rules to hunt bulls without any protection, resulting in a negative price.

In regards to the negative oil price, as will be discussed in the next section in relation to the so-called "best practice" rule in the financial industry, we believe that the proposed modification and quick implementation of CME's trading rules were key factors in promoting the negative oil price. In general, there is no problem in adjusting or updating new trading rules or functions for its information technology (IT) trading system, but the quick proposal and implementation of CME's new rule in such a short time created heavy shocks in the international community. The decisions made by CME during this event are against basic professional behavior as CME, one of the leading exchanges in the public sector, plays a significant international role and neglected the "best practice" rule by failing to implement a transition period or seek feedback from stakeholders for its new proposal to allow "negative oil price" on the IT trading system.

2.3 Applying the Best Practice Rule is the Core Requirement for Evolution of Corporate Governance in Practice

By following Stafford (see [1]), we know that a decade of economic turmoil, regulatory reform, and technological change has reshaped how corporations must do business today. Yet for directors, governance often proceeds in "business as usual" mode, so how can boards make use of new board mandates and technology to regain their oversight edge? In particular, it is always a challenging job to ensure transparent information and action in corporations' new reform policies to implement new regulatory requirements or compliances; to code new business processes or procedures; and to update or adjust any new trading rule for exchanges to public society, community, stakeholders, professional organizations, government/agencies, or related parties with a smooth transition in practice. These considerations are a key part of the evolution of corporate governance in practice.

Actually, during the evolution of corporate governance, **how** leaders understand and adapt governance to meet these new regulatory or compliance demands will in part determine how effective their companies are in the future. How companies approach corresponding new implementations and enforce regulatory compliance in corporate governance from the top-down (or bottom-up) so that their culture, technology, and processes fit better practices in compliance with industry standards, professional behavior, and ethics requirements is the so-called "best practice" rule in which corporate governance acts as a leading role model with industry benchmarks in practice.

In particular, those corporations, such as international exchanges, financial companies, and others with any nature of exposure to public communities, play a significant role as global financial intermediaries, by the nature of their businesses, and thus should subscribe to the "best practice" (rule) when it comes to implementing codes of professional integrity and ethics to act as role models in their practice.

Indeed, best practices are adopted by governments, too. For example, in order to conduct regulatory reform, the Australian government established the "best practice regulation handbook" in 2007 (see [2]); the government's goal was to enhance the regulatory framework with a focus on improving the quality of analysis applied to regulatory proposals through introducing a seven-step key concept called "Consultation Process".

On the other hand, in the professional industries for finance, trading, security, accounting, regulatory agency, and so on, each sector is always associated with the development of its "best practice" rule to all members with a focus on applying these rules as the baseline of their professional behaviors to maintain integrity in daily business. For example, since the establishment of the International Organization of Securities Commissions (IOSCO) in 1974, the body has conducted a number of guides for the best practice rules for its more than 200 members worldwide to follow-up or use as a guideline for their daily business behaviors in principle. One of IOSCO's recent guidelines is the so-called "CR03/2015" for *Mechanisms for Trading Venues to Effectively Manage Electronic Trading Risks and Plans for Business Continuity, Consultation Report* which was released in April 2015. On June 22, 2015, in response to this proposal ("CR03/2015") and IOSCO's assessment (see [3]), another global industry association WFE (World Federation of Exchanges), which represents more than 250 exchanges and CCPs (central counterparty clearing house) of all sizes worldwide, including CME group, commented on best practices in the area of risk management and business continuity by confirming a united goal to establish an environment which "[enabled] fair, orderly and transparent markets, and [reduced] systemic risk" by applying the best practice rule.

Another example is as follows: in 2013, IOSCO established the "19 Principles for Financial Benchmarks (Benchmarks)", which were endorsed by the Financial Stability Board as being the standards of best practice for Benchmarks administration. As the Federal Reserve Bank of New York is a component of the United States (US) Federal Reserve System and administers the Benchmarks for public policy purposes, the Federal Reserve Bank of New York is committed to administering the Benchmarks in a manner consistent with the 19 Principles (established by IOSCO) as "best practice" rules for the financial sector. From the 19 Principles, *No. 11 Principle on the Content of the Methodology, No. 12 Principle on the Changes to the Methodology*, and *No. 13 Principle on Transition* clearly explain how to structure a "transition period" by seeking feedback from stakeholders with a reasonable consultation time period if there are any changes or updates for issues such as "Changes to the Methodology, or Trading Methodology, or Adding Function" in practice — such as the updates executed by CME in April 2020.

In this way, both the International Federation of Accountants (IFAC) and Chartered Institute of Public Finance and Accountancy (CIPFA) also provide a good example on how to arrange the consultation process with a reasonable buffer transition time (from June 2013 to September 17, 2013) by seeking recommendations and suggestions for "Good Governance in the Public Sector — Consultation Draft for an International Framework" released in June 2013 (see [4]).

Of course, there are many other "best practice" rules established by IOSCO that are accepted by regulatory agencies and professional organizations; for example, "Prohibiting Market Manipulation" was adapted by US regulatory agencies of Commodity Futures Trading Commission (CFTC), and Securities and Exchange Commission (SEC) Regulation, too (see [5] for more related information).

Thus, it is crucial for the CME group, as members of WFE, to follow these best practices when introducing or updating new trading rules by planning for a consultation process with its stakeholders (indeed globally) by at least providing "transparent information" and allowing time for "translation period" to avoid "conflicts of interest" when applying or updating its function in the IT trading system. It seems that a better option for CME's execution would have been to first seek feedback from stakeholders internationally within a reasonable transition period before implementing the proposed new trading rules that became effective in the month of April 2020.

The action executed by CME in April 2020 sets up a bad example for the global exchange sector. In the next section, we elaborate by looking at other methods used by financial sectors under the same conditions of the COVID-19 strain since December 2019.

2.4 CME's Quick Action in Applying New Trading Rules Promoting the Occurrence of Negative Oil Price Events

2.4.1 *The timeline on CME's modification effectiveness of trading rules and the emergence of negative oil prices*

Due to the large-scale outbreak and intensification of the spread of COVID-19, the crude oil futures market increased in volatility; CME responded by raising the circuit breaker price threshold from 7% to 15% on March 19, 2020 (Eastern Time). On April 3, 2020, CME announced the "change for the code of the IT system to allow 'negative oil price' declarations and transactions to become effective from April 5 or April 8, 2020"; CME communicated with the CCPs and member units (also possibly including regulatory agencies of CFTC and SEC, too), while the market was repeatedly reminded of the possibility of negative oil price appearances. On April 15, 2020, CME conducted the function testing for its IT trading systems with negative price, and shared its testing report with the member units to verify what would happen to the market under negative oil prices. On April 20, there was a negative oil price on WTI2005 (crude oil futures contracts with maturity in May) and CME didn't intervene in the transaction; after the market closed on April 20 at 2:30 p.m. (Eastern Time), CME said that after the emergence of negative oil prices, the market operated normally. At 5:00 (EDT) on April 21, WTI2005 were finally pulled back to $10/barrel for delivery. After the negative oil price incident, in response to doubts in the market, CME responded on April 30, 2020 that the WTI2005 prices reflected the fundamentals of physical crude oil, and that they had notified the regulators and the market in advance before the WTI crude oil price fell to a negative value in early April so that customers could manage the risk in volatile prices while ensuring the convergence of futures and spot prices.

As we can see from the above timeline, CME modified the code of the IT system **on April 3, 2020**, to allow "negative oil price" declaration and transaction, and the code became effective **on April 5, 2020**. **The entire time span for CME to modify and implement the new trading rules[a] was only a couple of days — it is our opinion that this was definitely too short.** It was impossible to conduct any possible study on the impact of the changes in the trading rules or receive any opinions through a consultation process. CME's action to modify its IT trading system with a new function from the previous non-support of "price declarations below 0" to supporting "negative oil price" declarations and transactions falls under the categories of *No. 11 Principle on the Content of the Methodology* and *No. 12 Principle on the Changes to the Methodology* under the framework of the 19 Principles for best practices elaborated in the previous section; and thus, the action on *No. 13 Principle on* "Transition" should have been considered. Note that the modification of the trading rules (allowing for "negative oil price" declarations and transactions) is a major change in the trading mechanism; it would have been expected that the new trading rules would

---

[a]speaking loosely, "the updating the function of existing rule".

only take effect after a full impact assessment and complete consensus after consultations with stakeholders' opinions and feedback. On this topic, CME asserted that the possibility of trading negative prices for crude oil futures had been notified to the regulators and the market in advance before the price truly fell to a negative value, but this possibility was announced after the new trading rules had been officially adopted, and the negative prices appeared in a short period of time after the new rules had taken effect. We conclude that the action executed by CME in April 2020 set up a very irresponsible example for the global exchange sector.

2.4.2 *CME not applying best practice by planning the consultation process through a lack of disclosure and transparency of information which may have resulted in conflicts of interest*

The function of good governance in the public sector is to ensure that entities act in the public interest at all times consistent with the requirements of legislation and government policies, avoiding self-interest and, if necessary, acting against a perceived organizational interest (see [6]).

IOSCO's given principles for governance are intended to ensure that the public sector has appropriate governance arrangements in place in order to protect the integrity of the Benchmark determination process and to address conflicts of interest (see [6] or [7]).

Although the US Commodity Futures Trading Commission (CFTC) rules, which became effective on August 15, 2011, prohibit manipulation of commodity markets (see [5]), they cannot prevent traders from taking advantage of loopholes and information asymmetry for their own benefits. CME allowed such an opportunity because of its rapid implementation of new trading rules. The modification and quick enforcement of trading rules permitted parties to manipulate the market by using information asymmetry and led to the conflicts of interest between related parties. Shortly after the new rules came into effect, there was a negative oil price event, which seems closely linked to the asymmetric information misused among different related parties; although there is no evidence available, the lack of disclosure and transparency of information for the change in trading rule may have resulted in conflicts of interest for related parties involved in the negative price trading on April 20, 2020.

2.4.3 Significant changes in administrative regulations, rules, and trading mechanisms require extensive consultation

We would like to first point out that significant changes in administrative regulations, rules, and trading mechanisms require extensive consultation. It is a common practice in the industry to go through the consultation phase or to set up adequate transitional arrangements.

Based on best industry practices, the possible impact of the modification of the trading rules needs to be fully evaluated and disclosed. The changes to the rules and the possible impacts must be transparent to all related parties, and sufficient transition time is required before the rules come into effect, so that all related parties can adequately prepare for the change of rules and avoid information asymmetry among different related parties.

Significant changes in administrative regulations, rules, and trading mechanisms usually affect the interests of various stakeholders. It is common practice in the industry to set up a consultation stage or transition period to fully listen to feedback and also publish quantitative calculations or impact analysis for stakeholders to fully understand the possible impacts of the revised rules or mechanisms; after forming a consensus based on the feedback of various stakeholders, the changes would formally take effect.

Reforming the rules to follow good industry practices help avoid potential conflicts of interest as much as possible. For good practices in reform of rules, we can refer to the relevant literature (see [2]), which illustrate the regulatory reform process (see [8]) as we discussed in the previous section.

In the following example, we look to a similar situation affected by the spread of COVID-19 handled by the banking sector in which best practices allowed for a new translation period by the Basel Committee's Basel Agreement III market risk module. We also look to the example of the application of best practices by the International Accounting Standards Board (IASB) in dealing with the amendments to accounting standards to take effect.

Example 1: The revision of Basel III market risk module by the Basel Committee

After the financial crisis that was triggered by the subprime mortgage crisis in 2009, the Basel Committee discovered from the financial crisis that the original capital requirements of the banks' trading book were insufficient to absorb losses. The Basel Committee on Banking Supervision (BCBS) issued a revised opinion on market risk capital requirements (Basel 2.5). However, because the entire framework still had shortcomings, BCBS decided to comprehensively revise the capital requirements framework of the trading account and introduced the FRTB (Fundamental Review of the Trading Book: A Revised Market Risk Framework) to solicit feedback from various stakeholders. After several rounds of consultations and quantitative impact studies, FRTB finalized the draft in January 2019, and the Basel Committee formally published the "Minimum capital requirements for market risk", requiring banks to fully implement it by January 2022. From the solicitation draft published in 2012 to the formal finalization of the draft in 2019, FRTB has gone through several rounds of consultations and quantitative calculations, and has reserved corresponding transitional arrangements for the banks to fully implement (see [9]) with the specific timeline as shown in Fig. 2.1.

However, accounting for the outbreak of COVID-19 in December 2019 as it continues to spread around the world (even today as of August 12, 2020) and considering the virus's impact on the global banking system, the Basel Committee supervision agency **on March 27, 2020** postponed the implementation of Basel III for **one year until January 1, 2023** (see [10]). This is one typical example established by the Bank for International Settlements (BIS) on how to handle a transition period under duress of unexpected events in contrast to CME's reaction to the pandemic in April 2020 though

Fig. 2.1. Timeline of reform about Basel III's market risk.

under even more pressure than CME from the outbreak of COVID-19 in December 2019!

Example 2: The amendments to the International Accounting Standards Board (IASB) standards on financial instruments

The financial crisis in 2009 exposed the deficiencies of IAS 39–Financial Instruments: Recognition and Measurement (IAS 39) in the classification of financial assets, impairment provisions, and hedge accounting. IASB has revised the standard since 2009, and six consultation drafts, one supplementary document, and one discussion draft were issued successively. After six years of feedback and revision, it officially issued International Financial Reporting Standard No. 9 — Financial instruments (IFRS 9) in July 2014. From the reform of IAS 39 to the formal implementation of IFRS 9, IASB has gone through many rounds of consultations and revisions before its final iteration; in addition, the full implementation of IFRS 9 also sets a corresponding transition period (see [11]). This is another example of how to deal with the amendments to accounting standards before they take effect in practice.

2.4.4 *CME's lack of stakeholder feedback resulting in no consensus forming*

The stakeholders involved in the crude oil futures market in CME include crude oil producers (drillers, refiners, and physical crude oil shippers), crude oil demand parties, and investors (including institutional investors and retail investors, such as individual investors, ETFs, commercial banks' crude oil investment accounts for individual customers, and on-site and off-site funds for individual customers), the regulatory agencies such as CFTC, clearing companies, and third-party service agencies. These steps were remedial measures taken after the hasty coming into force of the new trading rules, a method inconsistent with the industry practice of fully consulting and forming a consensus among all stakeholders before the new rules come into force.

Although CME communicated and tested with clearing companies and member units after the new trading rules came into effect and prompted the possibility of negative oil prices, CME's stakeholders are not only clearing companies and member units but also individual investors and commercial banks' crude oil investment accounts for individual customers, and their comparative limited access to information, especially in allowing commodity futures to trade in a negative range, disrupting a common sense of previous trading cognition. It takes time for investors to understand the risks contained in the new rules. The new trading rules came into effect on April 5, and the negative oil price appeared on the market on April 20. This was different from CME's modification of the trading rules and its rapid effect, which led to a huge difference in risk perception of different stakeholders under the new trading rules. From April 20, we examine the event of negative pricing along with the time interval of oil prices and trading volume (see the volume in Table 2.1).[b] Due to asymmetric information, we see how different information allows certain traders to take advantage of new trading rules in a very short period of time, while other traders have not yet realized the huge risk under the new trading rules (instead of operating under the new risk from the trading rules modification, some traders operate under a cognitive bias towards the previous transaction risk until the market presents an extremely negative price). This reflects that the new trading rules came into effect too quickly with an absence of necessary consultations and transitional arrangements for adoption of the new rules. The modification and quick entry of the new trading rules greatly exacerbated the occurrences of the negative price.

2.5 Summary

The negative oil price event has brought unprecedented impact and shock to the financial market, which has refreshed the traders' understanding of the risk of the crude oil futures' market. Allowing commodity futures trading in a negative range breaks through the common sense of previous futures' market transactions and is a

---

[b]Please note that the trading data used in this table may be slightly different from others due to the difference of the time-buckets, time frequency, and related other criteria, but this difference will not impact the conclusion and question we address here.

Table 2.1. Trading volume on April 20, 2020.

Date	Trading volume	Trading volume with negative price	Last trading closing price	Proportion of trading volume with trading closing price determined on April 20	Proportion of negative prices traded on April 20
4/20/2020	247,947	4,814	−37.63	0.142%	1.94%

Trading volume in the last 3 minutes on April 20	Closing price based on the last 3 minutes of trading	Volume percentage of closing price determined in the last three minutes (based on three transactions) of April 20	All transactions with negative volume on April 20	Proportion of negative price on April 20	Trading volume on April 20
352	−37.63	0.142%	4,814	1.94%	247,947

Source: Bloomberg.

significant change in trading rules. Based on industry's best practices as discussed above, from the government to various professional organizations internationally in the field, significant changes in trading rules usually require fully seeking the opinions and feedback of stakeholders and setting a long transition period that allows for a full evaluation of the impact of significant changes in trading rules in which the changes and possible impacts are transparent to all related parties; this, along with a sufficient transition time before the rules come into effect, provides all related parties with preparation adequate for the implementation of the new rules and avoids information asymmetry among different related parties.

However, CME did not follow best practices by not planning a consultation process, lacking disclosure and transparency of information to stakeholders internationally, and allowing the new trading rules to take effect quickly. As a result, some traders did not fully understand the potential risks under the new trading rules. Although CME has communicated and tested with the clearing companies and member units after the new trading rules became effective, and prompted the possibility of negative oil prices, this is a remedy after the new trading rules have become effective. In view of the insufficient risk education under the new trading rules, different traders had different perceptions of the risks contained in the new trading rules. Some traders still carried the same risk bias cognition from before the modification of the trading rules over to the new rules. There is a big deviation which provides the space for some traders to use the new trading rules. Since the modification and quick implementation of these new trading rules was followed within half a month with the appearance of negative oil prices, we conclude that CME's modification of the trading rules took effect too quickly without properly consulting the feedback of various stakeholders and appropriate transitional arrangements, which to a large extent promoted the emergence of the negative oil price.

This negative oil price event has provided a vivid risk education course for market participants. When they participate in financial market transactions, market traders need to keep a high vigilance on the revision and quick entry into force of major market transaction rules, and have a full understanding of the risks involved.

The event of CME's negative oil clearing price on April 20, 2020, in which commodity futures traded in a negative range, is significant to the financial community worldwide, and even touches the fundamental issues of basic fair value of human rights by devaluation of labor's production (see [12] for more discussion in detail). By examining the so-called "best practice" rule for professional behaviors in practice, it seems that a better option for CME's execution would have been to first seek feedback from international stakeholders within a reasonable transition period before implementing the proposed new trading rule that became effective in the month of April 2020. Thus, as one of the most important financial intermediaries globally, CME should play a leading role by applying the best practices in financial industries, which is not how they acted in April 2020.

Before closing the discussion in this chapter, we like to recall that on May 7, 2020, the CFTC commissioner Mr. Dan M. Berkovitz stated, "The CFTC and the CME should continue working to analyze the causes of the divergence in the May contract. Based upon that analysis, CME and the CFTC should take whatever measures may be appropriate to ensure that trading in the WTI futures contract is orderly and supports convergence of the futures and physical markets." (see [13]) This is exactly one of the many fundamental issues we must face today after the event of April 20 with negative price happened, by understanding what went wrong with the current running engine operated by CME in practice.

The irony is that on August 13, 2020, CME made the following new announcement:

"Further to Clearing Advisory 20–171 dated April 21, 2020, CME Clearing will revert its options pricing and valuation methodology, currently based on the Bachelier model, effective for trade date on Monday, August 31, 2020. Products will transition from Bachelier back to Whaley or Black 76, depending on the products" (of 62 kinds of options, see [14] for more in details).

This action means that CME now only allows positive prices for underlying, so they (CME) moved back to positive (prices) from allowing negative prices on April 13, 2020 for underlyings. This was another bad behavior as the transition time allowed was only 17 days (including weekend time).

Finally, we would like to mention here that as of August 4, 2020, Bloomberg Business Week (see [15] for more details) reported that a small group of traders (called Vega Capital London Ltd.) in London made a fortune on oil's unprecedented plunge into negative territory (related to CME's movement by allowing negative prices in April 2020). They are now being scrutinized by regulators. Currently US Commodity Futures Trading Commission, the United Kingdom's Financial Conduct Authority, and CME Group Inc., owner of the Nymex exchange where the trading took place, are examining whether Vega's actions may have breached rules on trading around settlement periods and contributed to oil's precipitous fall, according to people with knowledge of the probes. Lets see what would come out soon.

References

[1] B. Stafford, The evolution of corporate governance. *The Corporate Board* (November/December), 10–13, 2015.

[2]   The Commonwealth of Australian Government: Best practice regulation handbook (available from www.regulatoryform.com), 2007.

[3]   CME Clearing. Testing opportunities in CME's "New Release" environment for negative prices and strikes for certain NYMEX energy contracts. Advisory #20–160, Advisory Notice, CME Group, April 15, 2020.

[4]   International Federation of Accountants (IFAC). Good governance in the public sector — Consultation draft for an international framework, (available from https://www.ifac.org/system/files/publicatio ns/files/Good-Governance-in-the-Public-Sector.pdf), June, 2013.

[5]   A. Lurton, W. Massey, and R. S. Fleishman, CFTC issues final rules prohibiting market manipulation. *Journal of Investment Compliance*, 12(4): 18–20, 2011.

[6]   International Organization of Securities Commissions (IOSCO). Principles for financial benchmarks (available from https://www.iosco.or g/library/pubdocs/pdf/IOSCOPD415.pdf), 2013.

[7]   International Organization of Securities Commissions (IOSCO). Statement of compliance with the IOSCO principles for financial benchmarks, 2020.

[8]   Australian Governments. Best practice guide for preparing regulatory impact statements (available from http://www.treasury.act.gov.au/ documents/regulatory_impact_statement_guide.pdf), 2003.

[9]   Basel Committee on Banking Supervision. Minimum capital requirements for market risk (see https://www.bis.org/bcbs/publ/d457.ht m), 2019.

[10] Basel Committee on Banking Supervision. Governors and heads of supervision announce deferral of Basel III implementation to increase operational capacity of banks and supervisors to respond to Covid-19, (available from https://www.bis.org/press/p200327.htm), 2020.

[11] IAS. IFRS 9 — Financial Instruments (available from https://www. iasplus.com/en/standards/ifrs/ifrs9).

[12] G. Yuan, (ed.), The fundamental challenge by CME's allowing negative trading price of crude oil future. In the book: The CME Vulnerability: The impact of negative oil futures trading, World Scientific Publishing, Singapore, 2020.

[13] D. M. Berkovitz, Statement of commissioner Dan M. Berkovitz on recent trading in the WTI futures contract before the energy and environmental markets advisory committee meeting, May 7, 2020 (available from https://www.cftc.gov/PressRoom/SpeechesTestimo ny/berkovitzstatement050720), 2020.

[14] CME Clearing. Transition Back to Whaley and Black 76 Options Pricing Methodology - Effective Trade Date August 31,

2020 (https://www.cmegroup.com/notices/clearing/2020/08/Chadv 20-320.html).

[15] L. Vaugham, K. Chellel, and B. Bain. London traders hit $500 million jackpot when oil went negative. Bloomberg Business week. August 4, 2020 (https://www.bloomberg.com/news/articles/2020-0 8-04/oil-s-plunge-below-zero-was-500-million-jackpot-for-a-few-lond on-traders).

Chapter 3

Impact of Negative Oil Price on Risk Measuring*

James Zhan

BMO Financial Group, Toronto, ON, M5X1A1, Canada
yi.zhan@bmo.com

Abstract

This chapter briefly discusses the impact of the recent negative West Texas Intermediate (WTI) oil price incident on the fundamental relationships between WTI futures and spot prices, options pricing, risk measuring, hedging strategy, and regulatory rules. It emphasizes the importance of promoting best practice in oil price-discovery, the robustness of valuation, risk modeling, and system development with improved rules and processes.

Keywords: Negative WTI futures price, negative WTI spot price, Black model, Bachelier model, VaR, CCR, FRTB

3.1 Introduction

Traditional options models assume underlying prices to be positive, but the oil's plunge below zero on April 20, 2020 for the first time in history has not only broken the co-movement relationship between West Texas Intermediate (WTI) futures price, spot price, and other oil products, but also the models that the institutions

---

*The views in this article belong solely to the author, and not necessarily to the author's affiliated employer, organization, or other group or individual.

rely on to calculate risks, including Greeks, Value-at-Risk (VaR), Counterparty-Credit-Risk (CCR), etc. for risk monitoring and regulatory capital calculation purposes. In what follows, I will briefly review the impacts on the fundamental relationship between futures and spot prices, WTI and Brent prices, options models, risk measuring, hedging strategy, as well as regulatory rules. Finally, lessons are learned to promote more sound price-discovery processes in oil pricing to maintain WTI's benchmark role and encourage stakeholders, especially risk professionals, to review and identify the gaps in existing models, systems, processes, and rules; better understand the risk profile of products in the new world of negative price; and build more robust risk management systems to support investment and hedging strategies.

3.2   Impacts

3.2.1   *Broken co-movement of WTI futures, spot, and Brent futures prices*

Traditionally, as the delivery period for a futures contract is approaching, the futures price converges to the spot price — this is supported by the futures pricing model and the no-arbitrage argument.

In a complete market, under assumptions of constant risk-free interest rate r, storage costs per unit being a constant proportion u of the spot price S_0, and constant convenience yield y, the oil futures price F_0 can be derived as follows (see [1]):

$$F_0 = S_0 e^{(r+u-y)T}.$$

This implies that as the contract maturity is approached ($T \to 0$), the futures price F_0 converges to the spot price S_0.

WTI spot price is the price for immediate delivery of West Texas Intermediate grade oil. It usually refers to "Cushing, OK WTI Spot Price FOB (DCOILWTICO)" linked to Cushing, Oklahoma, a major trading hub for crude oil that has been the delivery point for crude contracts, and therefore the price settlement point for WTI on the New York Mercantile Exchange. The data is available on the United States Energy Information Administration website.

However, there are other ways to trade oil, e.g. WTI/USD — "Crude Oil WTI Spot US Dollar" traded on retail forex trading

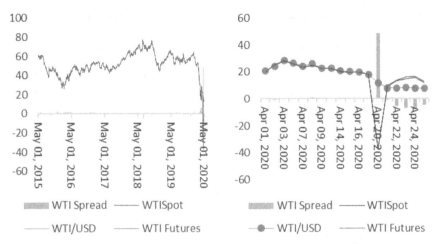

Fig. 3.1. WTI prompt futures price vs. WTI Spot vs. WTI/USD Spot vs. WTI Spread (=WTI/USD − WTI Spot) (Daily: Left: 5/1/2015–4/27/2020, right: zoomed 4/1/2020–4/27/2020).

Source: WTI Futures and Spot: eia.gov; WTI/USD Spot: Investing.com.

platforms (e.g. OANDA Corporation), representing the crude oil price expressed in USD per barrel of crude oil; theoretically it should be equal to the above WTI spot price with no-arbitrage assumption.

This is the case for WTI prompt futures, WTI spot, and WTI/USD spot price for long history until April 20, 2020, when the price for May 2020 delivery of WTI crude (i.e. the prompt contract price) collapsed into the negative zone. The consistent pattern between WTI futures, WTI spot, and WTI/USD spot is broken, as shown in Fig. 3.1 and Table 3.1: on April 20, 2020, the prompt WTI futures contract price plunged to \$−37.63, WTI spot to \$−36.98, while WTI/USD spot was around \$11.96.

The negative WTI price on April 20, 2020 might be attributed to the drained out oil demand from the stalled economy due to the COVID-19 pandemic, storage shortage, and limited trading liquidity. However, the Chicago Merchant Exchange's (CME) intervention in the approaching delivery period of the contract might also have some role, because relaxing price limit to allow negative numbers opened the possibility of negative price. CME might try to prevent speculators from making possible huge profits if WTI futures price continued to decrease, but was floored by zero. The large disparities between WTI prompt futures, WTI spot, and WTI/USD spot

Table 3.1. WTI prompt futures, WTI spot, and WTI/USD spot price (Daily: 4/16/2020–4/24/2020).

Date	Prompt futures	WTI spot	WTI/USD spot	Spread (WTI/USD-WTI spot)
Apr 16, 2020	19.87	19.82	19.88	0.06
Apr 17, 2020	18.27	18.31	18.16	−0.15
Apr 20, 2020	−37.63	−36.98	11.96	48.94
Apr 21, 2020	10.01	8.91	7.98	−0.93
Apr 22, 2020	13.78	13.64	8.05	−5.59
Apr 23, 2020	16.5	15.06	8.21	−6.85
Apr 24, 2020	16.94	15.99	7.99	−8

Sources: WTI Futures, WTI Spot: eia.gov; WTI/USD Spot: Investing.com).

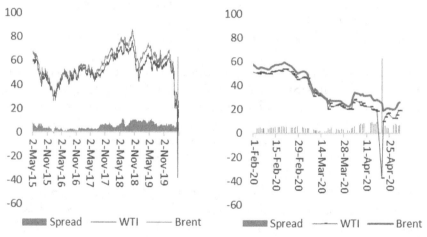

Fig. 3.2. Prompt contract prices for WTI, Brent, and Spread (=Brent − WTI) (Daily: Left: 5/2/2015–5/1/2020, right: zoomed 2/1/2020–5/1/2020).
Source: Investing.com.

on April 20, 2020 exposed significant arbitrage opportunity and indicated the extreme condition of the market and artificial intervention. The representativeness of the negative price and associated volume are also under question.

The negative prompt WTI futures price also broke its co-movement pattern with Brent prompt futures prices since April 20, 2020, as shown by Fig. 3.2 and the rolling correlation between

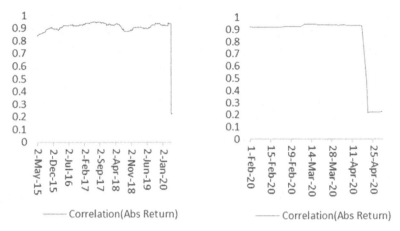

Fig. 3.3. Rolling correlation between WTI and Brent prompt contract prices (Left: 5/2/2015–5/1/2020, right: zoomed 2/1/2020–5/1/2020).
Source: Investing.com.

WTI and Brent prompt futures contract price (Fig. 3.3), which decreased to below 46% since April 20, 2020 from the average 90% before that date.

Due to WTI oil's benchmark role in global energy pricing and its close relationship with all other economic factors like interest rates, currency, gold, bonds, and stocks, any such unusual violation of historical relationship or fundamental no-arbitrage argument should be investigated and closely monitored to avoid a possible big impact on the financial market and economic activities. It is also suggested to revisit the price-discovery process with comprehensive factors considered, especially liquidity (volume) and wider market views from more market makers in order to get fair price.

3.2.2 *Option pricing model switch and significant risk profile changes*

The implications of negative price are significant. It has made some positions much riskier, exposing some banks and traders to potentially big losses and triggering a rush to remediate pricing engines and risk systems to recalibrate the more volatile market.

The traditional Black model used for options can't allow negative prices.

To address the issue, CME issued an advisory note on April 8, 2020 to switch the option pricing model to Bachelier model while WTI price is below \$8/bbl (barrel of oil).[a] and issued a further notice on April 21, 2020 to allow negative strikes for specified list of products.[b]

The Bachelier model resolves the negative price issue by assuming normal distribution of underlying price. However, it also introduces some new risk features which may need extra attention.

3.2.2.1 *Unbounded option price*

Under the Black model, due to positive price assumption, call option never exceeds the future price and put option never exceeds the strike.

Under the Bachelier model, because the underlying price can be in $(-\infty, +\infty)$, neither call option nor put option is bounded from above. Take an ATM (At-The-Money) call option as an example. Under the Bachelier model, call option price is (see notations in Appendix I):

$$C = e^{-r(T-t)} \frac{\sigma \sqrt{(T-t)}}{\sqrt{2\pi}}.$$

It is proportional to the implied volatility σ (absolute in dollar) and can go to infinity as $\sigma \to +\infty$, as shown by Fig. 3.5. On the other hand, under the Black model, the ATM call option price is:

$$C = e^{-r(T-t)} F[2N(d_1) - 1] \le F[2*1 - 1] = F.$$

It depends on the Black implied volatility nonlinearly, and is bounded by current future price F (since the normal cumulative distribution function $N(d_1) \le 1$ and assuming that risk-free rate is non-negative or close to zero here) (Fig. 3.4).

This alarms us that, with the potentially limitless decline in oil prices, there is no longer a cap on the potential losses for selling put options, e.g. if a bank had sold a put option that gave its clients the right to sell oil at \$10 a barrel, it would no longer be guaranteed that the bank couldn't lose more than \$10 a barrel on the deal because

---

[a]https://www.cmegroup.com/content/dam/cmegroup/notices/clearing/2020/04/Chadv20-152.pdf.

[b]https://www.cmegroup.com/content/dam/cmegroup/notices/clearing/2020/04/Chadv20-171.pdf.

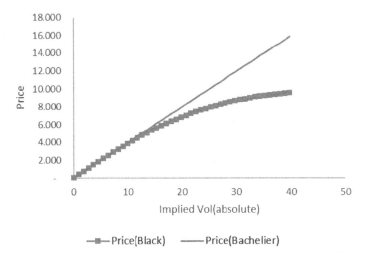

Fig. 3.4. ATM call option price vs. Implied Vol (absolute) (Black vs. Bachelier model). The deal settings: strike = \$10, future price = \$10, term = 1 year; risk-free rate = 0%.

oil prices can go below zero. This will deter banks from participating in any large hedges for their clients and press banks to adjust trading limits to their relevant positions to monitor more detailed information (e.g. storage capacity, etc).

3.2.2.2 *Greeks profile changes*

In terms of delta and vega, their disparities between the Black and Bachelier models are also significant. Take again the ATM call option above as an example: when the log-normal volatility increases, its Black model delta rises and its vega decreases, while the curves of the Bachelier model hold flat, as shown by Fig. 3.5.

More comparisons can be found in Appendix (Tables 3A.1 and 3A.2).

3.2.2.3 *Relationship between the Black and Bachelier implied volatility*

Because both the Black model and Bachelier model are increasing functions with respect to corresponding implied volatility, it is possible to convert between the Black and Bachelier implied volatilities in their overlapped price interval by solving the equation of the Black

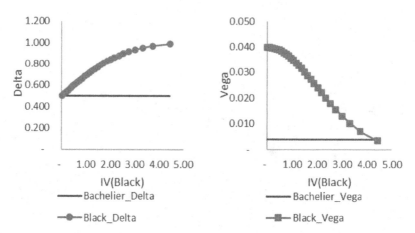

Fig. 3.5. Left: Delta: Black vs. Bachelier Model; Right: Vega: Black vs. Bachelier Model.

call option price and the Bachelier call option price, using ATM call option as an example (see notations in Appendix I):

$$e^{-r(T-t)}\frac{\sigma_B\sqrt{(T-t)}}{\sqrt{2\pi}} = e^{-r(T-t)}F\left[2N\left(d_1\right)-1\right],$$

with $d_1 = \frac{\sigma_{BS}}{2}\sqrt{(T-t)}$, then the Bachelier implied volatility is:

$$\sigma_B = \frac{\sqrt{2\pi}}{\sqrt{(T-t)}}F[2N(d_1)-1], \qquad\qquad (*)$$

and the Black implied volatility is:

$$\sigma_{BS} = \frac{2}{\sqrt{(T-t)}}N^{-1}\left[\frac{\sigma_B\sqrt{(T-t)}}{2F\sqrt{2\pi}}+\frac{1}{2}\right]$$

with constraint: $\frac{\sigma_B\sqrt{(T-t)}}{2F\sqrt{2\pi}}+\frac{1}{2}\leq 1$ and $F>0$.

Note that, if $d_1 = \frac{\sigma_{BS}}{2}\sqrt{(T-t)}$ is small, we may do a Taylor expansion for $N(d_1) = \frac{1}{2}+\frac{1}{\sqrt{2\pi}}d_1 + O(d_1^3)$.

Dropping the higher order term $O(d_1^3)$ and plugging $N(d_1)$ into (*), we have:

$$\sigma_B \approx \frac{\sqrt{2\pi}}{\sqrt{(T-t)}}F\left[\frac{2}{\sqrt{2\pi}}\frac{\sigma_{BS}}{2}\sqrt{(T-t)}\right] = F\sigma_{BS}.$$

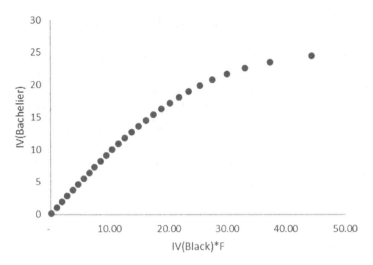

Fig. 3.6. Implied Vol (Bachelier) vs. derived.

This gives a simple relationship between the Bachelier implied volatility and Black implied volatility, which is consistent with the distribution assumption on the underlying price under the Black and Bachelier models, i.e.

Black: $dF = \sigma_{BS} \cdot F \cdot dW$ and Bachelier: $dF = \sigma_B \cdot dW$.

$F\sigma_{BS}$ is a good proxy to the Bachelier implied volatility σ_B solved from the pricing model when d_1 is small and future price is positive, as shown in Fig. 3.6 for comparison between the Bachelier implied volatility and those derived from the Black implied volatility * future price, in the short end, the dot line is close to linear (with 45 degree slope).

3.3 Risk Simulation

Consistent with pricing model switch, risk simulation models used for VaR, CCR, and stress testing should also be switched to be able to handle negative prices, i.e. from a log-normal model to normal model:

$$dF = \sigma \cdot dW$$

and the calibration of σ should be based on absolute return of historical data $\Delta F_t = F_{t+1} - F_t$.

Compared with a log-normal model (which produces scenarios in $(0, +\infty)$), a normal model will produce scenarios in a larger range $(-\infty, +\infty)$. The simulated scenarios may be acceptable for a VaR model because the simulation horizon is relatively short (in general, one day). However, for CCR, the simulation horizon may be years or tens of years and unreasonably large negative price may be generated, so it is more appropriate to use a displaced log-normal assumption to limit the price with lower bound $(-s)$ with incorporation of other techniques (e.g. mean reversion structure, not presented here):

$$d(F + s) = \sigma_{BS} \cdot (F + s) \cdot dW.$$

3.4   Regulatory Rule

Not only were many financial institutions caught off guard because of the negative WTI price, the regulators didn't expect it as well. In its latest version of Basel accord (FRTB — Fundamental Review of the Trading Book) [3], the commodity delta for SBA (sensitivity-based approach) is defined in relative terms and risk weights are calibrated accordingly, which essentially assumes that the commodity price can't go negative. To clarify, assume that the value $P(F)$ of a commodity derivative is a function of future price F, then the first-order Taylor expansion gives

$$dP = \frac{\partial P}{\partial F} dF \qquad\qquad (1)$$

$$= \left[\frac{\partial P}{\partial F} F\right] \left[\frac{dF}{F}\right]. \qquad\qquad (2)$$

Then the delta VaR under (1) and normal distribution assumption is

$$VaR_1 = 2.33 \cdot \left|\frac{\partial P}{\partial F}\right| \cdot HVol_{dF} \qquad\qquad \text{(I)}$$

and the delta VaR under (2) and log-normal distribution assumption is

$$VaR_2 = 2.33 \cdot \left|\frac{\partial P}{\partial F} F\right| \cdot HVol_{\left(\frac{dF}{F}\right)} \qquad\qquad \text{(II)}$$

where the historical volatility $HVol_{dF}$ is calibrated under a normal distribution (absolute return) assumption, and $HVol_{(\frac{dF}{F})}$ is calibrated under a log-normal (relative return) assumption, which requires a positive price assumption. Note that the HVols are used to derive the risk weight by incorporating the liquidity horizon (LH) (e.g. through scaling the 10-day HVol by square-root of LH). (II) is presumably the form accommodating the current rule in FRTB. With the possible negative commodity price from now on, (I) will be appropriate for the VaR calculation and should be used in the rule. Commodity delta definition and risk weight calibration should be amended accordingly. It is also suggested to review and enhance the definition of "the representative real price observations" related to the modelable risk factor definition. In our case, for WTI spot price on April 20, 2020, which is more representative, the negative price of Cushing, OK WTI spot price, or the positive price of WTI/USD spot?

3.5 Lessons

The negative WTI price may be largely attributed to the market conditions (drained out demand and storage shortage) due to the dire economic environment resulting from the COVID-19 pandemic and price-discovery with poor liquidity (low volume). However, CME's handling of the issue (timing of allowing negative price and switching option model) also attracted criticism, as seen from an article which stated "four of CME's largest clearing members have criticized the timing of the model switch, with some suggesting that a delay in receiving accompanying margin instructions from the central counterparty exposed them to undue risk"[c] The negative WTI price caused hefty losses for investors in futures and exchange traded funds (ETFs) (e.g. USO — United States Oil Fund) and CME's WTI related products may lose attraction to investors and hurt CME's revenue, and WTI's benchmarking role in pricing will also be under question. To avoid significant impact on financial market and risk

---

[c]https://www.risk.net/risk-management/7532031/cme-was-ill-prepared-for-negative-oil-prices-fcms-say.

management practice in the future, it is reasonable to unite all stake-holders to review the CME's decision-making process and rationale, improve the price-discovery process and transparency (e.g. involving more market makers), and ensure clients have enough time to respond to the changes with no big surprises.

On the financial institutions side, although CME issued advisory notes in early April and immediately after the negative incident, not enough attention was paid until "the wolf" really came on April 20, 2020 when many valuing and risk measuring systems ran into problems due to the inability to handle negative oil prices. The institutions were supposed to proactively challenge CME's decision and provide constructive feedback on their experience in handling the negative interest rates issued back in the 2008–2012 Euro-bond crisis, for which comprehensive review, remediation, and tests were done on pricing engines and risk systems, and all stakeholders (traders, risk managers, modelers, infrastructure business analysts, information technology (IT) developers, vetting, auditing staff, and regulators) were motivated to minimize fallout of misgauging the impacts. The institutions should be able to advise CME on potential impacts and efforts needed to respond for better decisions.

What's more, risk practitioners can learn the following lessons:

(1) Pay attention to all models' assumptions and conditions and monitor market and rule changes to capture the trend and violation of assumptions and conditions, otherwise risk systems may fail unexpectedly.

(2) Think with an open mind: anything is possible — negative interest rate, commodity price, and what's next? Probably negative dividend... people should review existing models, systems, and rules to identify gaps for improvement.

(3) Be prudent and prepared for swiftly handling the challenges:

   (a) Investigate/develop valuation and simulation models under various assumptions for vanilla and exotic options.
   (b) Collect/calibrate historical data for the different models (e.g. convert between Black–Scholes implied volatility and Bachelier model implied volatility in overlapped price zone).
   (c) Design/implement flexible risk systems to handle various models.

3.6 Appendix

For readers' convenience, notations and some basic properties for the Black model and Bachelier model for options on futures are summarized as follows. Details can be found in [1] and [2].

I. Black Model and Bachelier Model for Options on Futures

Black Model

Call option:

$$C = e^{-r(T-t)}[FN(d_1) - KN(d_2)]$$

Put option:

$$P = e^{-r(T-t)}[KN(-d_2) - FN(-d_1)]$$

$$d_1 = \frac{\ln(\frac{F}{K}) + \frac{\sigma^2}{2}(T-t)}{\sigma\sqrt{(T-t)}}, \quad d_2 = d_1 - \sigma\sqrt{(T-t)}$$

Notations:

r: risk-free interest rate
T: maturity
t: valuation time
F: futures price at time t
K: strike
σ: implied volatility
$N(\cdot)$: normal cumulative probability density function

Bachelier Model

Call option:

$$C = e^{-r(T-t)}[(F-K)N(d_1) + \sigma\sqrt{(T-t)}\,n(d_1)]$$

Put option:

$$P = e^{-r(T-t)}[(K-F)N(-d_1) - \sigma\sqrt{(T-t)}n(d_1)]$$

$$d_1 = \frac{F-K}{\sigma\sqrt{(T-t)}}$$

where $n(\cdot)$ is the normal probability density function and $N(\cdot)$ is the cumulative normal probability density function.

II. Bounds of Options

Table 3A.1. Comparison of bounds for call/put European options under the Black model and Bachelier model.

Bound	Black model	Bachelier model
Call Option Upper	F	unbounded
Call Option Lower	$e^{-r(T-t)}\max(F-K,0)$	$\max(F-K,0)$
Put Option Upper	K	unbounded
Put Option Lower	$e^{-r(T-t)}\max(K-F,0)$	$e^{-r(T-t)}\max(K-F,0)$

III. Greeks

Table 3A.2. Comparison of Greeks between the Black model and Bachelier model for European call options.

	Black model	Bachelier model
Delta	$e^{-r(T-t)}N(d_1)$	$e^{-r(T-t)}N(d_1)$
Gamma	$e^{-r(T-t)}\frac{N'(d_1)}{F\sigma\sqrt{(T-t)}}$	$e^{-r(T-t)}\frac{N'(d_1)}{\sigma\sqrt{(T-t)}}$
Vega	$e^{-r(T-t)}F\sqrt{(T-t)}\ N'(d_1)$	$e^{-r(T-t)}\sqrt{(T-t)}\ N'(d_1)$
Theta (w.r.t $T-t$)	$-rC + e^{-r(T-t)}\frac{F\sigma N'(d_1)}{2\sqrt{(T-t)}}$	$-rC + e^{-r(T-t)}\frac{\sigma N'(d_1)}{2\sqrt{(T-t)}}$

Note: (1) Notations follow each model's settings in the above Section I, respectively.
(2) Put option Greeks can be derived from put–call parity: $P = C - e^{-r(T-t)}(F-K)$.

References

[1]   John C. Hull, *Options, Futures, and Other Derivatives*, 9th Ed. (Pearson Education, Inc, USA), 2015.

[2]   D. Freddy and S. Walter, *The Mathematics of Arbitrage* (Springer-Verlag Berlin Heidelberg, Germany), 2006.

[3]   Basel Committee on Banking Supervision, *Minimum Capital Requirements for Market Risk* (BIS, Germany), 2019.

Chapter 4

Three Legal Reflections on the "Crude Oil Treasure" Incident: Starting with the CME Rule Change[*]

Duoqi Xu[†,‡,§], Peiran Wang[†,¶], and Yicheng Wang[†,∥]

[†]*Fudan University Law School, China*
[‡]*Shanghai Advanced Institute of Finance, China*
[§]*xuduoqi@fudan.edu.cn*
[¶]*peiranw@yahoo.com*
[∥]*wangyicheng@wustl.edu*

Abstract

The fall of crude oil futures into extreme negative prices has raised concerns globally. On the one hand, although the negative price mechanism facilitates market price discovery to some extent, in the delivery month it can trigger serious consequences such as abnormal market price fluctuations due to insufficient liquidity, which creates extreme market injustice and raises suspicion of manipulation. On the other hand, the reckless change of programs, which allow negative prices, lacks necessary legitimacy at the procedural level. Market participants who have been treated unfairly should actively defend their rights, and United States regulators and the Chicago Mercantile Exchange Group Inc. (CME) should explain to the market with thorough investigations and credible conclusions. The negative oil price incident is a profound warning and lesson for financial institutions and regulators in China.

---

[*]Please note that the views expressed here are those of the authors and do not represent the views of Fudan University and Shanghai Advanced Institute of Finance. The corresponding author is Duoqi Xu.

Keywords: CME, crude oil futures, negative price, market manipulation, rule-making procedure, legal responsibility

4.1   Introduction

On April 20 Eastern Standard Time (EST), the West Texas Intermediate (WTI) prompt month May (20) (WTI2005) crude oil futures prices hovered at $-35.00 to $-40.00 per barrel in the three minutes before the close, which finally set at $-37.63/barrel, triggering a great shock in the market. In China, the "Crude Oil Treasure" incident related to negative oil prices has sparked a debate on risk control and investor protection for financial products, and a series of consequences are fermenting from the fall of crude oil futures' prices into the negative territory. To date, however, few analyses and evaluations have been conducted from a market justice perspective on the behavior of the Chicago Mercantile Exchange Group Inc. (CME) changing mechanisms that allow negative prices. In fact, immediately after the prices of crude oil futures closed the day in extreme negative territory, they quickly rebounded back into positive territory and settled at $10.01 per barrel on April 21, the final trading day of the contract. This dramatic and abnormal price movement begs the question: can these extreme prices in just three minutes before the close on April 20 really "worked to perfection" (see [1]) as CME claimed, to reflect the market supply and demand conditions? This chapter starts from the reality of the harm caused by negative prices, i.e. intensifying market manipulation, debunks the lies of CME from both the substantive and procedural dimensions, and provides legal perspective and advice for market participants who have suffered damages in the event of negative oil prices.

4.2   Real Harm: Negative Price Mechanism Exacerbates the Serious Consequences of High Market Volatility

Just 20 minutes before the close, the prices of WTI crude oil futures fell below $0, all the way to $-40.3 per barrel by the short-selling. Not only did the long positions lose big, but they also carried a

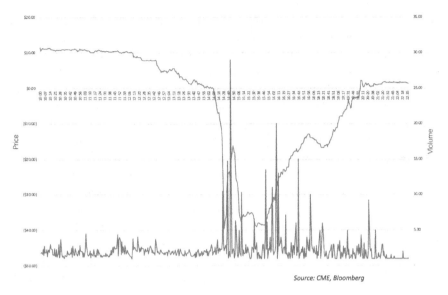

Fig. 4.1. Dramatic tumble within a few minutes.
Data Source: CME, Bloomberg.

heavy debt. One has to wonder: are these extreme prices really an "objective reflection" of the so-called market supply and demand relationship? Or is it an obvious intentional "corner"? The exchange, as the "watchdog", has not only failed to prevent and deter suspected market manipulation but has instead fueled the momentum of price distortion by short-selling forces through a "bottomless" negative price mechanism, with serious adverse consequences.

4.2.1 *Pondering over market manipulation: "Corners" just before the closing bell*

Market manipulation is not clearly defined in United States statutory law, and this concept varies among court decisions and scholarly opinions. After all, "manipulation cases are fact-intensive and that the law in this area will continue to evolve largely on a case-by-case basis" [2]. In general, market manipulation refers to "conduct intended to induce people to trade a security or force its price to an artificial level" [3]. Accordingly, malicious and profiteering market manipulation falls into two categories: fraud-based manipulation and market power-based manipulation. The former includes schemes such as spreading a false rumor [4] and "pumping and dumping", while the latter is a "corner" or a "squeeze" using positions and spot market advantages [5]. By contrast, the latter act is more insidious and difficult to identify. The framework for the identification of such manipulation is: (1) that the accused had the ability to influence market prices; (2) that they specifically intended to do so; (3) that artificial prices existed; and (4) that the accused caused the artificial prices [6]. Market power-based manipulation has conventionally been more of a "long market power" approach: a large buyer (the "large long") keeps accumulating futures contracts that those who have sold futures contracts (the "shorts") are simply incapable of delivery, forcing the shorts into a dilemma — either to bear the penalty of an undeliverable default or to buy back the futures positions at a very high price. To achieve this predatory exploitation, manipulators control long positions in futures contracts, on the one hand, and control the supply of contracted commodities in the spot market, on the other, preventing the delivery of the shorts, thus enabling deliberate price gouging during the performance or liquidation of futures contracts [7].

In fact, how a "short market power" works, as opposed to the above-mentioned scenario, is logically identical. Because the probability of an "inability to deliver" scenario is much greater than an "inability to receive" scenario, the latter has received relatively little discussion. In the manipulation of a short market power, a "large short" is constantly selling positions, making excessive deliveries that the longs cannot take, and thus futures prices are constantly being depressed, allowing the large short to repurchase his futures' positions at prices below normal competitive levels [8]. Given that the global demand for crude oil sharply decreased due to the COVID-19 pandemic, if the large short forces in the market, collaboratively abusing the advantageous position in controlling warehousing and transportation resources, as well as short positions, making use of the unrestricted downward movement of price after CME revised the rules, were able to continuously depress the prices before the close and eventually trade at an extreme negative price to reap huge profits, then it would be a typical market manipulation causing serious price distortion. It is worth noting that a small group of veteran traders at a tiny London firm called Vega Capital London Ltd. pocketed as much as $500 million that day, and are now being scrutinized by regulators whether they have breached rules and contributed to the drastic slump [9].

Market manipulation causes futures market's prices to deviate significantly from the true supply and demand, disrupts the normal function and order of the market, and produces extremely unfair results in the distribution of benefits between the two sides of the game, and is the object of a severe legal crackdown. It is worth mentioning that in the United States, market manipulation is a felony punishable by a fine up to $1,000,000 or imprisonment up to 10 years [10].

4.2.2   The market-oriented trap: Negative price mechanisms with "no bottom line"

According to the CME settlement procedure, the daily WTI crude oil futures settlement is based on the Volume Weighted Average Price (VWAP) of the last three minutes before the close of trading at 14:28–14:30 EST [10]. This settlement mechanism leaves room for market manipulation using the short time before the close, such as "banging the close", an act of buying or selling a large number of futures contracts during the closing period of a futures contract (that is, the period during which the futures settlement price is determined) [12]. Such acts do not need to be fraudulent to constitute market manipulation under the Commodity Exchange Act (CEA) as long as there is an intent to manipulate prices [13].

On April 20, the daily WTI crude oil futures fell by about $55 per contract, but lost about $40 just 20 minutes before the close, accounting for 73% of the total decline throughout the day; among them, just within the three minutes before the daily settlement time ranges (14:24–14:27), the decline reached $25, accounting for 45% of the total decline throughout the day — it can be seen that the large short, in addition to the moves of "corners", undoubtedly also has the characteristics of "banging the close" in the use of key time before the closing period to quickly distort prices, the combination of the two forming into a new and covert market manipulation. Unlike the traditional "banging the close", the suspected manipulation of the crude oil futures market is not through a large number of trading contracts to control the price, but the use of the aforementioned "corners", with a small volume of trading to force the price of the settlement time ranges of three minutes to the lowest point.

The question is, who gave the large short in the market the opportunity to manipulate the market by "corners", so that the prices of the contracts, which had been already very low, were easily suppressed to the bottomless pit in such a short period of time?

CME's new mechanism of allowing negative prices must take a share of the blame. Once again, we can tear down the lie of CME that the "negative price reflects the real supply and demand": on April 20, 219 lots were traded at a negative price, representing only 14.38% of the total volume of the day; the settlement price of $-37.63 per barrel, determined in the last three minutes, was based on only three transactions, with a total volume of 352 lots, representing only 0.25% of the total volume of the day [14]! Do distorted prices formed by such a small number of transactions in such a short period of time really reflect the true supply and demand relationship? It is important to note that the WTI spot market price on April 20 was $11.96 per barrel, while the "$-37.63 per barrel" futures contract settlement price was a far cry from that — how did the spot and futures prices diverge so much as they approached their expiry date? Furthermore, the WTI2005 contract closed the next trading day (April 21, the last trading day of the contract) at a settlement price of $10.1 per barrel, which is the price of real delivery crude oil. It can be seen that the settlement price on April 20 was distorted to the extreme.

In fact, before the advent of the negative price mechanism, a "long market power" was more of a concern than a "short market power" because there was no limit on the price of the contract upward, meaning that there was no ceiling on the losses of the shorts caused by the large long, while the price in a "short market power" situation always had a floor of zero — whether it was 20 minutes or 200 minutes, the losses of the squeeze of the long contracts downward were always limited. This has done the damage caused by the "short market power" less serious than that of the "long market power", thus escaping the scrutiny and suspicion of most people. However, CME's sudden change of the price mechanism to allow negative values changed all that: the losses suffered by the longs due to the squeeze of the short power are entirely possible to be bottomless. As a result, the large short was able to take advantage of the loopholes to manipulate the WTI2005 futures contract price into a frenzied downward spiral in the negative range within a short period of time before the close.

Under the United States CEA, the board of trade "shall have the capacity and responsibility to prevent manipulation, price distortion, and disruptions of the delivery or cash-settlement process" [15]. And, "to reduce the potential threat of market manipulation or congestion (especially during trading in the delivery month), the board of trade shall adopt for each contract of the board of trade, as is necessary and appropriate, position limitations or position accountability for speculators" [16]. There have also been instances in history where the exchanges have suspended trading due to market manipulation in the form of cornering — the directors of the Chicago Board of Trade voted to end the technical corner resulting from the inability of shorts to obtain corn to deliver in accordance with their contracts [17]. It can be seen that the exchanges should act as watchdogs of the futures market, create a fair and orderly trading environment, and prevent the phenomena of market manipulation and price distortion. However, in this negative oil price incident, CME did not take timely measures to prevent or stop market manipulation in accordance with the law. On the contrary, by rapidly changing the rules to allow negative prices, it expanded the space for malicious market manipulation and increased the possibility of heavy losses for those who were preyed upon. The negative oil price incident has raised doubts about CME even in the United States. On April 21, Harold Hamm, executive chairman of Continental Resources Inc. wrote to the United States Commodity Futures Trading Commission (CFTC), the agency responsible for regulating CME, requesting an investigation into whether the drop in crude oil futures prices below zero was caused by "potential market manipulation, failed systems, or computer programming failures," while Continental Resources also filed a lawsuit against CME [18]. If credible and in-depth findings confirm that market manipulation was behind negative oil prices, then CME's negative price mechanism is undoubtedly an evil helping hand.

It seems that CME itself also recognized the flaws of this mechanism. On August 13, 2020, CME made an announcement that they will move back to the Whaley and Black 76 Options Pricing Methodology, which no longer allows negative prices [19].

4.3 Procedural Defect: Unfair Decision-Making Process without Consultation

Negative prices create significant externalities, and CME's failure to control for adverse effects through a scientific decision-making process when changing the program to support negative prices sets the stage for potentially serious consequences. This rule change, which did not listen to the voices of different interest groups and did not alert the market to risks, demonstrates the irresponsible attitude of CME.

4.3.1 *"Pull one hair and the whole body moves": The importance of procedural control in rule-making*

The futures exchange is at the center of the futures market and must formulate scientific and reasonable trading rules to ensure the orderly participation and fair competition of the market players. The rules set by the exchange guide the behavior of market participants, on the one hand, and influence the distribution of benefits, on the other, so it is important to ensure certainty and predictability of the rules so that market participants can plan their behavior in advance in accordance with the rules. Futures trading is a zero-sum game (or, more accurately, a negative-sum game, since the exchange also collects a fee from each transaction that is borne by both parties), where one party's gains necessarily mean the other party's losses, and where the margin system multiplies the size of both parties' gains and losses. With such a context in mind, the stability of exchange-related rules becomes even more important. Any rule changes that may have a potentially material impact on the interests of market participants should be undertaken under a well-developed and reasonable procedure to adequately safeguard the interests of market participants.

CME changing the mechanism and allowing negative prices for crude oil futures lacked the necessary consultation procedures, public transition procedures, and exit notification procedures, which not only reduced the scientific reasonableness of the decision outcome but also undermined the value of the process itself.

Firstly, during the whole process, CME had never publicly consulted clearing members, industry associations, crude oil producers, and end-customers, and has not allowed the subjects with different positions to fully demonstrate their views and reasons. In practice, it is not difficult to collect options; it is true that CME had the right to set its own rules, but in contrast, other exchanges have more equitable rules for reference. In changing the documentary requirements relating to listed issuers in 2019, the Stock Exchange of Hong Kong (HKEX) extensively solicited the views of listed companies, structured products issuers, law firms, accountancy firms, professional bodies, industry associations, and individuals through questionnaires and other means [20], respecting the voices of different participants and ensuring that the impact of the changed rules on each subject would be within an acceptable range. The significance of the process lies not only in promoting good results but also in ensuring equal and full participation and demonstrating respect for market subjects.

Second, before the formal implementation of the negative price mechanism, CME had not set enough public transition period and had not left a buffer time for market participants to respond to technical changes. In the April 8 advisory notice, CME mentioned, "If any WTI Crude Oil futures prices settle, in any month, to a level below \$8.00/bbl, CME Clearing WILL move to the Bachelier model for all WTI Crude oil options contracts as well as all related crude oil options contracts effective the following trade date. CME Clearing will send out an advisory notice with one day notice before any implementation occurs with all appropriate details." "Please note that all existing CME Clearing message and file formats already support, without modification, negative futures prices as well as negative strike prices. We will publish additional information shortly regarding the details of potentially affected products and sample files" [21]. On the one hand, this notice emphasized the negative price mechanism of options contracts, which only incidentally suggested the possibility of negative prices for the futures contracts. CME, on the other hand, spoke vaguely and left "appropriate details" and "potentially affected products" to subsequent notifications, and thus it was only a forewarning reminder and did not have the substance to attract the attention of market members. Also, literally, there shall be a one-day buffer for changes to the option price mechanism, rather than switching price models as soon as the \$8/bbl condition is triggered. These factors combined to make it difficult to imagine that market participants would be able to make full preparations immediately. It was not until April 15, two trading days before April 20, that CME released a "test environment" for negative futures prices [22].

Third, CME not only failed to collect opinions before making decisions, but also failed to adequately publicize them before implementation, and even failed to warn interested stakeholders of the risks. As will be discussed later, not all participants would be able to deal with negative prices, and this mechanism would produce large negative externalities, with a wide range of implicated subjects. At the very least, risk warnings and explanations should be given to the majority of market participants, so that those who cannot handle and accept negative prices can exit the transactions as soon as possible. In contrast, the fact that the CME price mechanism was changed so stealthily and abruptly led to the situation where one party benefited significantly and the other lost severely, lacking the due sense of responsibility to maintain a fair and orderly market.

4.3.2   *An endless recipe for troubles from rash decision-making: The externalities of negative prices*

As an important financial infrastructure, whether a futures exchange can provide sound and reliable services not only concerns the interests of hundreds of millions of investors but also has an important impact on the stability of the entire financial system. The behavior of exchanges in adjusting their mechanisms and rules often generates externalities far beyond their control, and these externalities are difficult to internalize in a timely manner because of the long transmission pathways. If not carefully investigated and handled with care, the severe consequences of CME's reckless decisions will ultimately be borne by the many innocent victims.

CME should at least take into account, before formally changing the rules, that there are many investment instruments in the financial markets tied to crude oil futures, and if negative prices are allowed to occur, it is likely to lead to serious disruptions in this part of the market. In the case of ETF (exchange-traded fund) investment funds linked to crude oil futures, as a security, they cannot be traded at prices below zero, so a fall in the price of crude oil futures into a negative range would cause these financial instruments to malfunction and, in extreme cases, create systemic financial risk. Terminal ETF financial customers will have no way to use negative prices to carry out trading operations in their favor, but will have to bear the full loss of principal and incur huge debts as a result of the negative price of crude oil futures, which is an inequality of rights and obligations that implies extreme inequality in both substance and form. Once those customers with unfair debts are unable or refuse to pay (and they do have good reason to do so), the futures brokers or clearing houses will eventually swallow the loss, which in serious cases will trigger a credit or insolvency crisis for the financial enterprises concerned, with unimaginable knock-on consequences. Another example is that some exchanges operating contracts linked to WTI crude oil futures are facing the negative impact of being unable to handle the negative price trading. When futures prices fell into negative territory, the Moscow Bourse had to suspend trading for technical reasons, which prevented many traders from closing their positions and led to losses of nearly a billion rubles, and now many Russian brokers have joined individual investors in preparing a lawsuit against the Moscow Bourse [23]. "The resulting negative on the NYMEX (New York Mercantile Exchange) settlement price on April 20, created a risk to continue trading on the Moscow exchange on April 21, as the brokerage and clearing systems are not able to work with negative prices and their appearance could lead to problems across the market" [24].

CME did not adequately consider the possible negative externalities of their actions and did not listen to the views or suggestions of different interested parties through procedural measures to control the negative consequences of their decisions, laying the root for potentially serious impacts.

4.4   The Assertion of Rights: An Analysis of Rules and Law

In this negative oil price incident, those with the heaviest losses are undoubtedly the Bank of China "Crude Oil Treasure" customers. But judging by the concerned attitude of China's financial regulators, this segment of investors will not bear the full cost of the loss, and the market has also heard word that Bank of China will bear the negative price portion of the loss [25]. "Crude Oil Treasure" is a simulation board linked to the futures market, and investors in "Crude Oil Treasure" in China have a legal relationship with Bank of China, rather than directly holding crude oil futures contracts traded on CME [26]. The entity actually involved in trading

WTI crude oil futures is BOC International (BOCI) Commodities and Futures (USA) LLC., a Bank-of-China-controlled entity that is a clearing member of CME, which has genuinely and directly suffered losses as a result of WTI futures contracts falling into negative prices. BOCI should be proactive in finding ways to investigate and hold alleged market manipulators accountable. And can this difficult and long process be preceded by measures to maximize recovery of losses within the legal framework, taking action against CME that has allowed negative prices?

4.4.1   Require CME to adjust the WTI2005 contract daily settlement price in accordance with settlement rules

Based on the analysis of this chapter, WTI2005 crude oil futures settlement price of April 20 seriously deviated from the true market price, and thus the relevant market subjects have the right to request CME to correct. According to the CME Rulebook, when determining the daily settlement price, "in the event the Exchange determines that the settlement price derived by one of the methods set forth above is not an accurate representation of the relevant market, the Exchange may determine the settlement price based on other market prices, including settlement prices for similar contracts trading on other exchanges" [27]. In addition, although CME sets forth a number of rules for determining the settlement price, "in the case of inaccuracy or unavailability of a settlement price, or if a settlement price creates risk management concerns for the Clearing House, the Clearing House reserves the right to calculate settlement variation using an alternate price determined by the Clearing House." [28]. Given that the settlement price of "$-37.63 per barrel" is most likely a price that has been significantly distorted as a result of market manipulation, CME should, on the basis of an in-depth investigation, consider making the necessary adjustments to the settlement price of the day in order to maintain fairness and justice in the futures market. Although CME does not explicitly provide for market manipulation as a condition for adjusting settlement prices [29], the aforementioned provisions certainly provide CME with reliable authority. BOIC can maintain close communication with the CFTC to request CME to adjust the daily settlement price of the WTI2005 contract in accordance with the settlement rules.

4.4.2 A lawsuit: The debate of feasibility and non-feasibility

If negotiations with CME are unsuccessful, could BOCI consider filing a lawsuit against CME to seek rescission of the relevant transactions in the context of the price distortion of the day, based on the principle of fairness?

On the surface, both the Chinese law and the American law seem to have relevant provisions at the substantive level that can serve as a basis for claiming rights. Article 153 of the General Provisions of the Civil Law of the People's Republic of China (General Provisions of the Civil Law) provides that: "A civil juristic act which is in violation of the mandatory provisions of law or administrative regulations is invalid, except that such mandatory provisions do not invalidate the civil juristic act. A civil juristic act that undermines public order or moral decency is invalid." Market manipulation is, of course, prohibited by law, and transactions in this context should be invalidated. To take a step back, even if it cannot be fully recognized that the market has been manipulated or the time required is too long, according to Article 151 of the General Provisions of the Civil Law, "where a party takes advantage of another party that is in jeopardy or lacks the ability of judgment, which leads to unfairness when a civil juristic act is established, the injured party shall have the right to request the people's court or an arbitration institution to revoke the civil juristic act," the relevant transaction could be requested to be rescinded on the grounds that the settlement price has been seriously distorted and the fair trade has been damaged. Applying US law, UCC §2–302 also provides for the doctrine of manifest injustice: "If the court as a matter of law finds the contractor any clause of the contract to have been unconscionable at the time it was made, the court may refuse to enforce the contract, or it may enforce the remainder of the contract without the unconscionable clause, or it may so limit the application of any unconscionable clause as to avoid any unconscionable result."

However, it can be difficult to recover losses through civil litigation, and there are many issues that require more in-depth analysis. On the one hand, if a tort claim is filed, it is difficult to name CME, which has not actively participated in the transaction, as a defendant, while the actual market manipulator is unidentified and has to wait for a long time for investigation and identification, and it is also very difficult to obtain evidence. On the other hand, if a contractual claim is brought, there is the problem of identifying the counterparty to the transaction. In substance, short and long are true parties to the transaction; in form, CME, as the central counterparty, is the seller of all buyers and buyer of all sellers. Whether the law of contracts can be perfectly applied in this futures market-specific trading model remains to be explored. If CME were to be sued, one possible approach would be to assert that the futures transaction took place between BOCI (as the clearing member) and CME (as the central counterparty), and that the futures contract was settled at a price so distorted that the transaction was unconscionable. However, it should be noted that when BOCI acquired a clearing membership of CME, it was likely that the parties had agreed on an arbitration clause or a forum clause for settling disputes, or even other clauses that limit the liability or loss of CME to the clearing member. Moreover, BOCI, as a clearing member, needs to consider other potential long-term implications of the litigation.

There is no direct legal relationship between Bank of China and CME, and BOCI is a clearing member of CME — few precedents for members suing exchanges. To turn the situation around by filing a lawsuit against CME seems like facing a dilemma.

4.5   Conclusion

Financial market shocks triggered by negative crude oil futures prices could have far-reaching implications. While market transactions follow the principle of freedom, markets can also fail, and settlement prices determined by trading in just a few minutes may not necessarily reflect the true supply and demand conditions in the market, especially in the case of abnormal price fluctuations. The introduction of a negative price mechanism by CME has failed to reflect justice at the procedural level and equity at the substantive level. Market participants who have been unfairly treated should actively defend their rights, and United States regulators and CME should explain to the market with thorough investigations and credible conclusions.

From the consequences of loss and the difficulties of defending rights, the negative oil price incident is a profound warning and lesson: China's financial institutions should participate in trading after having a deep understanding of other countries' market rules and trading mechanisms in order to prevent this kind of fall into the financial "game trap." At the same time, the "Crude Oil Treasure" incident has put forward new requirements for the regulators: High-risk overseas linked products, as a kind of financial innovation under the regulatory arbitrage, stretching over fields of banking, futures, and securities, and different regulatory departments cannot easily form a combined force — in this context, the role of the Financial Stability and Development Committee to "strengthen financial regulatory coordination and supplement regulatory shortcomings" should be highlighted.

References

[1]   CME Group Chairman and CEO Terry Duffy said "The futures market worked to perfection" in an interview regarding the negative prices, see CNBC, April 22, 2020, https://www.cnbc.com/ 2020/04/22/cme-boss-says-his-exchange-is-not-for-retail-investors-a nd-its-no-secret-futures-can-go-negative.html, last visited May 1, 2020.

[2]   CFTC, Proposed rules: Prohibition of market manipulation, [fr doc 2010-27541], 75 (2010): 67660, 2010.

[3]   S. Thel, The Original Conception of Section 10(b) of the Securities Exchange Act. *Stanford Law Review*, 42(2): 393, 1990.

[4]   See Commodity Exchange Act §6 (c1A), 7 USC. §9 (2020).

[5]   C. Pirrong, Energy market manipulation: Definition, diagnosis, and deterrence. *Energy Law Journal*, 31(1): 1–5, 2010.

[6]   CFTC, supra note 2, at 67660-67661.

[7]   E. T. McDermott, Defining manipulation in commodity futures trading: The futures squeeze. *Northwestern University Law Review*, 74(2): 205, (1979–1980).

[8]   C. Pirrong, supra note 5, at 4.

[9]   See L. Vaugham, K. Chellel, and B. Bain, London Traders Hit $500 Million Jackpot When Oil Went Negative, Bloomberg Businessweek, August 4, 2020, https://www.bloomberg.com/news/articles/2020-0 8-04/oil-s-plunge-below-zero-was-500-million-jackpot-for-a-few-lond on-traders, last visited September 16, 2020.

[10] Commodity Exchange Act §9, 7 USC. §13 (2020).

[11] See CME Light Sweet Crude Oil (CL) Futures Daily Settlement Procedure, https://www.cmegroup.com/confluence/display/EPICS ANDBOX/NYMEX+Crude+Oil, last visited May 1, 2020. Comparatively, Shanghai International Energy Exchange takes the Volume Weighted Average Price in the whole day as the daily settlement price, so the sudden one-way price fluctuation in a short time is not likely to affect the settlement price on a large scale.

[12] See CFTC Glossary, "Banging the Close", https://www.cftc.gov/L earnAndProtect/EducationCenter/CFTCGlossary/glossary_b.html, last visited May 1, 2020.

[13] CFTC v. Amaranth, 554 F. Supp. 2d 523, at 534.

[14] The trading volume of WTI2005 on April 20, 2020 is 140,605 lots. Data Source: CME home page based on the report in 5 minutes for WTI May Futures Contract.

[15] Commodity Exchange Act §5(d4), 7 U. S. C. §7 (2020).

[16] Commodity Exchange Act §5(d5), 7 U. S. C. §7 (2020).

[17] See Corn Trading Halt Forced by Squeeze, The New York Times, Sept. 26, 1937, https://www.nytimes.com/1937/09/26/archives/ corn-trading-halt-forced-by-squeeze-chicago-exchange-orders-110-12. html, last visited May 2, 2020.

[18] Chris Prentice, Oil Exec and Trump Ally Hamm Seeks US Probe of Oil Price Crash, Reuters, April 23, 2020, https://www.reuters.com/ article/us-global-oil-cftc-hamm-idUSKCN2242UO, last visited May 4, 2020.

[19] See CME Clearing, Transition Back to Whaley and Black 76 Options Pricing Methodology — Effective Trade Date August 31, 2020, August 13, 2020, https://www.cmegroup.com/notices/clearing/202 0/08/Chadv20-320.html, last visited September 16, 2020.

[20] See HKEX, Responses: Consultation Paper on Proposed Changes to Documentary Requirements relating to Listed Issuers and Other Minor Rule Amendments, Feb, 2019, https://www.hkex.com.hk/Ne ws/Market-Consultations/2016-to-Present/Responses_February_201 9?sc_lang=en, last visited May 5, 2020.

[21] CME Clearing, CME Clearing Plan to Address the Potential of a Negative Underlying in Certain Energy Options Contracts, April 8, 2020, https://www.cmegroup.com/notices/clearing/2020/04/Chadv 20-152.html#pageNumber=1, last visited May 5, 2020.

[22] See CME Clearing, Testing Opportunities in CM's "New Release" Environment for Negative Prices and Strikes for Certain NYMEX Energy Contracts, April 15, 2020, https://www.cmegroup.com/not ices/clearing/2020/04/Chadv20-160.html#pageNumber=1, last visited May 5, 2020.

[23] A. Marrow, Russian Brokerages Seek Compensation from Moscow Bourse over Suspended Oil Futures Trading, Reuters, April 29, 2020, https://www.reuters.com/article/russia-moex-lawsuit-idUSL5 N2CG674, last visited May 4, 2020.

[24] N. Kumar, Mobira suspended trading in futures on WTI has consulted with CME Group, The Times Hub, April 21, 2020, https://thetimeshub.in/mobira-suspended-trading-in-futures-on-wti -has-consulted-with-cme-group/9055/, last visited May 4, 2020.

[25] J. Lin and A. Yi, "Crude Oil Treasure" Tries Settlement, BOC to Bear the Negative Price Loss and Compensate 20% Margin (in Chinese), Securities Times, May 6, 2020, https://news.stcn.com/news/2 02005/t20200506_1740066.html, last visited May 6, 2020.

[26] See Bank of China, Crude Oil Treasure (Individual account crude oil service) (in Chinese), https://www.boc.cn/pbservice/pb3/201712/t2 0171218_10998217.html, last visited May 8, 2020.

[27] CME Rulebook §813.6.

[28] CME Rulebook §813.11.

[29] Comparatively, the Shanghai International Energy Exchange explicitly provides that in cases where "futures market participants buy and sell futures contracts on their own or on the basis of an account under their actual control, which seriously affects the settlement price" or "other irregularities cause abnormal fluctuations in futures trading prices or substantial deviations from market prices in an instant, which seriously affect the settlement price," "the Exchange may adjust the daily settlement price and the settlement price for delivery." See Article 35 of the Settlement Rules of the Shanghai International Energy Exchange.

PART II
Why Oil Prices Plunged and Settled Negative

Chapter 5

Why Oil Prices Plunged and Settled Negative: A Game-Theoretical Perspective[*]

Chenghu Ma[†,‡] and Xianzhen Wang[†,§]

[†] *School of Management, Fudan University,*
220 Handan Rd., Shanghai 200433, China
[‡] *machenghu@fudan.edu.cn*
[§] *xzwang19@fudan.edu.cn*

Abstract

We provide a game-theoretical explanation to the negative prices event of WTI2005 on April 20, 2020, in the context of a battery of economic phenomena. First, in the wake of the petropolitical maneuvering among several of the largest oil producers and the outbreak of the COVID-19 pandemic over the world, the global oversupply has caused tremendous pressure on oil prices. Second, speculative activities and the physical delivery mechanism led to a significant long-short imbalance, especially as the Cushing storage was reaching its capacity. Third, the Chicago Mercantile Exchange's (CME) introducing of the negative price scheme stimulated strategic interactions among futures traders. The negative prices were triggered by the existing long buyers, while their counterparties showed little resistance, reflecting the fact that the market was vulnerable and highly susceptible to manipulation, and some active long/short investors may form a coalition to exploit the specific trader(s).

Keywords: Negative oil prices; petropolitics; COVID-19; coalition game

---

[*]The views expressed in this paper are those of the authors and do not represent the views of the affiliated institution.

> If you stick around long enough, you'll see everything in markets.

—Warren Buffett, March 11, 2020

5.1   Introduction

On March 9, 2020, the United States (U.S.) stock market indices plummeted and triggered the circuit breaker system of the New York Stock Exchange (NYSE) for the first time since 1997. The next day, in an interview about the stock market crash, Warren Buffett, the chairman and CEO of Berkshire Hathaway, said that the market overreacted to the news (COVID-19), and "if you stick around long enough, you'll see everything in markets."

Buffett was right. The marketwide circuit breakers of the NYSE were triggered another three times in the next two weeks. Most astonishingly, the Chicago Mercantile Exchange Group (CME) announced that its trading and clearing systems began to support negative futures and/or strike prices on April 15; five days later, the May WTI (West Texas Intermediate) contract traded on the New York Mercantile Exchange (NYMEX) (hereinafter WTI2005 or CLK20), which was the U.S. benchmark of crude oil that would be delivered in May, fell as low as \$−40.32 per barrel on April 20, with a record high volatility and decline.

It is generally known that the oil price collapse in 2020 began with the outbreak of COVID-19, but things aren't that simple in a long-term perspective. As Fig. 5.1 shows, the downward trend of oil price in 2020 can be traced back to the fourth quarter of 2018, and could be viewed as the continuation of the oil price downturn cycle since the second quarter of 2011. For the long-period fluctuations, we can draw some clues from the perspective of petropolitics, including geopolitical and strategic plays or strategic maneuvering mainly among countries of crude oil suppliers. For the recent crash of the crude oil futures price, a credible explanation is that the COVID-19 pandemic has resulted in a sharply shrinking demand.

As for the rare phenomenon of (deep) negative prices of WTI2005 on April 20, it caused a serious challenge to modern asset pricing theory built upon some idealistic assumptions on the well-being of the financial market, namely, a perfect competitive and frictionless

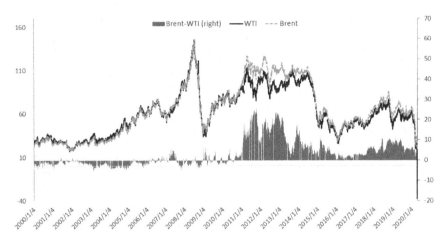

Fig. 5.1. Oil futures price since 2000.
Source: Wind.

market environment, and individual rationality. To explain the negative price event, it requires us to dig into the market micro-structure perspective. We believe that in the case of the physical delivery mechanism, the presence of frictions on futures trading, in addition to the strategic plays among traders on both sides of the futures contract, contributed greatly to the outbreak of the negative price event. Without doubt, CME's introducing of a negative price scheme should also account for it.

The remainder of this chapter is organized as follows. In Section 5.2, we explore the macro-level factors that caused the plunging of oil prices. Section 5.3 presents the arguments from the angle of the physical delivery mechanism of the NYMEX WTI crude oil futures. Section 5.4 describes the micro-level observations of WTI2005, and provides a game-theoretical illustration of the negative pricing mechanism. We conclude in Section 5.5.

5.2 Imbalance of Demand and Supply: Petropolitics and COVID-19

Crude oil is indispensable in modern society, mainly as the most important production input for manufacturing; as an intermediary good for many other real sectors of the economy such as transportation, aircraft industry, etc.; and its close relationship with politics. Thus, its price fluctuations are not pure economic phenomena. [1–3] Here we will explore the reasons for the current oil price downturn from the perspectives of petropolitics and supply–demand imbalance (economy).

5.2.1 *America as an oil producer*

In the context of the disintegration of the Bretton Woods system and the oil crisis, U.S. and Saudi Arabia established the petrodollar system in the 1970s. For decades to come, U.S. has taken care of Saudi Arabia's national security and political interests, and in return, Saudi Arabia (OPEC (Organization of the Petroleum Exporting Countries)) has guaranteed the energy security of U.S. Moreover, U.S. can enforce its foreign policy through the system, and vast petrodollars are recycled into U.S. through sovereign wealth funds of oil-exporting countries, which have promoted the development of high tech enterprises.

The win–win cooperation between U.S. and Saudi Arabia (OPEC) maintained the relative stability of the oil price for decades, but things changed following the 2008 financial crisis triggered by the U.S. subprime mortgage crisis. Because of the success of the development of shale oil and gas, U.S. oil production has continued to rise since 2009, as shown in Fig. 5.2. In 2018, U.S. surpassed Saudi Arabia

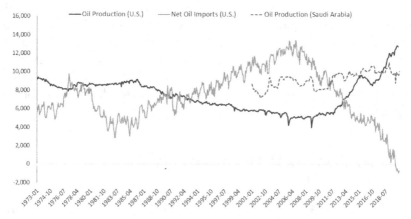

Fig. 5.2. U.S. crude oil production and net oil imports (thousand barrels/day). *Source*: EIA, Wind.

and Russia to become the largest oil producer on Earth, accounting for nearly 15% of the world's oil production. Eventually, U.S., used to being the largest net importer of oil, became a net exporter since September 2019.

The great change of the world energy picture has had a profound impact on geopolitics and international relations. From an American perspective, the maintenance of oil prices within a certain range is preferred. On the one hand, the impact of high oil prices on the economy is mitigated by its energy self-sufficiency, though this comes at the cost of its political influence on oil-exporting countries which would be weakening in such case. [4, 5] On the other hand, low oil prices could result in harm being caused to the (shale) oil industry, energy security, and overall economy, but it is relatively easy to exert political influence on the OPEC countries and other oil producers in this scenario. From the angle of Saudi Arabia, U.S.'s turning from one of its largest crude oil customers into a potential competitor has led to the disappearance of the power-balancing between the two countries; that is, Saudi Arabia has lost its confidence in U.S. to fulfill its commitments. Therefore, Saudi Arabia needs to build good relationships with other oil net importers, such as China, India, and Japan; meanwhile, it also has to come into contact with some powers (e.g. Russia) that affect its peripheral security environment. As a result, the conflict and balance between U.S. and Russia in the Middle East has become increasingly complex and intense, [6] while the "dollar-oil" relationship between U.S. and Saudi Arabia has also changed. As shown in the following paragraph, the fluctuations in oil prices of recent years are closely related to the political interactions among these countries.

Following the entry into the Syrian civil war in 2015, Russia has earned its growing influence in the Middle East through military operations in Syria. Consequently, Israel and Saudi Arabia, which are traditional allies of U.S., have to keep close contact with Russia on regional security issues [6]. Also, in 2015, Saudi royalty experienced a regime change. Two years later, King Salman and his son Prince Salman took full power, and launched a long-running corruption investigation resulting in a number of arrests. Most Western countries expressed concerns over Salman's administration, which eventually came to a head when the journalist Jamal Khashoggi was murdered in October 2018. Finally, to soothe the tempers of the

Western world, Saudi Arabia signed a massive arms deal with U.S., and terminated the rising trend of oil prices since 2016 by pumping more oil.[a] In fact, U.S. President Trump already accused OPEC of artificially pushing up oil prices on Twitter in April 2018. As mentioned above, U.S. seeks to avoid high oil prices, especially when the prices far exceed the costs of its shale oil industry. Low oil prices could not only weaken the financial stability and national power of oil producers, [7] such as Russia and Saudi Arabia, but could also increase the chance that the petrolist countries would move toward democracy, according to the First Law of Petropolitics presented in Refs. 5.

OPEC+ brought oil prices back to about $60 from $40 through two production cuts in December 2018 and December 2019, respectively. But during this period, U.S. oil production continued to rise and took market share from Saudi Arabia and Russia. To strike back the free rider, Russia refused to deepen oil output cuts on March 6, 2020, and started an oil price war with Saudi Arabia by increasing their production, thereby setting off a domino effect of collapsing global asset prices. One consequence of the extremely low oil prices is that the U.S. shale oil industry has been hit hard since its costs are much higher than Russia and Saudi Arabia (see Fig. 5.3).[b] For instance, Whiting Petroleum, one of the U.S. leading shale oil producers, filed for bankruptcy on April 1. After days of marathon negotiations, OPEC, Russia, and U.S. finally reached an agreement with the largest slash to production in history on April 12.

Through a brief review of history, we learn that in addition to the supply and demand theory discussed later, petropolitics plays an important role in oil prices.[c] As a matter of fact, the petrodollar system implies that the USD exchange rate is a crucial factor in

---

[a]https://abcnews.go.com/Politics/kushner-pushed-inflate-saudi-arms-deal-110 -billion/story?id=59418244.

[b]The average production costs of U.S. shale oil range from $27 to $37 per barrel, and the average breakeven price is about $50 per barrel, according to the March 2019 Dallas Fed Energy Survey (https://www.dallasfed.org/research/surveys/d es/2019/1901.aspx#tab-report).

[c]We don't know the details of the negotiations, but it is certain that there must be a lot of political compromise. For example, according to some news reports (https://www.reuters.com/article/us-global-oil-trump-saudi-specialrepo rt-idUSKBN22C1V4) in an April 2 phone call, President Trump put pressure

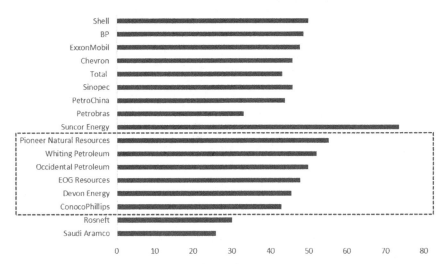

Fig. 5.3. Breakeven prices (dollar/barrel) of some leading oil companies around the world, derived from financial reports.

Source: Refs. [8].

the setting of oil prices, while the exchange rate itself is strongly influenced by politics as well. [9]

5.2.2 *Outbreak of COVID-19*

The outbreak of the coronavirus disease (COVID-19) pandemic in late 2019 has spread to 216 different countries, areas, and territories, and the number of confirmed cases is about 5 million globally as of May 22, 2020. [10] Following the experience of China's fight against COVID-19, a number of countries have launched their own versions of the "lockdown" policy, including forced quarantines, business shutdowns, and travel restrictions. The resulting hit to economic activity from the pandemic has caused a deep recession. According to the forecasts of the International Monetary Fund (IMF) in *World Economic Outlook (April 2020)*, the global economy is projected to contract sharply by −3% in 2020, whereas in its January report, the world output was projected to rise 3.3% in 2020.

---

on Prince Salman to cut oil production by withdrawing U.S. troops from the kingdom.

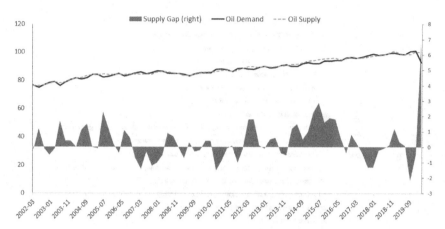

Fig. 5.4.   Crude oil demand and supply (million barrels/day).
Source: OPEC, Wind.

The halt of global economic activity has led the oil demand to shrink sharply, all while the oil supply in April had reached a record high, thanks to the price war between Saudi Arabia and Russia discussed earlier. As Fig. 5.4 shows, in the first quarter of 2020, especially after Europe and U.S. adopted the "lockdown" policy, the oil supply had far outstripped demand. Furthermore, Ref. [11] reckons that oil demand in April is 29 mb/d (millions of barrels per day) lower than a year ago, and 23.1 mb/d below for year-ago levels in the second quarter of 2020; taking the historic OPEC+ production cut deal into consideration, oil supply is set to plunge by 12 mb/d in May. Obviously, the reduction of supply is far behind the contraction of demand. Even if the production cut agreement is fully implemented in May, the excess supply is still about 10% of the total demand in 2019.

Generally, inventory is a good way to absorb uneven rates of demand or supply. As we can see from Fig. 5.5, U.S. crude oil inventories reached 1.16 billion barrels in late April, up 9.3% from the beginning of the year; the commercial oil inventories (excluding those in the Strategic Petroleum Reserve) were 528 million barrels, an increase of 22.7% over the beginning of the year, and close to the historical highest levels in March 2017, while the net stocks (held at refineries and tank farms) in percentage of working storage capacity was greater than 60% in late April. However, there appears to be no clear answer about the relationship between oil prices and the

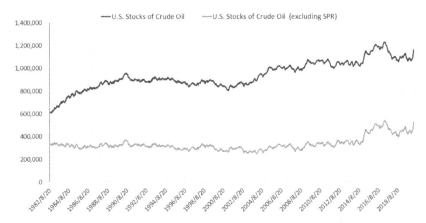

Fig. 5.5. Weekly U.S. ending stocks of crude oil (thousand barrels).
Source: The U.S. Energy Information Administration (EIA).

U.S. commercial inventories. As illustrated in Figs. 5.1 and 5.5, also referred to Ref. [12], there was a strong negative relationship prior to 2003, which turned significantly positive from 2004 to 2007, and then negative again since 2014. What is certain is that inventory accumulation is associated with speculative activity, [12, 13] and changes in the fundamentals driving supply and demand are essential.

As for oil inventory information concerning futures delivery locations, we will discuss it later. To sum up, under the supply–demand analysis framework, [14] the supply-demand imbalance and high stocks can be seen as the triggers of the oil price crash in 2020. As the previous lines already suggest, aside from the pandemic, petropolitics is a critical factor that caused the imbalance between oil supply and demand. In the April edition of *Short-Term Energy Outlook*, the U.S. Energy Information Administration (EIA) forecasts that U.S. will return to being a net oil importer in the third quarter of 2020 due to a significant decline of production. [15] To some extent, this can be viewed as one of the consequences of the petropolitics among OPEC, Russia, and U.S.

5.3 Limitations of Cushing Storage: A Delivery Mechanism Explanation

The petropolitics and outbreak of COVID-19 are indeed decisive factors in the collapse of oil price, but only the price changing trend can be derived accordingly, and the movements of prices in derivatives markets do not always follow the logic at the macro-level. Therefore, to better understand the negative price of WTI2005 on April 20, we should resort to examination at the micro-level, such as with regards to delivery mechanism.

The standard delivery procedure for the NYMEX (WTI) oil futures contracts is physical delivery,[d] which requires the seller (short position) to provide qualified crude oil to "any pipeline or storage facility in Cushing, Oklahoma, with pipeline access to Enterprise, Cushing storage or Enbridge, Cushing storage" in the delivery month, while the buyer (long position) must offer the "outgoing pipeline or storage facility with access to the incoming pipeline or storage facility" on the second business day after the final day of trading (Chapter 200 in Ref. 16). Otherwise, if the buyer is unable to transfer the oil delivered by the seller into a designated pipeline or storage facility, it is considered an "unexcused failure to make delivery", and they shall be penalized according to the damages assessed by the Clearing House Risk Committee (Chapter 7 in Ref. 16).

In most cases, physical delivery ensures the convergence of the futures contract price and the spot price of the underlying asset. Nevertheless, this would result in disaster in extreme instances. Suppose the futures contract sellers are oil producers, whose wellhead spot price is p_w, and the delivery cost is c_s, including transportation, warehousing, insurance, etc. Thus, the bottom futures price they would accept (for selling) is $f_s = p_w + c_s$ regardless of time cost. Assuming the buyers are refiners, they have two ways to acquire crude oil. Firstly, they can buy the oil directly from the sellers with total cost of $p_w + c_t$, where c_t is the transportation cost from the well to their refineries. Alternatively, they could long futures contracts at price f_b and purchase oil through the physical delivery mechanism; now the total cost is $f_b + c_b + c_e$, where c_b is the delivery cost for the buyers, and c_e is the transportation cost from the delivery location (say Cushing) to their refineries. Hence, the top price the buyers would pay for a futures contract is $f_b = p_w + c_t - c_b - c_e = p_w + c_s - c_b$, if $c_t = c_s + c_e$. Under normal market conditions, c_b can be neglected

---

[d]Investors have several options, such as Alternative Delivery Procedure (ADP), and Exchange of Futures for Physicals (EFPs).

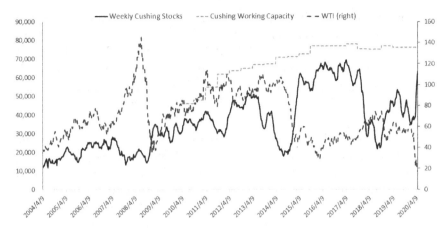

Fig. 5.6. Cushing crude oil stocks and storage capacity (thousand barrels). *Source*: EIA.

relative to $p_w + c_s$ and c_s, therefore we have $f_s = f_b \approx p_w + c_s$, which is exactly the convergence mechanism of the spot price and the futures contract price under the physical delivery system.[e] However, what would happen if $c_s < c_b$?

On the basis of delivery rules introduced by NYMEX, c_s can be regarded as fixed, relatively speaking. Rather, c_b could be huge if buyers fail to find the required "outgoing pipeline or storage facility". Consequently, f_b could be negative, which may partly explain the negative prices of WTI2005 on April 20. To illustrate, Fig. 5.6 shows the weekly Cushing crude oil stocks and storage capacity, where we can observe that oil stocks have skyrocketed since March, and that capacity utilization rate exceeded 80% in late April. The same situation can be found in 2014–2015, when oil prices were also falling rapidly. Given this, many people from media and industry believe that the high level of inventory in Cushing is the core reason for the negative oil futures price on April 20. However, before we can accept the limitations of Cushing storage capacity as the final answer, there are still several unsolved problems to consider.

---

[e]In textbooks, the price of a commodity for future delivery should be equal to the present spot (cash) price plus carrying charges, including storage, insurance, and interest rates.

For one thing, high level of inventory in 2015–2017 didn't result in negative futures prices. One may argue that this time was different as a result of the petropolitics and COVID-19 pandemic discussed earlier, but we can only arrive at the limited conclusion that oil prices were under downward pressure, and that the pressure may be much greater this time, while the negative prices problem is still pending.

For another, the Brent oil prices were positive during the same period, implying that $p_w > 0$. The final settlement price of WTI2005 on April 21 was $10.01, and the delivery dilemma obviously could not be addressed overnight, then why would sellers (oil producers) accept a deep negative price on April 20? Put another way, what disinclined them from closing out within the last 22 minutes before settlement on that day?

In actuality, following the delivery cost mechanism, f_b has the real potential to be negative, though f_s should always be positive in the context of a positive p_w. This indicates that the negative prices of WTI2005 on April 20 were triggered by the buyers, since they should have found that $c_b > p_w + c_s$, and would have had to liquidate their long positions by selling. Thus, the problem arising from such a situation is why the oil producers were so reluctant to unwind their short positions at negative prices, and is also why we believe that apart from the Cushing inventory capacity explanation, there must be some deeper causes.

5.4   Coalition Game: A Market Micro-Structure Explanation

Here, we attempt to provide a market micro-structure explanation to the negative price event on April 20, 2020. First, in Section 5.4.1 we look into the basic information on the WTI2005 futures contract, mainly concerning regulations on settlement and delivery, along with restrictions on market participants. Then, in Sections 5.4.2 and 5.4.3 we dig into the trading information from data on different frequencies. We shall draw some conjectures on what happened on that day, with particular focus on what drove the price to the negative zone. Finally, in Section 5.4.4, we provide a theoretical framework to illustrate the negative price event, and the causality effect of CME's introducing of the negative pricing scheme on the event.

5.4.1 *Basics on WTI2005*

WTI2005 is a crude oil futures contract traded on CME Globex and CME ClearPort. It requires physical delivery of a pre-specified quality of light sweet crude oil on any calendar days in May 2020 at a designated location arranged by the Exchange. The contract is measured in units of 1,000 U.S. barrels, or equivalently 42,000 U.S. gallons. For a precise description of the contract, please refer to Appendix A.

Besides the long and short division, participants of futures contract on either side can be further classified into three categories: active settlers, passive settlers, and deliverers, depending on how they settle their contracts.

Investors who engage in physical delivery of the crude oil contract must have a license issued in advance by CME. Investors without a license were obliged to close their positions by the expiration date of the contract, which was Tuesday, April 21, 2020.

Investors who could not, or did not wish to, engage in physical deliveries could close their positions by Tuesday, April 21, 2020, either at a market price (TAM: trade at market) during active trading times, or at the final settlement price (TAS: trade at settlement), which is the volume-weighted average price (VWAP) based on the three minutes tick-by-tick transactions between 2:28 p.m. and 2:30 p.m. Eastern Time (ET).

Those who failed to close their positions at TAM by Monday, April 20, 2020, and who were not to engage in physical deliveries, their contracts would be cleared at the prescribed TAS or at TAM on the final trading day, that is April 21, 2020.

The trading volume on a trading day measures the number of contracts that changed hands during the trading day. The trading volume measures trading intensity. The ratio between the daily trading volume relative to the semi-monthly (15 days) average volume (SMAVG) can be treated as a liquidity measure of daily trading activity. Figure 5.7 shows a consistent deterioration of liquidity when it moves closer to the expiration date of the contract.

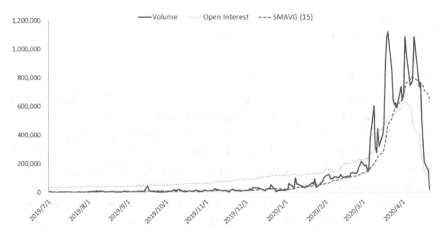

Fig. 5.7. Trading volume and open interest of WTI2005.
Source: Wind.

The open interest on a trading day measures the number of out-standing contracts unsettled (long or short) by the end of a trading day. On April 21, the expiration date of the contract, the open interest was 2,427. This constitutes the net number of contracts that will engage in physical deliveries in the calendar days of May.

When advancing towards the expiration date of a contract, the open interest serves particularly well as an indicator of selling pressure in a bear market, since the long side of a futures contract has a tendency to close their long positions by conducting selling orders, thus creating downward pressure on the price. When in a bull market, it serves as an indicator of upward pressure as short sellers tend to close their positions by buying back the contract, and pushing the price up.

5.4.2 *Long-short imbalance*

The (day-end) open interests on April 20 and April 21 were 13,044 and 2,427, respectively. So, it is reasonable to guess that the number of contracts that could be physically delivered is somewhere between 13,044 and 2,427, given the negative TAS price on April 20. Meanwhile, the open interest on April 17 was 108,953, suggesting that only 12% of the long positions could engage in the delivery procedure at the most. This is perhaps unsurprising as most traders do not have a license to conduct physical delivery, or they have the license to deliver, but are short of capacity/facility to carry out the physical transaction.

Most short sellers, on the other hand, are usually on the supply side of the crude oil industry. They have the license and storage capacity to carry out physical delivery. Since they have been enjoying continuous decline in WTI2005 futures price over the past months, they have no pressure to clear their short positions unless TAM or TAS falls substantially below its "fundamental value", for instance, when it becomes negative. In this last scenario, the short sellers may choose not to carry out physical delivery, instead of clearing their contract by purchasing back at negative TAS or TAM.

Moreover, in the last days of WTI2005, there existed a strong speculative atmosphere. The average open interest of the last 10 days of WTI2005 was 50% greater than that of WTI2004; and during the trading hours of April 19–20, there were more than 154,000 contracts changing hands, with about 60% traded above $10, as shown in Fig. 5.9. It implies that most traders on the long side of the contract could close their positions before the big afternoon crash on April 20, unless they were inclined to close out at the TAS price, such as Bank of China (BoC), which we will discuss later.

So, in conclusion, there was a long–short imbalance on April 20. With urgent demand of clearance from investors on the long side of the futures contract, and with virtually no pressure of clearance from the short sellers, it is not surprising to see futures prices drop to a level near the marginal cost of production by some of the most efficient producers (of crude oil) on this planet, e.g. OPEC countries. In economics, the marginal cost constitutes the Bertrand competition equilibrium price, below which virtually no producer can make a profit. The marginal cost is thus treated as the most conservative measure of fundamental value of production goods.

5.4.3   *2:00 p.m.–2:30 p.m. ET*

It is puzzling that the futures price actually dropped substantially below zero with TAS = $−37.63 on the settlement day April 20. As illustrated in Fig. 5.8, WTI futures contract opened at $17.73

The CME Vulnerability

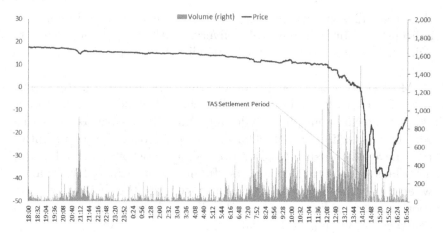

Fig. 5.8. WTI2005 prices from April 19, 6:00 p.m. to April 20, 5:00 p.m. (ET). *Source*: Bloomberg.

with a daily high of $17.85 achieved during the early trading, and a historic low of $-40.32 achieved around the settlement time at 2:29 p.m. The closing price for the day was $-13.10 with TAS = $-37.63.

Digging into the 30-minutes frequency trading data reveals that the TAM plugged into the negative zone in the last 30 minutes before the settlement time. Additionally, the 1-minute frequency trading data within 2:00 p.m.–2:30 p.m. ET, shows that the futures price dropped below zero at around 2:08 p.m. ET with a trading volume of 1,132, before diving into final (TAS) at closure $-37.11 at 2:30 p.m. within the span of 22 minutes.[f]

The total volume in the negative zone in the last 22 minutes before settlement was merely 5,403. Therefore we can say that, we could not observe strong resistance from short sellers who presumably would be expected to urge into the bidding process, clear their short positions, and claim differential profits with a huge profit margin (contract price plus $37.63). This obviously did not happen at or

---

[f]The 1-minute intraday data we discuss here is drawn from Bloomberg. It should be noted that the trading volume on April 20 obtained from the 1-minute data was less than that from the daily data. We conjecture that the difference may be due to the NYMEX WTI crude oil futures having two trading platforms. Nevertheless, our discussions and conclusions remain intact.

before the settlement time as short sellers played very passive roles in supporting the futures price in the positive zone and reluctantly let it drop deep into the negative zone. Of course, short sellers are the only beneficiaries of negative price trading.

We also observe the vulnerability of traders on the long side, even though merely 5,403 units of the contract were "on sale" in the negative price zone within the last 22 minutes before settlement. As with the 9/11 event, it is a dramatic (and irrational) sacrifice for traders who hold long positions in the futures contract to sell (goods of positive value) at a negative price, particularly if they have the license to carry out physical delivery, and do have access to a storage facility.

It nevertheless remains open to interpretation as to what drove them to making such a sacrifice. The marginal trader who initiated negative sales at 2:08 p.m. ET or so is, in our opinion, majorly suspect and likely guilty of participating in market manipulation. We shall provide a game-theoretical argument in supporting our conjecture.

Incidentally, as the entire trading day terminated at 5:00 p.m. ET, trading volume in the negative zone was 9,586, primarily consisting of short sellers who would otherwise have had to carry out physical deliveries. It is especially eye-catching and almost entirely unbelievable that short sellers would not rush into the market in the first 22 minutes of the negative price zone to close their positions (by buying) when the futures price dropped below zero. If they had, the negative price event would probably have been largely avoidable.

The futures price reversed back to a final settlement price of \$10.01 on April 21, the final trading day of the WTI2005 contract.

The price volume distribution could tell us more. As shown in Fig. 5.9, most of the changing hands were above zero, and nearly half of those were distributed between \$10 and \$15, consistent with CME's defense.[g] Meanwhile, of the about 10% trading in the negative price zone, almost 20% traded near the bottom (below \$−35), just a little more than 2% of the total trading volume. Nevertheless, this

---

[g]https://www.cnbc.com/2020/04/22/cme-boss-says-his-exchange-is-not-for-retail-investors-and-its-no-secret-futures-can-go-negative.html.

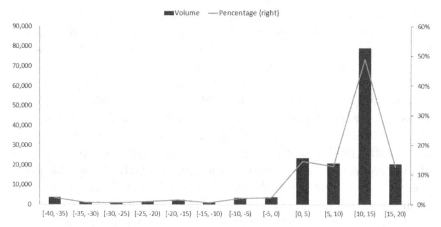

Fig. 5.9. Price volume distribution of WTI2005 from April 19, 6:00 p.m. to April 20, 5:00 p.m. (ET).

Source: Bloomberg.

minority of trading determined the settlement price, which put the open interest of WTI2005 in great exposure to a margin call risk. For example, "Yuan You Bao", a structured crude oil product sold by BoC, held more than 24,000 long positions with an estimated total loss of $1.4 billion in the WTI2005 collapse.[h]

Therefore, we conjecture that the historic crash of WTI2005 was not just "a function of supply and demand", as CME Group Chairman and CEO, Terry Duffy, argued. It is highly possible that certain predatory actors on Wall Street may already have had eyes on preys such as "Yuan You Bao". While we do not have access to tick-by-tick trading information to find out the truth, we can only elaborate on our conjecture through a theoretical model.

5.4.4   *A game-theoretical illustration*

We consider a simple three-player game in which PL and AL each has one unit "goods" to clean up, and SS is a potential buyer, and

---

[h]https://www.caixinglobal.com/2020-04-27/in-depth-a-bitter-14-billion-lesson-on-commodity-price-speculation-101547398.html.

demands for one unit goods only. The reservation value of the goods to all three players is the same: $v = 1$. Each player may propose a price within an admissible quotation set $A \subseteq [-1, 1]$, and it is always feasible for the players not to submit a quote, i.e. $\varnothing$.

The goods change hands when the buyer bids, when at least one of the potential sellers submits a quote, and when the price submitted by SS is no less than the minimum effective asking quotes submitted by the sellers; in that case, we say that a match is made. When a match is made, the settlement price p is set to be the bidding price submitted by SS, and the final payoffs to the three players will be $(p - v, p - v, v - p)$. If no matches were made, the payoffs will be $(-1, -1, -1)$.

We are only interested in pure strategy Nash equilibria.

A price $p \in A$ is said to be an *equilibrium* if it is supported as an outcome to a Nash equilibrium of the game. [17] And, $p \in A$ is said to be a *stable equilibrium* if it is supported as an outcome to a coalition-proof Nash equilibrium of the game; [18] that is, there exists no coalition among the three players which can induce a new equilibrium outcome that improves the payoffs to all coalition members.

For the special case $A = [0, 1]$, it is straightforward to verify that any price in the interval $[0, 1]$ can be supported as an equilibrium. However, $p = 1$ is the only stable equilibrium. For instance, $p = 0$ is an equilibrium because, when all players quote 0, no individual player can deviate with an alternative bid, or no-bid, to improve its final payoffs $(-1, -1, 1)$. However, when the two sellers form a coalition and ask for $p' = 1$, SS' best response is to take the offer since, otherwise, there will be no match, with final outcome $(-1, -1, -1)$. So, by forming a coalition, the two sellers can always induce a stable equilibrium with outcome $(0, 0, 0)$ that strictly benefits both coalition members. Following the same argument, all $p \in (0, 1)$ can be supported as an equilibrium, but none are stable.

Now, we expand the admissible set by allowing negative bids, say $A = [-1, 1]$. Again, we can easily verify that each point in the interval $[-1, 1]$ can be supported as an equilibrium. And, $p = 1$ is the only stable equilibrium.

To illustrate the negative price equilibrium settlement, we take the extreme quotation $p = -1$. It is a Nash equilibrium with all three players quoted at $p = -1$. The final payoffs are $(-2, -2, 2)$.[i] When both sellers ask for $p = -1$, SS certainly takes the offer. And, knowing that the other seller (say, AL) and SS match at $p = -1$, any deviation by PL, with an alternative ask strictly greater than -1 or by keeping silent $\varnothing$, can neither change the settlement, nor the final payoffs.

The equilibrium settlement $p = -1$ is, however, non-stable. When the two sellers form a coalition and ask for $p = 1$, they can always induce a stable equilibrium with final payoffs $(0, 0, 0)$.

So, expanding the admissible set to include negative quotes can indeed narrate the negative settlement prices as equilibria. These equilibria are, however, non-stable — it requires strategic calibration (mutual suicide) between the two potential sellers, and requires determination by SS to stick to the extreme greedy bid of $p = -1$. It should also be recognized that $p = -1$ cannot be supported as an equilibrium settlement when one of the sellers, say PL, is passive (with no bidding), or is active, but bids a higher price. In this case, even though a match is made between AL and SS with $p = -1$, any deviation from $p = -1$ by AL will induce an outcome that is strictly higher than -2. Therefore, the extreme negative equilibrium price $p = -1$ requires mutually suicidal calibration by the sellers.

Following these same arguments, we can show that all negative equilibrium prices in the negative zone $[-1, 0)$ would require suicidal calibration between the two potential sellers, and are non-stable.

One may ask: Is there an alternative explanation in supporting $p = -1$ as a strategic equilibrium outcome? Can the buyer form a coalition with one of the sellers, say AL, to make a match at $p = -1$?

One way to make SS and AL a stable coalition is to introduce a side-payment agreement between the two parties, say, for instance, by sticking to a $p = -1$ quote, SS would fully cover up AL's payoff

---

[i]With only one seller (say, AL), in addition to the buyer, submitting quote $p = -1$ does not constitute a Nash equilibrium — AL can always submit alternative bids, or keep silent, to improve his final payoff.

loss relative to the stable equilibrium outcome at $p = 1$. This would induce an equilibrium final outcome $(-2, 0, 0)$, and make PL the only loser in the game. This, of course, changes the nature of the game. It changes the payoff structure, as well as the equilibrium outcomes.

In the above illustrative three-player game, one may treat PL and AL as investors on the long side of a futures contract who wish to clear (sell) their positions before expiration. PL may play a role as Passive Long, and AL plays a role as Active Long. SS can be treated as a Short Seller who also wishes to close her position (buy) before expiration. There is a long-short imbalance in this game — more investors on the long side of the contract, in comparison to the short sellers, must clear their positions before expiration.

Now, let us go back to April 20, 2020, on the WTI2005 contract. This is what, we believe, had happened. The liquidity in the futures trading had been low throughout the entire trading day. Traders on the long side futures market found it difficult to close their positions even when the futures price dropped below the fundamental value. As it moved into the last 30 minutes before settlement, some active traders initiated a wave of sales, while some other traders had held long positions (e.g. Yuan You Bao) stayed passive. The futures price broke into the negative zone at 2:08 p.m. ET, and dropped to a historic low of -40.32 in the last minute of the settlement time on the trading day.

There was little resistance from existing short sellers. They were very patient, with no urge to clear their short positions and claim their huge profit margin. The trading volume in the negative price zone within the last 22 minutes before settlement was merely 5,403 units. Throughout the entire trading day that terminated at 5:00 p.m. ET, trading volume in the negative zone was 9,586, mainly coming from short sellers who might, otherwise, carry out physical deliveries, and who might participate earlier.

Had these short sellers entered the market earlier, within the last 30 minutes before settlement, the negative price event could have been avoided because there would have been no resistance for investors on the long side of the market to sell in the negative price zone. In fact, for the most efficient crude oil producers worldwide, it would be even irrational for them to sell below the marginal cost. The marginal cost corresponds to the Bertrand equilibrium price from the real sector of the economy. Indeed, the Bertrand equilibrium price can be supported as a stable equilibrium settlement price should short sellers play a relatively active role, and should active traders on the long side of futures contract avoid initiating a wave of (suicidal) sales within the last 30 minutes before the final settlement time.

At the end of the day, the only major winners are those short sellers; all investors on the long side of the futures contract, particularly those who cannot conduct physical deliveries, suffered the most unimaginable loss ever recorded in the history of futures trading.

The negative price event was short-lived, and bounced back to the range above $10 at final settlement on April 21, 2020. This is fully consistent with our prediction on the instability of the negative price equilibria.

The motivation behind the sacrificial sale by active traders on the long side of the market within the last 30 minutes before settlement is not justified, particularly in the presence of massive (and passive) traders on the same side. It is not a stable outcome, not even a Nash outcome.

In accordance with our game-theoretical arguments above, a convincing explanation of the event is that some of the active traders on the long side of the futures contract formed a coalition with some existing short sellers or some arbitragers, and reached a side-payment agreement with the latter to cover up their losses. If this is the case, some parties must be guilty of participating in illegal market manipulation. The introducing of a negative pricing scheme by CME just a few days before the negative price event, which makes negative price quotations possible from a technical point of view, is certainly a key stimuli. The legitimacy of the negative pricing scheme for any commodity goods traded on the Futures Exchange, mainly concerning its implications for the well-being of the financial market, must be re-assessed.

5.5   Concluding Remarks

Modern asset pricing theory has been built upon several key assumptions on the effectiveness of the market economy in terms of individual rationality, no frictions, and perfect competition. These conform perfectly to Adam Smith's invisible hand phenomenon and are advocated by the notion of equilibrium and no-arbitrage. In an idealistic frictionless and perfect competitive market environment, the equilibrium security prices must fulfill the no-arbitrage condition, namely a security with a positive value must be associated with a positive equilibrium price.

The recent WTI2005 negative price event casts a serious challenge to modern asset pricing theory. In this chapter, we provided a tentative theoretical explanation for the event mainly based on a series of economic events from both the macro and micro perspectives. The presence of frictions on futures trading, in addition to the strategic plays among traders on both sides of the futures contract, contributed greatly to the outbreak of the negative price event.

Firstly, the market failure took place at a time of the worldwide spread of COVID-19 starting from late 2019, which had a dramatic negative impact on the demand side of crude oil, mainly as a production input and intermediary goods.

Secondly, the petropolitical maneuvering, involving several of the most powerful countries on the planet that control the supply side of crude oil, resulted in a failure to reach a production reduction agreement between Russia and Saudi Arab on March 6, 2020, which was followed by an oil price war, with the addition of the introduction of a policy advocated by the U.S. government in strengthening the market share of U.S.'s crude oil production by maintaining crude oil production even in a time of severe decline in demand. The imbalance of demand and supply on the aggregated economy caused tremendous pressure on oil prices, as well as on crude oil storage capacity.

Thirdly, from a micro perspective, when the oil price dropped below the marginal cost of production, particularly, when OPEC+ countries reached a crude oil production-agreement on April 12, 2020, it attracted short-term speculators rushing into the futures market, mainly on the most active WTI2005 contracts that would expire on April 21, 2020. Most speculators taking long positions bet that oil price would bounce back to the normal fundamental level. Many of these short-term speculators did not plan to conduct physical delivery of the crude oil product, and may not even have had the license to do so. Even to those who have the license for delivery, the shortage of U.S. crude oil storage capacity caused severe friction for them in actually carrying out physical delivery in May. This, consequentially, caused a long-short imbalance in futures trading, and imposed huge pressure on the futures price, particularly when it moved closer to the final settlement date of the contract, that is, April 20–21, 2020.

Finally, CME's introducing of a negative price scheme for crude oil products and its derivative products, which became effective immediately after its announcement on April 15, greatly stimulated strategic interactions among traders on both sides of the futures contract. This, as we believe, eventually led to the outbreak of the negative price settlement event on April 20–21, 2020.

To be sure, we make no claim that the coalition-game theory is the only explanation for the WTI2005 negative price event. Not surprisingly, the margin call could also trigger selling no matter the price. However, this narrative can't explain the great patience of the existing short sellers on that day.

Acknowledgments

We would like to thank Zhu Songping, Yuan Xianzhi, Yuan Xi, Li Ping, and Liu Luchuan for stimulating conversations on the subject. We would also like to thank Yang Jingping, Yu Wenguang, and Yuan Xianzhi for organizing the CSIAM online conference on April 26, 2020. We are grateful to Paul Ma for English proofreading. Additional thanks are given to Xie Cheng for his work as research assistant and Li Ying for her useful comments and suggestions. And finally, we thank Ms. Ann Lai, the editor from World Scientific in Singapore, for her professional guidance.

Appendix A. WTI Contract

Table 5A.1 illustrates some key specifications of the NYMEX WTI crude oil futures contract. More details can be found on the CME website.[j]

---

[j]https://www.cmegroup.com/trading/energy/crude-oil/light-sweet-crude_contract_specifications.html.

Table 5A.1. NYMEX WTI crude oil futures contract specs.

Contract Unit	1,000 barrels
Product Code	CME Globex: CL; CME ClearPort: CL; Clearing: CL; TAS: CLT; TAM: CLS
Price Quotation	U.S. dollars and cents per barrel
Minimum Price Fluctuation	0.01 per barrel = $10.00 TAS: Zero or +/−10 ticks in the minimum tick increment
Trading Hours	CME Globex: Sunday–Friday 6:00 pm.–5:00 pm ET; TAS: Sunday–Friday 6:00 pm–2:30 pm. ET CME ClearPort: Sunday–Friday 6:00 pm.–5:00 pm ET
Listed Contracts	Monthly contracts listed for the current year and the next 10 calendar years and 2 additional contract months
Settlement Method	Deliverable
Termination of Trading	3 business day prior to the 25th calendar day of the month prior to the contract month. If the 25th calendar day is not a business day, trading terminates 4 business days prior to the 25th calendar day.
TAM or TAS Rules	Subject to the requirements of Rule 524.A in *NYMEX Rulebook*
Settlement Procedures	Based on the trading activity on CME Globex during the settlement period, defined as: 14:28:00 to 14:30:00 ET for the Active Month and 14:00:00–14:30:00 ET on the day of expiration. Refer to CME Group Settlements in *Client Systems Wiki* for details.
Delivery Procedure	Delivery shall be made free-on-board ("F.O.B.") at any pipeline or storage facility in Cushing, Oklahoma with pipeline access to Enterprise, Cushing storage or Enbridge, Cushing storage. See Chapter 200 in *NYMEX Rulebook*.
Delivery Period	No earlier than the first calendar day of the delivery month and no later than the last calendar day of the delivery month.

Source: CME.

References

[1]   E. L. Morse, (1986). After the fall: The politics of oil. *Foreign Affairs*, 64(4), 792–811.

[2]   W. Engdahl, (2004). *A Century of War: Anglo-American Oil Politics and the New World Order*. Pluto Press, London.

[3]   J. Baffes, M. A. Kose, F. Ohnsorge, and M. Stocker, (2015). The great plunge in oil prices: Causes, consequences, and policy responses. *Policy Research Notes*, World Bank Group.

[4]   M. L. Ross, (2001). Does oil hinder democracy? *World Politics*, 53(3), 325–361.

[5]   T. L. Friedman, (2006). The first law of petropolitics. *Foreign Policy*, 154, 28–36.

[6]   B. B. Wu, (2018). The big-power politics, geo-strategic competition and strategic patterns in the middle east. *Foreign Affairs Review* (in Chinese), 5, 42–70.

[7]   IMF (2020). *World Economic Outlook Reports*. Available at: https://www.imf.org/en/Publications/WEO.

[8]   Y. Deng, *et al.*, (2020). The cost curve of crude oil derived from some leading oil companies over the world (in Chinese). *Industry Tracking Report*, Haitong Securities.

[9]   J. A. Frieden, (2014). *Currency Politics: The Political Economy of Exchange Rate Policy*. Princeton University Press, New Jersey.

[10] WHO (2020). *Coronavirus Disease Situation Report*. Available at: https://www.who.int/emergencies/diseases/novel-coronavirus-2019/situation-reports/.

[11] IEA (2020). *Oil Market Report*. Available at: https://www.iea.org/reports/oil-market-report-april-2020.

[12] K. J. Singleton, (2013). Investor Flows and the 2008 Boom/Bust in Oil Prices. *Management Science*, 60(2), 300–318.

[13] L. Kilian, and D. P. Murphy, (2014). The role of inventories and speculative trading in the global market for crude oil. *Journal of Applied Econometrics*, 29(3), 454–478.

[14] L. H. Ederington, C. S. Fernando, T. K. Lee, S. C. Linn, and A. D. May, (2011). Factors influencing oil prices: A survey of the current state of knowledge in the context of the 2007–08 Oil Price Volatility. Working paper, EIA.

[15] EIA (2020). *Short-Term Energy Outlook*. Available at: https://www.eia.gov/outlooks/steo/report/global_oil.php.

[16] NYMEX, *NYMEX Rulebook*. Available at: https://www.cmegroup.com/rulebook/NYMEX/.

[17] J. Nash, (1951). Non-cooperative games. *Annals of Mathematics*, 54(2), 286–295.

[18] D. Bernheim, B. Peleg, and M. Winston, (1987). Coalition-Proof Nash Equilibria I. Concepts. *Journal of Economic Theory*, 42(1), 1–12.

Chapter 6

Tanker Shipping and Negative Oil Prices: More Than Just the Freight Rates[*]

Cong Sui[†,§] and Mo Yang[‡,¶,‖]

† Collaborative Innovation Center for Transport Studies,
School of Maritime Economics and Management,
Dalian Maritime University, Dalian, China
‡ School of Finance,
Dongbei University of Finance and Economics,
Dalian, China
§ suicong2004@163.com
¶ mo.yang@hotmail.com

Abstract

On April 20, 2020, the West Texas Intermediate crude oil futures contracts for May were traded at as low as -40.32 per barrel on the Chicago Mercantile Exchange. This was a very unusual mispricing. First, the mismatch between supply and demand had caused a slump in oil prices. Second, the rise in oil storage led to increased cost of inventory and shipping, which had further impact on oil prices. Third, the trading principles and features of oil futures on exchanges triggered the mispricing of crude oil futures. However, when faced with such huge mispricing,

---

[*]The views expressed in this paper are those of the authors and do not represent the views of the affiliated institutions.
[‖]Corresponding author.

arbitragers did not take the arbitrage opportunity initially due to constraints of holding tankers or tankships. Retrospectively, arbitragers did take action, but with a one-day delay. The post-event performance of the shipping market indicates that holding tankships is of vital importance in the arbitrage of crude oil mispricing.

Keywords: Crude oil price, tanker ship market, arbitrage

6.1   Can Crude Oil Prices be Negative?

On April 20, 2020, the West Texas Intermediate (WTI) crude oil futures contract for May (referred to as May WTI contract hereinafter) traded on the Chicago Mercantile Exchange (CME) plummeted by $55.90 per barrel. The lowest trading price was $$-40.32$ per barrel and the closing price was $$-13.10$ per barrel. The final settlement price was $$-37.63$ per barrel. This occurred just five days after CME's announcement that energy futures contracts can be traded at zero or negative prices on the New York Mercantile Exchange (NYMEX), and trading and settlement on CME will be conducted normally.

Negative prices seemingly go against fundamental economics. To understand what is happening, we need to start from the commodity and the futures markets. Under the assumption of risk-neutral and frictionless market, the commodity price and the futures price should satisfy the following equation [7]:

$$F = (S + U)e^{rt} \tag{1}$$

where F denotes the futures price, S denotes the commodity spot price, U denotes the cost of inventory and shipping, r denotes the risk-free interest rate, and t denotes the duration of the futures. For the sake of simplicity, and without loss of generality, if the time value of money is ignored, then an approximate relationship between the commodity price and the futures price can be expressed as

$$S \approx F - U. \tag{2}$$

Assume that the whole market reaches a consensus on the current price (the commodity price, i.e. S) and price to be paid in one month (the futures price, i.e. F) of a product. Disregarding trading purposes, the approximate relationship (2) holds when the market reaches the equilibrium. If $S < F - U$, buyers will prefer immediate purchase (purchasing commodities), and sellers will prefer sale in one month (selling futures). Conversely, if $S > F - U$, buyers will prefer purchase in one month (purchasing futures), and sellers will prefer immediate sale (selling commodities).

April 20, 2020 is the second last trading day for the May WTI oil futures contracts traded on CME. If these futures contracts are taken as approximate commodity contracts, then the occurrence of negative prices is theoretically possible. However, two conditions must be met before negative prices come to be real: First, the crude oil market has very low expectation for future prices, that is, the prices of June WTI contracts are very low. Second, the cost of inventory and shipping is relatively high. That is, negative prices may only occur when the cost of inventory and shipping (i.e., U) is higher than the futures prices (i.e., F).

Crude oil prices have long-term relationships with economic activities [8]. As the benchmark of the United States (US) oil prices, WTI crude oil futures prices have drawn academia's attention [3, 6]. The mismatch between supply and demand in the crude oil market has become increasingly severe since the beginning of 2020. On the one hand, due to the impact of the coronavirus pandemic, the global economy suffered significant recession, and the crude oil demand has reduced dramatically. On the other hand, main oil-producing countries cannot reach a consensus on the reduction in production, and the resulting price war on crude oil has raised the supply dramatically. The mismatch between supply and demand has led to the slump of crude oil prices. By April 20, 2020, crude oil quotes in all major markets dropped to approximately \$20 per barrel.

6.2 Were Cost of Inventory and Shipping the Cause for Negative Prices?

The mismatch between supply and demand continuously pushed down the market's expectation for crude oil prices. The first condition for the occurrence of negative prices is almost satisfied. Meanwhile, there is analysis asserting that the inventory of crude oil is reaching the limit and the cost of inventory is increasing dramatically. Have

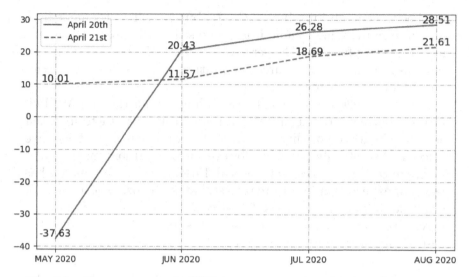

Fig. 6.1. Term structures for WTI futures contracts on April 20 and 21. *Source*: CME and WIND.

the cost of inventory and shipping already surpassed the expected crude oil price?

From previous analysis, if the May WTI contract is taken approximately as a commodity, then the difference in price between the May and June contracts should be approximately the cost of inventory and shipping for one month. On April 20, the one-month price differences for crude oil futures contracts from May to August were \$−58.06, \$−5.85, and \$−2.23, per barrel, respectively. On the next day, the corresponding one-month price differences turned to \$−1.56, \$−7.85, and \$−2.93, per barrel, respectively. Figure 6.1 exhibits the term structures of the WTI contracts discussed.

Then, following the analysis above, the monthly cost of inventory was predicted to be \$58.06 per barrel on April 20, which dropped to \$1.56 per barrel on the next day. Obviously, such dramatic intraday change in the cost of inventory and shipping is extremely unlikely.

In fact, the inventory of crude oil has not reached the limit. Cushing, Oklahoma is the designated delivery point for WTI futures contracts. With a centralized location, Cushing is the most significant crude oil trading hub in the US. The most direct inventory cost is storing crude oil at Cushing. It is true that the storage of crude oil

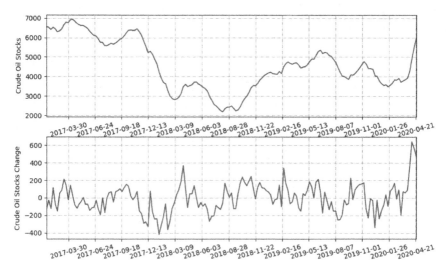

Fig. 6.2. Crude oil stocks and stock changes at Cushing, Oklahoma.
Source: Data of crude oil stock changes (bottom) is from the Energy Information Administration (EIA). Crude oil stocks (top) are calculated based on changes in stocks.

at Cushing has increased significantly since April. However, based on historical statistics, the inventory had not reached the limit on April 22, and is even lower than the level in 2016 and 2017 (as shown in Fig. 6.2).

There was some sources of information asserting that, although the crude oil inventory at Cushing had not reached the limit, all tankers had been rented by producers and merchandisers, who would fill up the tankers soon. Some analysts predicted that all tankers at Cushing would be filled up in late May. Even the rush in purchasing crude oil inventory cannot explain how the difference in price between May and June WTI contracts reduced to $1.56 per barrel.

Let's temporarily put aside the question of whether the inventory at Cushing had reached the limit. Even if all tankers at Cushing have been filled up, can't WTI crude oil be physically delivered? Despite the fact that Cushing is located at central inner land, there is still the option of tanker shipping for crude oil. The seaway pipelines provide a direct connection between Cushing, Oklahoma and the export market at Houston, Texas. Ever since the abolition of the export ban on crude oil, WTI crude oil has become seaway crude oil, and

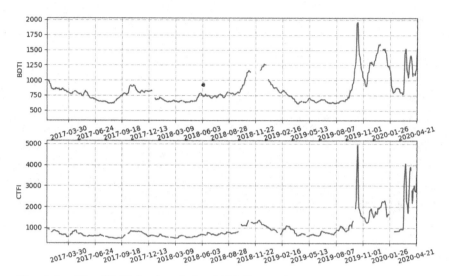

Fig. 6.3.   The BDTI (top) and the CTFI (bottom).
Source: iFinD.

has huge export capacity. Therefore, inventory is not the only factor of concern. A comprehensive analysis on both inventory and shipping is needed to get the whole picture [1]. Now let's look at the shipping market. With the mismatch between supply and demand in 2020, needs for crude oil shipping have gradually pushed up the shipping price. Figure 6.3 displays the changing trends of the Baltic Exchange Dirty Tanker Index (BDTI) and the China Import Crude Oil Tanker Freight Index (CTFI) since 2017. Two observations can be made: First, although the tanker shipping price has been increasing, it has not surpassed the peak in 2019. Second, the shipping market has been in a downturn since the 2008 financial crisis. Even the peak in 2019 did not reach the pre-financial crisis level. Therefore, there is still a long way to go before the shipping market reaches its limit.

Rough calculation of costs of inventory and shipping. On April 16, 2020 the Shanghai International Energy Exchange made the announcement to adjust the daily inventory cost of crude oil to 0.4 RMB per barrel. On April 22, 2020, the rent for a very large crude carrier (VLCC) was approximately 0.2 million dollars per day, which was equivalent to approximately $0.1 per barrel (the cargo volume of a VLCC is between 0.2 and 0.3 million ton, which is approximately the volume of 2 million barrels). Based on the market price, the cost of shipping was higher than the cost of inventory. If calculated at the peak price on April 22, the monthly shipping cost of crude oil was approximately $3 per barrel. It is worth noting that the BDTI and the CTFI dropped from 1525 and 3566.64 on April 22 to 1236 and 2099.86 in 8 days, respectively. The post-event performance of the shipping market confirms that the market is far away from its limit.

If we date back to April 20, the settlement price of June WTI was $20.43 per barrel. Taking the monthly shipping cost of $3 per barrel into account, the May WTI contract should be approximately $17.43 per barrel, which is far from being negative.

Based on the analysis above, the rise in the cost of inventory and shipping can push down crude oil prices. However, the cost was not high enough to cause negative prices on April 20. So, what was the decisive factor that triggered the negative price?

6.3 Why Do Exchanges Allow Negative Price Trading?

On April 15, 2020, CME made the announcement to allow for listing of energy futures contracts with zero or negative strikes on NYMEX, which means negative price trading for WTI futures is supported by CME's pricing and valuation model.

But why do exchanges allow negative price trading? Both the mismatch between supply and demand and the rise in cost of inventory and shipping have increased the likelihood of negative prices. Under this circumstance, if exchanges do not allow for trading at zero or negative prices, trades are to stop when prices slump to the minimum quoting unit. As a consequence, long futures positions cannot close out but have to conduct physical delivery and suffer the loss. Also, there will be no out-of-money futures options in the market, which restrains hedging through futures options. Therefore, for the sake of ordinary trading and hedging needs, exchanges allow negative price trading.

The participants of the futures market can be largely categorized as hedgers, speculators, and arbitragers. Most market participants will choose to close out before maturity, instead of conducting physical delivery. There are two main reasons for this. First, unwillingness of physical delivery. For all types of market

Table 6.1. Trading volumes and open interests for May and June WTI contracts on April 20 and 21.

	Trading volume		Open interest	
	April 20	April 21	April 20	April 21
May 2020	32.50	18.44	10.86	1.30
June 2020	145.82	241.21	53.80	58.16
Ratio	1:4.5	1:13	1:5	1:45

Source: CME and WIND (minor differences in numbers for data from different sources).

participants, in most cases, their purpose of trading can be achieved by closing out before maturity, and the troubles brought by physical delivery can be avoided. Second, incapability of physical delivery. Not all market participants are qualified for physical delivery. For those who cannot conduct physical delivery, their position must be closed out before maturity. For futures contracts that are nearly matured, market participants who are unqualified for physical delivery can only close position but not open position. Therefore, the allowance of negative price trading by CME ensured these market participants can close out to leave the market.

In fact, only a small proportion of futures contracts ends with physical delivery. Most futures contracts are closed out before maturity. This is a common feature for all futures contracts traded on exchanges. May WTI contracts are no exception. April 20 was the second last trading day for May WTI contracts. At this point of time, most traders had headed for June WTI contracts. Table 6.1, Figs. 6.4 and 6.5 show the trading volume and the open interest of May and June WTI contracts on April 20 and 21. On April 20, the ratio of the trading volume of May contracts to June contracts was 1:4.5, and became 1:13 just one day after, while the ratios of the open interest were 1:5 and 1:45 for the two days, respectively.

6.4 The Mispricing Caused by Illiquidity

Mispricing is commonly found in financial and commodity markets. The negative trading prices of May WTI contracts on April

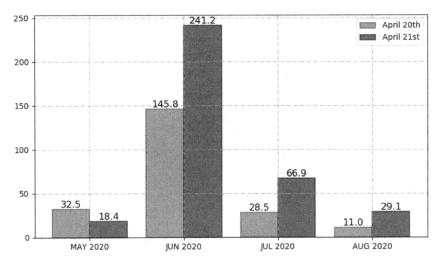

Fig. 6.4. Trading volumes of WTI contracts on April 20 and 21.
Source: CME and WIND.

20 constituted a typical mispricing event.[a] First, May futures were close to maturity, with inactive trading and insufficient liquidity. This is easily observable from the above comparison of trading volumes and open interests between May and June contracts. Second, traders holding May contracts could only close position and not open position if they were unqualified for physical delivery. Therefore, under the circumstance of insufficient liquidity and buying quotes, the occurrence of massive selling quotes could lead to immediate illiquidity, which could likely cause the price slump.

Where were the massive selling quotes on April 20 coming from? There were two main sources for the last-minute selling quotes of WTI contracts on that day. First, long positions without qualification for physical delivery were margin closed-out by brokers. Traders have to close their position before maturity if they cannot conduct physical delivery. If traders fail to do so, brokers have the right to conduct margin close-out. It is worth noting that brokers will conduct margin close-out regardless of the price. This leads to fire sales, which are

---

[a]For a long time, main crude oil prices of the world are strongly interrelated [3,9]. However, on April 20, 2020, only the WTI crude oil futures contracts traded on CME were traded at negative prices.

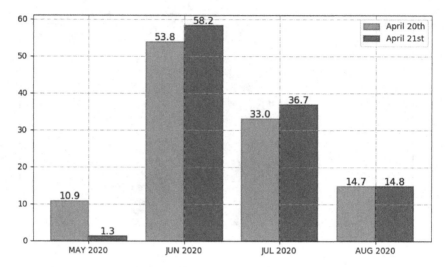

Fig. 6.5.   Open interests of WTI contracts on April 20 and 21.
Source: CME and WIND.

forced sales commonly seen in financial markets and can be found in almost all markets.

Second, there was a possibility of market corner through suppressing prices,[b] Several conditions must be satisfied before this can happen: (1) *Easy control.* On the one hand, futures contracts have insufficient liquidity when close to maturity. On the other hand, the settlement price is determined in a short time interval. The settlement price for the WTI crude oil futures contract is calculated as the weighted average of the strike prices between 2:28 pm and 2:30 pm, New York Time. (2) *Huge space.* On April 15, CME announced that negative price trading was allowed, which led to unlimited downside space for prices. (3) *Profitability.* Trading of WTI crude oil futures contracts supports trading at settlement, which means that futures contracts are traded at the daily settlement price. To conclude, speculators have both motivation and capability to corner the market.

---

[b]Hache and Lantz [6] conclude that speculative trading is a key factor for market instability and the oil bubble.

6.5   Where were the Arbitragers (Function of Tankers and Tanker Ships)?

Why were there no buyers? There is one type of trader: arbitragers. Arbitragers seek opportunities of arbitrage from mispricing in markets to achieve profits, which in turn pushes the market price towards normal. When such massive mispricing occurs in a market, arbitragers will normally take the chance of arbitrage in the first place, and the price will go back to normal in a short period of time. However, under this circumstance, the arbitrager must be qualified for physical delivery (which should be hedgers) so as to open position. There is also a key reason why arbitragers did not take action on April 20: They needed to hold tankers or tanker ships. Notably, April 20 was the second last trading day for May WTI contracts. With negative price occurring at closing quotation, April 21 was the only day to open position for arbitrage. Therefore, arbitrage on May contracts is very likely to be taken as commodity arbitrage, which requires tankers or tanker ships for physical delivery of crude oil. In other words, there was a huge arbitrage risk if no tanker or tanker ship was on hold.

From the perspective of post-event performance, arbitragers did take actions but with a one-day delay. Let's take a closer look at the shipping market after April 20. The BDTI was increased by 16.5% on April 21, with a 30% two-day increase. Similarly, the CTFI was increased by 21.2% on April 22, with a 31% two-day increase. As for the time-zone difference, Beijing, China is seven hours ahead of London, United Kingdom, and the latter is five hours ahead of New York, US. Table 6.2 and Fig. 6.6 show the settlement prices of May WTI contracts and the BDTI and the CTFI.

To have a closer look at the timeline: On April 20, May WTI contracts dropped to negative trading prices when it was close to closing quotation, with a price difference of $58.06 compared to June contracts. Over the next two days, the BDTI and the CTFI rose by approximately 30% (taking the time-zone difference into consideration, there was an overlapping period between the increase in shipping prices and the last trading day of May WTI contracts). Just one day after, which was the last trading day of May WTI contracts, the price difference between May and June contracts returned to normal level.

Table 6.2. The settlement prices of May WTI contracts and the BDTI and the CTFI.

| Date | BDTI | | CTFI | | Settlement prices |
	Index	Daily growth	Index	Daily growth	
2020-04-20	1,182.00	2.43%	2,717.32	−1.55%	−37.63
2020-04-21	1,377.00	16.50%	2,942.88	8.30%	10.01
2020-04-22	1,525.00	10.75%	3,566.64	21.20%	—

Source: iFinD and WIND.

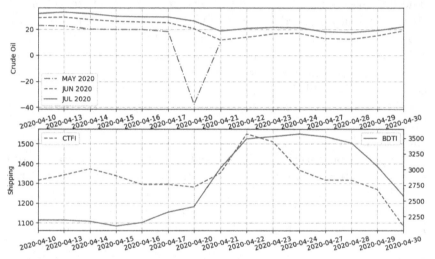

Fig. 6.6. The settlement prices of May, June, and July WTI contracts (top) and the BDTI and the CTFI (bottom).
Source: iFinD and WIND.

Therefore, we propose a reasonable conjecture: When it was close to closing quotation, May WTI contracts were under negative price trading. Many arbitragers found this mispricing to be an opportunity for arbitrage, and began to search for tankers and tanker ships. As a consequence, shipping prices were pushed up by massive orders. At the same time, arbitragers holding tanks and tanker ships opened positions in the futures market to take arbitrage from May WTI contracts, which contributed to the recovery of the market from mispricing. Searching for tanker shipping for the purpose of arbitrage mainly happened on April 21, New York Time.

6.6 The Reason Behind the Occurrence of Negative Oil Prices

From the analysis above, we can conclude that the negative settlement price of May WTI contracts on April 20 was a mispricing event. The mispricing was the consequence of several factors.

First, on the macro level, the global economy had been in recession due to the impact of the coronavirus pandemic, and oil demand had reduced greatly. The main oil-producing countries could not agree on reduction in production, with the result that oil supply had been increasing continuously. The mismatch between demand and supply caused the slump in oil prices. Second, on the meso level, the rise in oil storage had led to increased cost of inventory and shipping, which had further impact on oil prices. It is worth noting that, by April 2020, the situation was insufficient to bring negative oil prices; however, the necessary conditions for the occurrence of negative oil prices were all met. Third, on the micro level, the trading principles and features of oil futures on exchanges became the last piece in the puzzle for the resulting negative oil prices. (1) The CME announcement on April 15 that allowed negative price trading provided technical support. (2) The fact that the futures contracts were close to maturity, and most traders had closed their position to leave the market was the natural feature for insufficient liquidity. (3) Closing to delivery, traders unqualified for physical delivery cannot open position, which further worsened the problem of illiquidity. (4) The delay in response of arbitragers left the mispricing for one day before the market recovered from it.

6.7 The Shipping Market in View of the Oil Pricing Mechanism

Fuel oil is the main cost of shipping. As crude oil prices have direct influence on fuel oil prices, the fact that the crude oil market can have

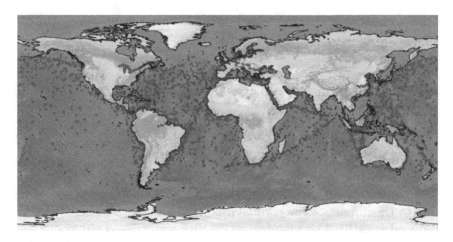

Fig. 6.7. Real-time allocation of selected ships worldwide.
Source: Collaborative Innovation Center for Transport Studies, De Montfort University (DMU).

an impact on shipping price is easily understandable.[c] Conversely, the influence of the shipping market on the crude oil market is rarely analyzed.[d] There are many futures-commodity arbitragers in the market, who will contribute to the convergence of futures prices to commodity prices when contracts are close to maturity. As for crude oil, it is crucial for the futures–commodity arbitragers to hold tankers or tanker ships. The negative settlement prices of May WTI contracts on April 20 was a typical mispricing. The occurrence of such a huge mispricing in the global market is quite unusual. This indicates that the function of the shipping market in the oil pricing mechanism has long been overly underestimated.

With trading wars and oil wars adding to the global impact of the coronavirus pandemic, the global market has been subject to

---

[c]Volatilities of crude oil prices and exchange rates are the main risks faced by shipping markets [5].

[d]Agerton and Upton [1] analyze the price discount of WTI crude oils to Brent crude oils from 1990 to 2015 from the perspective of crude oil shipping (by means of pipeline, barge, and rail). They conclude that the limit in shipping causes the price discount. In contrast, most of studies focus on the influencing factors of tanker shipping prices [2, 4].

dramatic volatility with one mispricing following another. The battle for pricing may be a long-lasting feature of the global economy in the near future. Shipping markets, financial markets, and commodity markets are the three pillars of the modernized global economy, managing resource allocation for logistics, capitals, and commodities, respectively. Shipping is the foundation for the global industrial chain (see Figure 6.7). According to the *Trade and Development Report 2019* by the United National Conference on Trade and Development, the global total amount of trade for 2019 is approximately 19 trillion dollars. When measured by product weight, the total amount of trade by shipping takes up to 90% of the global total amount of trade, and the number becomes 70% when measured by product value. The negative oil prices event on April 20 reminds us of the vital importance of shipping markets in the global economy.

Acknowledgement

The authors would like to acknowledge financial support from the National Natural Science Foundation of China (71971034, 71571034) and the Humanities and Social Science Youth Project of Ministry of Education of China (19YJC790171).

References

[1] M. Agerton and Jr. G. B. Upton, Decomposing crude price differentials: Domestic shipping constraints or the crude oil export ban? *Energy Journal*, 40(3): 155–172, 2019.

[2] A. H. Alizadeh and W. K. Talley, Vessel and voyage determinants of tanker freight rates and contract times. *Transport Policy (Oxf)*, 18(5): 665–675, 2011.

[3] S. Coronado, Jr. T. M. Fullerton, and O. Rojas, Causality patterns for Brent, WTI, and Argus oil prices. *Applied Economics Letters*, 24(14): 982–986, 2017.

[4] J. Dinwoodie and J. Morris, Tanker forward freight agreements: The future for freight futures? *Maritime Policy & Management*, 30(1): 45–58, 2003.

[5] A. A. El-Masry, M. Olugbode, and J. Pointon, The exposure of shipping firms' stock returns to financial risks and oil prices: A global perspective. *Maritime Policy & Management*, 37(5): 453–473, 2010.

[6] E. Hache and F. Lantz, Speculative trading and oil price dynamic: A study of the WTI market. *Energy Economics*, 36: 334–340, 2013.

[7] J. C. Hull, *Options, Futures, and Other Derivatives*, 6th Ed. (Prentice Hall, USA).

[8] L. Sandrine and V. Mignon, Oil prices and economic activity: An asymmetric cointegration approach, *Energy Economics*, 30(3): 847–855, 2008.

[9] J. C. Reboredo, How do crude oil prices co-move? A Copula approach, *Energy Economics*, 33(5): 948–955, 2011.

Chapter 7

Option Pricing with Shifted Lognormal Model for Negative Oil Prices*

Henry Yang

MBA '19, Cornell University, Ithaca, NY 14853-0099, USA

py87@cornell.edu

Abstract

Fischer Black and Myron Scholes (1973) assumed asset prices follow lognormal distributions and derived the famous Black–Scholes option pricing formula. The lognormal assumption implies the asset price will never be negative and has zero as its lower bound. By relaxing the negative and zero bound, we derive a Black–Scholes-like option pricing formula for asset prices following a shifted lognormal distribution with a lower bound. The formula can be applied to price options with negative prices and negative strikes.

Keywords: Black–Scholes, negative price, negative strike, option pricing, shifted lognormal distribution

7.1 Introduction

Oil prices made history on April 20, 2020, crashing into the negative price territory for the first time amid the coronavirus pandemic, which reduced global oil demand by 24% while oil production remained at its peak.

---

*The views expressed in this article are those of the author and do not represent the affiliated institution.

United States (US) oil benchmark West Texas Intermediate (WTI) light sweet crude oil futures crashed below US$0/barrel on April 20, 2020 for the first time in history, closing the day at negative US$37.63 a barrel as desperate traders rushed to liquidate their expiring contracts.

WTI monthly futures contracts are traded on the Chicago Mercantile Exchange (CME), each contract expiring around the 20th of each month. When a contract expires, all long position holders (who bought WIT contracts) and short position holders (who sold WIT contracts) would exchange physical oil in Cushing, Oklahoma, US. In general, majority of the futures contracts are closed before the expiration day, leaving just a small percentage of open contracts ending up with physical delivery. Due to lack of liquidity when a contract nears its expiration day, large and professional trading houses often require their traders to close their open positions by selling long positions or buying back their short positions three to five days before the expiration day.

Trading volume for WTI May contracts started to decline from April 16, indicating that large traders had finished their trading activities. Realizing that liquidity was drying out and physical demand was crashing, the remaining traders fled from the expiring May WTI oil futures contracts in a frenzy on April 20, just one day ahead of the expiration day April 21 with no place to put the crude, but the June WTI contracts settled at a much higher level of US$20.43 a barrel.

WTI starts a trading day session at 6:00 p.m., New York Time, and ends at 5:00 p.m. the next day. The trading is halted for one hour. The "normal" trading hours are between 9:00 a.m. to 2:30 p.m. The contract settlement price of the day is the volume-weighted average of the last three minutes before 2:30 p.m. WTI futures daily settlement prices are benchmark prices for WTI-linked financial derivatives including, but not limited to, commodity indices and exchange-traded funds (ETFs). Many over-the-counter (OTC) WTI-linked financial products are settled or traded at the daily settlement prices. Therefore, the oil prices display high volatility between 1:00 p.m. to 2:30 p.m. after traders return to the trading desks from lunch and before the normal market closing time at 2:30 p.m.

On April 15, 2020, CME announced "effective immediately" that their trading and clearing systems were ready for negative WTI prices and negative strike prices for WTI options. In mid-March, when oil prices dropped into the lower \$20 price range, we observed that many investors entered into the oil market, expecting to buy at the bottom. As May 20 contracts neared the expiration, the price continued to drop, and traders panicked to close their contracts, driving the prices below zero. The May US WTI contract fell by US\$55.90, to settle at negative US\$37.63 a barrel after touching an all-time low of negative US\$40.32 a barrel at 1:29 p.m. The spread between May and June at one point widened to US\$60.76, the widest in history for the two nearest monthly contracts. Investors bailed out of the May contracts ahead of expiry later on Monday because of the lack of demand for the actual oil.

When a futures contract expires, traders must decide whether to take delivery of the oil or roll their positions into another futures contract for a later month. This process is usually relatively uncomplicated, but this time there were very few counterparties that were willing buy from investors and take delivery of the oil. Storage was filling quickly at Cushing in Oklahoma, which is where the crude is delivered. "The storage is too full for speculators to buy this contract, and the refiners are running at low levels because we haven't lifted stay-at-home orders in most states... there's not a lot of hope that things are going to change in 24 hours," said an analyst.

7.2   Traders Rewrite Risk Models After Oil's Plunge Below Zero

The oil's plunge below zero has broken the models that many traders rely on to calculate risk. Banks need to recalculate the value and riskiness of their trading portfolios to account for a world in which the price of oil can go negative. The possibility of sub-zero prices has made some positions much riskier, exposing some financial institutions and traders to potentially significant losses and triggering a rush to recalibrate, exacerbating the wild swings in the markets.

Standard pricing models, used for options on futures and swaps, can't handle negative numbers, producing incorrect risk metrics. For example, banks use hedges to limit losses with \$0 as a floor, which is no longer there. The increase in volatility means an increase in "value-at-risk", the statistical metric many banks and trading houses use to estimate the probability of losses. Still, the speed at which oil has swung to sub-zero prices has left traders in shock and contributed to wild gyrations. In the options markets, for example, bid–ask spreads have widened drastically, a sign that fewer traders are willing to take on additional risk. One clearinghouse has switched the options pricing and valuation model from standard Merton–Black–Scholes to Bachelier to accommodate negative prices in the underlying futures and allow for listing of options contracts with negative strikes for a certain set of crude oil and energy products. Switching between Merton–Black–Scholes and Bachelier is currently artificially determined at a price point, though it can be calibrated when more data become available [3]. However, it is not natural to assume a single asset price follows two separate distributions.

In the following sections, we introduce a shifted lognormal option pricing formula, assuming the asset price follows a single shifted lognormal distribution. Based on this assumption, we derive a simple Black–Scholes-like option pricing formula.

7.3   Options on Asset with Shifted Lognormal Distributions

In traditional option pricing theory such as the Merton–Black–Scholes framework, the asset prices are assumed to follow a lognormal distribution. Therefore, the Merton–Black–Scholes option pricing formula is not applicable for negative prices and negative strikes [2]. In commodity trading, though the prices could become negative, as demonstrated by recent WTI prices, they have theoretical lower bounds which are supported by physical demand/supply. Examples are crude product spreads and calendar spreads where the spread prices could go negative with lower bounds theoretically determined by storage costs.

In this section, we model such asset prices as the following shifted lognormal distribution and derive Merton–Black–Scholes-type option pricing formula.

Let asset price S follow a shifted lognormal distribution:

$$S = a + b \cdot e^{(r-0.5\sigma^2)T+\sigma\sqrt{T}\cdot x},$$

where x is standard normal variable.

We will derive the option price formula on S. Let $f(x)$ be the density function of standard normal distribution:

$$f(x) = \frac{1}{\sqrt{2\pi}} e^{\frac{-x^2}{2\sigma^2}}$$

Let y be a monotonic function of x, $y = H(x)$, $g(y)$ be the density function of y, then the distribution of y is:

$$g(y) = f(x) \left| \frac{dx}{dy} \right|$$

In the following, we derive the call option price formula with brute force calculus. The payoff function of call with strike K is $\max(S - K, 0)$, then the call option price is the discounted expectation of payoff:

$$c = e^{-rT} E(\max(S - K, 0))$$

$$= e^{-rT} \int \max(S - K, 0) g(S) dS$$

We have two cases, $b > 0$ and $b < 0$. S is a monotonically increasing function of x when $b > 0$ and monotonically decreasing function when $b < 0$. When $b > 0$, a is the "floor" cut-off price, assuming $K > a$,

$$c = e^{-rT} \int \max(S - K, 0) g(S) dS$$

$$= e^{-rT} \int_K^\infty (S - K) g(S) dS$$

$$= e^{-rT} \int_K^\infty (S - K) f(x) \frac{dx}{dS} dS$$

$$= e^{-rT} \int_{X^*}^\infty (S - K) f(x) dx$$

Where X^* satisfies equation:

$$K = a + b \cdot e^{(r - 0.5\sigma^2)T + \sigma\sqrt{T} \cdot X^*}$$

Solving,

$$X^* = \frac{\ln(\frac{K-a}{b}) - (r - 0.5\sigma^2)T}{\sigma\sqrt{T}}$$

$$= -\frac{\ln(\frac{b}{K-a}) + (r - 0.5\sigma^2)T}{\sigma\sqrt{T}}$$

Continuing the integration of option formula:

$$c = e^{-rT} \int_{X^*}^{\infty} (S - K) f(x) dx$$

$$= e^{-rT} \int_{X^*}^{\infty} S \cdot f(x) dx - e^{-rT} \int_{X^*}^{\infty} K \cdot f(x) dx$$

$$= e^{-rT} \left(\int_{X^*}^{\infty} (a + b \cdot e^{(r-0.5\sigma^2)T + \sigma\sqrt{T} \cdot x}) f(x) dx - \int_{X^*}^{\infty} K \cdot f(x) dx \right)$$

$$= e^{-rT} \left(\int_{X^*}^{\infty} (b \cdot e^{(r-0.5\sigma^2)T + \sigma\sqrt{T} \cdot x}) f(x) dx - \int_{X^*}^{\infty} (K - a) \cdot f(x) dx \right)$$

$$= e^{-rT} (I_1 - I_2)$$

We carefully work out the integrations:

$$I_2 = \int_{X^*}^{\infty} (K - a) \cdot f(x) dx$$

$$= (K - a) \cdot N(-X^*)$$

And,

$$I_1 = \int_{X^*}^{\infty} (b \cdot e^{(r-0.5\sigma^2)T + \sigma\sqrt{T} \cdot x}) f(x) dx$$

$$= \int_{X^*}^{\infty} b \cdot e^{(r-0.5\sigma^2)T + \sigma\sqrt{T} \cdot x} \frac{1}{\sqrt{2\pi}} e^{-0.5x^2} dx$$

$$= \int_{X^*}^{\infty} b \cdot e^{(r-0.5\sigma^2)T} \cdot \frac{1}{\sqrt{2\pi}} e^{\sigma\sqrt{T} \cdot x - 0.5x^2} dx$$

$$= \int_{X^*}^{\infty} b \cdot e^{(r-0.5\sigma^2)T} \cdot \frac{1}{\sqrt{2\pi}} e^{-0.5(x - \sigma\sqrt{T})^2 + 0.5\sigma^2 T} dx$$

$$= \int_{X^*}^{\infty} b \cdot e^{rT} \cdot \frac{1}{\sqrt{2\pi}} e^{-0.5(x - \sigma\sqrt{T})^2} dx$$

$$= \int_{X^* + \sigma\sqrt{T}}^{\infty} b \cdot e^{rT} \cdot \frac{1}{\sqrt{2\pi}} e^{-0.5z^2} dz$$

$$= b \cdot e^{rT} \cdot N(X^* + \sigma\sqrt{T})$$

Call option price is:

$$c = e^{-rT}(I_1 - I_2)$$

$$= e^{-rT}\left[b \cdot e^{rT} \cdot N(X^* + \sigma\sqrt{T}) - (K-a)N(-X^*)\right]$$

$$= b \cdot N(X^* + \sigma\sqrt{T}) - (K-a)e^{-rT}N(-X^*)$$

$$= bN(d_1) - (K-a)e^{-rT}N(d_2)$$

$$d_2 = -X^* = \frac{\ln(\frac{b}{K-a}) + (r - 0.5\sigma^2)T}{\sigma\sqrt{T}}$$

$$d_1 = X^* + \sigma\sqrt{T} = \frac{\ln(\frac{b}{K-a}) + (r - 0.5\sigma^2)T}{\sigma\sqrt{T}}$$

When $b = S$ and $a = 0$, we get Black–Scholes formula.

By introducing an extra parameter for the one-sided price bound, we derived a Black–Scholes-like option pricing formula [1]. Theoretically, the bound can be determined by the physical constraints of the asset, such as storage cost, seasonality factors, and demand-supply constraints. Practically, the traders often have a very good sense of the bounds.

References

[1] W. Schachermayer and J. Teichmann, How Close Are the Option Pricing Formulas of Bachelier and Black–Merton–Scholes?, *Mathematical Finance*, 155–170, 2008.

[2] L. H. Frankena, Pricing and hedging options in a negative interest rate environment. *Thesis for master degree, Delft University of Technology*, 2018.

[3] M. Dong, Option pricing with a non-zero lower bound on stock price. *The Journal of Futures Markets*, 775–794, 2005.

Chapter 8

The Paradox of Negative Oil Prices*

Bin Zhu

Nanhua Futures Co. Ltd.,
193 West Lake Avenue,
Hangzhou 310002, China
gann888@nawaa.com

Abstract

2020 is definitely a year that will be remembered in history. The global outbreak of the COVID-19 pandemic has caused a huge impact on the global economy, in particular, the paradox of negative oil prices, which has raised huge challenges in the practice of commodity and related asset risk management.

Keywords: Paradox of negative oil prices, WTI futures, Black model, spot price, risk management

8.1 The Background for the Paradox of Negative Oil Prices

2020 is definitely a year that will be remembered in history. The global outbreak of the COVID-19 pandemic has caused a huge impact on the global economy. The index of the global stock market has declined repeatedly, and the stock markets of various countries have frequently been melted. The commodity market has also been

---

*The views expressed in this chapter are those of the author, and do not represent the affiliated company.

affected, as evidenced by the negative value of the West Texas Intermediate (WTI) oil prices, which has never been seen before in history.
On April 8, the Chicago Mercantile Exchange (CME) stated that it
was making adjustments to the software in response to the emergence
of negative prices on futures contracts. On April 15, CME Clearing
stated that if there is a negative price, all CME trading and clearing
systems can continue to operate normally. Then on April 21, Beijing
time, the WTI crude oil May futures contract price fell to a negative
value, the lowest point even fell below US$−40 per barrel, the settle-
ment price of that day finally locked in at US$−37.63 per barrel. The
emergence of negative oil prices has subverted everyone's perception
and is a challenge to the futures' pricing system. In my opinion, a
negative price in futures is definitely an unreasonable phenomenon.

8.2   The Difference Between Futures Price
and Spot Price

When it comes to spot trading, everyone will be more familiar with
it. It is a buying and selling behavior that immediately exchanges
money once the transaction is completed. The price formed during
this trading process is called the spot price. As spot trading has a
certain degree of closure or regionalism, there may be some information asymmetry in the transaction process, so the spot price will
usually be a regional price, or even a monopoly price, and may lack
universality and representativeness.

A futures contract, which is clearly defined in our textbooks [1], is
a standardized forward contract, a legal agreement to buy or sell an
underlying asset at a predetermined price at a specified time in the
future. This specific underlying asset can be a certain commodity,
such as gold, crude oil, copper, soybeans, etc., or can also be some
kind of financial assets, such as stocks, bonds, foreign exchange, etc.

Futures are the product of the spot market development to a
certain stage. Due to the mismatch of supply and demand in time,
the spot trading of hand-in-hand delivery may not always be realized.
The difference in time, location, and trading objects will lead to
fluctuations in transaction prices and thus generate risks. Therefore,
spot forward transactions have gradually been derived. At first, the
two parties of the transaction verbally promised to buy and sell a
certain amount of commodity at a specific time in the future.

However, in this process, on the one hand, there will be a credit risk of a party defaulting. On the other hand, there will be a demand for a party that no longer needs commodities and hopes to transfer them. Therefore, the trading contract has gradually appeared, and gradually evolved into a standardized futures contract, which can be freely circulated in the exchange. The price formed during the futures contract transaction is called the futures price, so the futures price is the market's expectation of the spot price at a certain point in the future.

But there are tens of thousands of spot markets and spot prices, which spot price does the futures price expect to match? This is closely related to the design of the futures system [1, 2]. The most critical core of the standardization of commodity futures contracts is the standardization of commodity delivery systems, such as the shape, weight, quality, packaging, transportation, storage, delivery warehouse, delivery time, etc., that is, delivery products must meet specific standards, which means futures prices are actually the prices of specific commodities that meet specific requirements, and the boundaries of this specific commodity are artificially drawn, coupled with various artificial trading rules, so we say that the futures market is an artificially designed market.

Therefore, the futures price is not equal to the spot price. The futures price can only represent a specific part of the spot price, but as the futures price is formed by the open market and has the characteristics of being open and efficient, the futures price is more likely to become a pricing benchmark. Other spot prices establish a connection with the futures price through this basis. But to check whether the futures price is reasonable and the pricing benchmark is effective, the most critical factor is whether the design of futures contracts and transaction delivery systems is perfect.

8.3   What is the Reasonable Basis of Futures Price?

When CME's WTI crude oil futures have a negative price, we think this is an unreasonable price, because it deviates too far from the spot price, which violates the basic logic of the regression of price difference between spot price and futures price. So what kind of futures price is a reasonable futures price, or what kind of spread between futures price and spot price is a reasonable spread? To answer this question, let us return to the most basic theory of futures price determination.

Currently, there are three well-known theories of futures price determination: Carrying Cost Theory, Risk Premium Theory, and Expectation Theory.

Carrying Cost Theory takes the commodity as the starting point, and believes that the futures price should be equal to the spot price plus the holding cost. The holding cost includes three parts: financing interest, storage expenses, and income. This theory can usually be used to explain the market structure of futures contango, because it is usually impossible for the holding cost to be negative.

Risk Premium Theory analyzes futures prices from the perspective of speculators, and regards futures as a similar risk asset to stocks. It believes that futures prices are equal to the expected value of spot prices plus risk premiums. Therefore, the higher the risk, the higher the required return. Under this theory, futures can be contango or have backwardation, depending on the relationship between expected returns and risk-free returns.

Expectation Theory believes that the current transaction price of futures contracts should be equal to the consensus spot price at the time of delivery made by the market. When the market expects that there is sufficient spot supply at the time of delivery, there will be more short hedgers, and more discounts need to be provided to lure speculators to act as longs to achieve the purpose of transferring risk, so futures will have discounts. A discount is a kind of compensation for speculators to bear the risks that hedgers are not willing to bear. Conversely, when the market expects spot supply to be tight at the time of delivery, there will be more long hedgers and futures will see a premium.

Considering the recent WTI crude oil market, we will find that none of the above theories can explain such a situation, let alone explain the emergence of negative prices.

No matter which one of the theories we follow, as the futures contract expires and the delivery date approaches, the expected future spot price becomes a reality step by step. Therefore, when the expiration date approaches, the futures price and the target spot price will always gradually get close until the time of delivery when the difference between the two prices tends to be zero or within the range of no-arbitrage.

So here comes the question, where does the anomaly in futures prices or the anomalies in spot-future spreads come from? In the final analysis, it depends on whether the design of the futures trading delivery system is reasonable.

On April 21, Beijing time, the WTI crude oil May contract's settlement price showed a negative value, and the next day was the contract's expiration date. The spot settlement price returned to more than US$10, and the price difference at that time had exceeded US$−40. In history, the spot–futures spread is basically within US$5. The crude oil market has changed drastically only a few times, when the price fluctuated sharply, the price difference exceeding US$5, but it is basically within US$10. The historical highest price of the New York Mercantile Exchange (NYMEX) crude oil futures appeared on July 11, 2008, at US$147.90 per barrel. The spot–futures spread at that time was about US$15, which was the historical extreme spread before the negative price appeared on April 21. This has fully explained the shortcomings of the CME crude oil trading delivery system. The system which allowed negative prices eventually caused market price distortions and subverted history.

Is it possible that the price of crude oil futures could approach US$200 per barrel, or even US$500 per barrel? Is it possible that a spot–futures spread of more than $40 or even hundreds of dollars could appear? Of course, it may occur under a specific system. For example, although various types of spot goods are abundant, there are very few deliverable commodities and delivery warehouses that meet the requirements of futures, which artificially causes the underlying commodity to be in extreme shortage.

Therefore, the distorted transaction delivery system will inevitably cause distorted transaction prices, which will lead to wrong pricing in the futures market.

8.4　The Impact of Unreasonable Futures Pricing on the Market

The two basic functions of the futures market are pricing and risk hedging, and risk hedging is actually based on reasonable pricing, so the rationality of futures market pricing is the foundation for the function and existence of the entire futures market. Unreasonable futures pricing will have a very adverse impact on the market.

Firstly, trade pricing will be inaccurate.

When the pricing of futures is relatively reasonable and effective, the pricing of the upstream and downstream of the industrial chain will basically adopt the "futures price + basis" pricing model, which is more common in the spot trade of crude oil [1].

As an exchange group with more than 170 years of operating history, investors have reason to believe that the design of CME's trading delivery system is reasonable, and the futures prices formed under this system are open, fair, and just. Based on this trust, WTI crude oil has become the global crude oil pricing benchmark. However, since 2008, WTI crude oil has continued to break investors' trust, and there have been significant deviations from spot market prices many times, until the emergence of negative oil prices on April 21 completely destroyed this trust. The value of WTI crude oil as a pricing benchmark is lost, so the "future price + basis" trade pricing model is also inaccurate. For the upstream and downstream of the industrial chain, we must find a new, more objective, and fair price benchmark. This is a real challenge for the practice of risk management for the financial industry (see [3] for more detailed discussions).

Secondly, the linked products will fail.

For a long time, the market has always used CME's WTI crude oil as the pricing benchmark, and considering the special position of crude oil in the national economy, there are many derivatives linked to it, such as some domestic or foreign exchange-traded funds (ETFs) or exchange-traded product (ETP) funds. For fund products that track certain commodity indexes, crude oil futures account for a large weight. Even more, some Chinese institutions have fund products like "crude oil treasure" (i.e. the name in Chinese is "Yuan You Bao") of Bank of China, or the "account crude oil" of Industrial and Commercial Bank of China (ICBC) and China Construction Bank (CCB). In the event of loss of the linked benchmark, these products will fail. As the saying goes, "with the skin gone, what can the hair adhere to".

Thirdly, hedging risk function will be lost.

One of the basic functions of the futures market is risk hedging. The reason why it can hedge risks is that it divides the attributes of commodity prices by time, and the division of the time axis does not split its price links. The price should be consistent in the direction of operation, and the difference between the spot price and futures price will eventually return when the futures expire. We can establish a futures position that is opposite to the spot, and use the profits of one market to hedge the losses of another market [4] for the general framework of financial risk management established by the Bank for International Settlements (BIS) since the 1980s.

But negative oil prices will lead to the loss of the risk hedging function in the futures market. For example, suppose that when the crude oil futures price is US$10, the long position entry for hedging, the settlement price of US$−37 makes the long futures position hedge loss reach US$47. At the same time, the oil price in the spot market has not changed much. It is still around US$10. When the bulls settle the futures position while purchasing in the spot market, it is equivalent to the purchase cost of up to US$57, several times the spot price! At this time, crude oil futures did not help the bulls to achieve the purpose of hedging risks, but aggravated the risk of the bulls. For bears, how do they hedge risks when facing negative oil prices? They do not need to enter the futures market to hedge risks at all! So it means that the crude oil futures market has lost the power of industrial shorts, leaving only speculative shorts. How many speculative shorts can bravely enter the short market under negative oil prices to undertake the risk transferred from the long hedgers? When the market power of a party is almost lost, the liquidity of the market is basically lost, all its functions can no longer be played, and the market loses its meaning for existing.

Therefore, the negative oil price is definitely not a normal price. It is a product of distortion caused by unreasonable system design. It should be obliterated in the long river of history and become an isolated case for the future.

References

[1] J. C. Hull, *Option, Futures, and Other Derivatives* (10th edn.) (Pearson Education, Inc, USA) 2019.

[2] H. R. Stoll, Commodity futures, and spot price determination and hedging in capital market equilibrium, *Journal of Financial Quantative Analysis*, 14(4): 873–894, 1979. doi: 10.2307/2330460.

[3] D. Freddy and S. Walter. *The Mathematics of Arbitrage*, (Springer-Verlag Berlin Heidelberg, Germany), 2006.

[4] BIS. Basel Committee on Banking Supervision: *Minimum Capital Requirements for Market Risk*. (BIS, Germany), 2019.

PART III

To Meet the Challenge with Negative Price and Management in Practice

Chapter 9

The Challenges of Negative Oil Future Price Posed to Risk Managers and Quants*

Michael Peng

Boston Consulting Group, Risk Practice,
10 Hudson Yard, New York, 10001
mkpeng2007@gmail.com

Abstract

The oil future's precipitous drop to the negative range on April 20, 2020 stunned and confounded many industry professionals and academics. It also posed a great challenge to risk managers and financial engineers responsible for the appropriate models for pricing and risk measurement. This chapter provides an extensive discussion about the rationale and mechanism behind the negative price as well as the related modeling issues. We generalized the situations and scenarios under which negative prices are economically reasonable; examples from past experiences in different markets in the world were discussed. Model choice in handling negative commodity price was discussed. Our analysis and simulation cast doubts on the appropriateness of the Bachelier option model the Chicago Mercantile Exchange (CME) hastily switched to before the big plunge. Specifically, we introduced the hyperbolic sine transformation method, whose output is amenable to the Vascecik model, as a viable alternative to the Bachelier model, and demonstrated its applicability in modeling negative oil price.

Keywords: Negative commodity price, hyperbolic sine transformation, Vascecik model, Bachelier model, CME option model, risk management, commodity pricing, Black model, oil future contract, financial engineering

---

*The views expressed in this paper are those of the author and do not represent the views of the affiliated institution.

9.1 Introduction

Oil was once called "black gold". People have even gone to war to get oil. On April 20, 2020, however, even if only briefly, they would have *paid* you to take it off their hands: oil prices plunged from $17.85 to *minus* $37.63, more than a 300% drop, the largest one-day drop for United States (US) crude in history — and it all happened in just 20 minutes! The history-making negative oil future price befuddled many market practitioners and sent shocking waves to investors and the industry as whole. Is this time just another aberration or a new norm in the futures market? Can it happen again? What are the challenges posed by the negative oil price for risk managers and quantitative modelers? Indeed, perhaps more significantly, the spectacle of oil prices falling below zero also demonstrates the outsize impact that various derivative financial products can exert in setting the price in markets.

The purpose of this chapter is to put negative price in perspective by analyzing the mechanism behind it and its impact on risk management and the commodity market. The exposition will proceed as follows: I first provide a brief recap on what happened in the US oil futures contracts and explain the micro structure that contributed to the negative prices by comparing different markets' reactions to the selling pressure, using Yuan You Bao, an oil-linked product marketed by Bank of China, as a show case. Next, I generalize the situations and scenarios under which negative prices are economically reasonable; examples of past experiences in different markets in the world are discussed. I then discuss the model choice in handling the negative commodity price by introducing the hyperbolic sine transformation method whose output is amenable to the Vascecik model. The conclusion will be summarized at the end.

9.2 The Formation of Negative Futures Price

9.2.1 *What happened: A brief recap*

Against the backdrop that the COVID-19 pandemic has stalled factories and shut down business around the world, causing a historic drop in oil demand just as production was reaching new highs, the oil futures were in a free fall earlier in April.

The panic was apparent in the futures market as the May contract expiry approached and traders deliberated on how they would take delivery of physical barrels of oil when storage sites were reaching full maximization. In contrast, the June contract traded at volumes 70 times higher and rose to $21, entering a super-contango futures market. This large front-month spread made traders not want to roll (i.e. sell May contracts and buy into June futures), nor did they want to hold and take delivery, hence they dumped the May futures instead. Figure 9.1 provides a vivid depiction of this dramatic price move.

Figure 9.1 shows the dramatic event that happened in April 20, when the May WTI futures precipitously dropped to the sub-zero zone in a very short period of time.

This expiration-squeezed sell-off further pushed down the price and augmented bearish market sentiment. All this occurred as driving season approached and producers were gearing up to increase production for the summer time, making it that much harder and unlikely for oil rigs to be turned off fast enough and protect against a further surplus. So a couple of days before the May WTI contracts expired, traders were faced with a dilemma: to either take physical delivery (which is impossible due to lack of storage) or to pay in order not to do that. The amount they were prepared to *pay* to get out of their contracts was as high as 40 US dollars per barrel of oil, which was still lower than the astronomic storage costs they would otherwise have encountered.

Crude Oil

Price per barrel of West Texas Intermediate

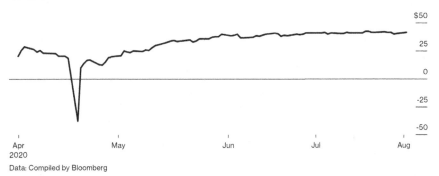

Data: Compiled by Bloomberg

Fig. 9.1. The dramatic price move on April 20, 2020.

The Chicago Mercantile Exchange (CME) first warned traders and brokers of the prospect of negative oil prices on April 8. It reiterated the possibility a week later. Intercontinental Exchange (ICE), which lists oil contracts in London, had also enabled its systems to permit negative prices. Terry Duffy, CME chief executive, told CNBC in late April that his company worked with regulators for two weeks before announcing that negative oil prices would be allowed. "So this was no secret that this was coming at us," he said. The CME and ICE clearing houses had also been preparing for negative pricing by switching the way they calculated the pricing for options on the West Texas Intermediate (WTI) benchmark.

9.2.2 *The micro structure of the US oil future market*

In addition to macro factors, there are some micro structures in the US oil futures market that could well be the institutional catalysts that beset the negative prices.

Location-specific requirement for physical oil delivery. It is worth noting that while the deep plunge happened in one US futures market (WTI), it did not happen in other markets. We only have to look at the price of Brent crude, the widely-used European benchmark, to see that things aren't so bad after all. Prices for Brent futures fell around 5% on Monday April 20, 2020, to approximately $27 a barrel. That's not far off from where the price was the previous Thursday. In other words, Brent futures traders more or less shrugged when WTI futures hit the skids — futures prices for light sweet crude oil, which is commonly known as West Texas Intermediate (WTI), plunged approximately 40% on the same day, to around $11 a barrel, a 20-year low.

Why the big difference? This difference can be attributed to one particular micro feature of US WTI: WTI May-dated futures contracts, which expired Tuesday, April 21, 2020, required futures buyers to take delivery of the oil at a specific location — Cushing, Oklahoma. But given that there was little, if any, storage space available in *that* location, the traders were forced to ditch their contracts. By contrast, none of these gyrations were happening with Brent crude futures. Brent crude can be delivered offshore to a *variety* of locations. If there isn't much storage in one place, then the oil can be delivered elsewhere. In simple terms, the flexibility of the Brent futures contract means that lack of storage in one place isn't forcing traders to dump futures contracts in the way that it is with WTI futures. Previously, it wasn't even regarded as a possibility that oil futures contracts could reach zero, let alone turn negative. Nevertheless, the virtual "impossible" happened, and the result has been general confusion.

Put option as the "synthetic storage". It is notable that the day before futures expiry, the price can often be volatile due to the expiry of calendar spread options and the settlement of various over-the-counter (OTC) derivatives products. This is why most investor products, such as exchange-traded funds (ETFs), roll their positions much earlier in the month. On April 20, open interest in the May contract — at 108,593 contracts — was fairly large. However, a closer look reveals open interest in put options on the May/June spread, known as *synthetic storage*, was equally large at 63,550. This means many puts were so deep in-the-money that options were effectively offsetting futures one-for-one. With these options converting into futures at settlement prices and netting against outstanding futures positions, large physical traders did not have to trade much at all, with futures price spiraling down sharply.

CME's trading at settlement (TAS) mechanism. CME's TAS mechanism allows OTC dealers to execute futures in advance at prices that will be determined later at settlement, offsetting dealers' bilateral exposure. Usually, the TAS market is fairly balanced between sellers and buyers. May, however, was an exception. Big players had already left the contract and TAS became offered at larger and larger discounts to the settlement price throughout the day. Increasingly desperate sellers pushed the discount out until it reached its maximum daily limit soon after 14:00 Eastern Standard Time (EST) and was closed by CME. Reaching this limit — set at 10 cents — was unprecedented for TAS, which ordinarily trades at a maximum of 1 or 2 cents above or below settlement.

With the price plunging, there was a growing panic among the few remaining traders, because whatever long positions could not be liquidated using TAS had to then be quickly sold in the open market. That day, 77,076 contracts traded in TAS. In contrast, it was only a very small number of contracts — closer to 10,000 lots or 10 million barrels of oil — that got caught in the bloodbath of the open market, illustrating clearly how relatively small positions can wreak havoc. For broader discussions on the background behind negative oil prices, see Bhansali [2], Constable [9], Chestney [10], and Harding [12].

9.2.3 *Assessing the damage*

The damages from negative oil futures prices were widely spread, from institutional investors to small, less sophisticated investors of structured oil product or oil ETF.

Case in point: Connecticut-based Interactive Brokers (IB) disclosed a $104 million loss as it compensated customers who were stuck in the previous month's trading around the May WTI contracts. Essentially, IB was compensating investor's loss beyond their equity caused by the negative price. G. H. Financials, another broker, has since required all traders to exit front-month energy contracts five days before expiry.

CME's WTI franchise was also hurt when investors turned sour on oil-focused ETFs. In particular, the price plunge caused hefty losses for investors in ETFs like the United States Oil Fund, a popular vehicle for betting on oil prices. Known by its ticker USO, the fund holds WTI futures and sometimes accounts for a significant chunk of activity in the contracts, lifting CME's fee revenue.

One week after the big plunge, USO held more than a quarter of outstanding contracts for June WTI futures, following massive inflows from investors. USO's operator, United States Commodity Funds LLC, said on Tuesday that it issued all its registered shares, an unusual event that effectively turns USO into a closed-end fund and could lead to further deviations between USO and oil prices. If WTI futures turn negative again, such deviations could continue, for the simple reason that an ETF — as a security — can't trade at prices below zero. "If the ETF is tied to the futures and the futures go negative while the ETF can't, there will be dislocations," Duffy said. "People should know that before they invest in these instruments." As a showcase of massive loss for small investors, I have to mention the case of Yuan You Bao, an oil-linked structured product sold by Bank of China.

9.2.4 The mysterious case of Yuan You Bao

One of the biggest participants remaining in the last moment was Bank of China (BoC). The state-owned bank's retail investor product, Yuan You Bao — "crude oil treasure" — still held positions for thousands of investors at the start of that fateful day and, as prices plunged into negative territory, went on to rack up massive losses (estimated to be $85 million up to a billion dollars). The case shows how much a large future market such as US can be moved by relatively small volumes, especially when they are driven by obscure structured products that fall outside of US regulations. There are quite a few questions still begging to be answered.

Why did the Yuan You Bao product allow investors to remain in the market right up to the penultimate day of the contract, thereby exposing them to high levels of volatility and potential calamitous risk? Why did the bank appear to be enticing more investors into its product even as prices were firmly on the slide, running an advertisement describing oil as "cheaper than water"?

The investment product itself appeared to be insulated from this risk due to the fact that customers had to prepay the entire notional amount of futures when opening the account. As long as futures prices stayed positive, keeping this notional amount as collateral would be safe. However, as soon as prices went into negative, it was not enough.

To be fair, given the lack of sophistication among many retail investors, BoC had prudently inserted an important risk mitigation clause into its policy, allowing it to liquidate the clients' position if the account balance dropped below 20% of the notional amount. In other words, the bank had the right, but not the obligation, to liquidate futures on behalf of clients.

The four and a half hours order-blocking window. It is worth noting that customers were not allowed to place any orders after 10:00 EST (22:00 Beijing time) on the penultimate day. This gave BoC traders an embedded optionality for four and a half hours between 10:00 EST and 14:30 EST when WTI on CME settled. Why didn't they use this to terminate their investors' accounts earlier when the balance fell below the contractual threshold?

If we set aside for a moment any rules of ethics or the dealer's fiduciary responsibilities, then the most rational decision at 10:00 EST for the market maker would be to do nothing and perhaps attempt to monetize this option rather than intervening and dealing with potentially unhappy customers. Since futures prices at the time were already very low, it was not unreasonable to expect some short-term bounce. If prices had returned to $20/bbl and BoC traders had terminated their clients' positions earlier at lower prices, they would undoubtedly have had many complaints. Doing nothing was also possibly easier from a legal perspective as, if the price continued to slide, the positions would just settle or roll at 14:30 EST as specified in the contract. In this case, the dealer's embedded option would expire worthless and the customer would pay for the loss. We may, of course, never know the whole truth about why BoC did not use its contractual right to liquidate the trades earlier when clients' accounts were already drained. Regulators may need to find the motives behind the behavior that led to painful losses that day.

9.3   The Nature of Negative Price

9.3.1   *How price can be negative*

Many people, including market professionals, are dumbfounded by the very idea of "negative price". These are actually fairly common — occurring everywhere from personal transaction of daily items to electricity markets (more details provided below) to stock exchanges that pay for order flow to boost liquidity.

Positive price is the cost you have to pay in order to *get* something ("asset") which you believe will generate immediate or future utility/benefit for you. Negative price is the cost you have to pay in order to dispose of something which you believe has become a liability or temporally lost its value. There are not many things you have to *pay* to get rid of: you pay to have your furniture taken away to a storage facility before your overseas assignment. You reimburse someone's transportation cost for coming to collect all the kids' toys you no longer need. But why oil? Surely an item of such obvious cost and utility as oil must always be worth something?

Human beings are prone to the cognitive bias of loss aversion, putting more psychological weight on a loss than an equivalent gain (i.e. you feel more pain for a dollar loss than the incremental happiness from a dollar gain). It is not surprising, therefore, that we feel a certain horror at negative prices, which suggests that your assets can turn to liabilities, losing *more than* everything you once owned!

The obvious question posed by negative prices is why a transaction occurs at all if the price is less than zero? Why not hold on to what you have? There are at least three different scenarios for negative price to happen.

The first is a storage problem familiar to anyone clearing a house for sale. The grand piano may be impressive to guests and bought at a high price; but if there is going to be nowhere to put it, it turns from an asset into a liability as the day of the move draws near with no buyer in sight. In US, the chances are you have to pay the thrift store to come to pick up the chunky furniture you pledge to donate. Even the negative interest rates can be explained by this storage problem discussed earlier: putting the money under the mattress is highly risky due to the likelihood of house fire or burglary; while buying a safe costs money, there is still a risk of theft and, furthermore, large transactions with cash are cumbersome and sometimes impossible — particularly in this e-commerce era. In the wake of the coronavirus pandemic (COVID-19), many stores only accept e-payment or card. Therefore, paying for storage in a bank deposit can make lots of sense.

US oil traders found themselves in a similar position in April 2020: owning a barrel of WTI at contract expiry means taking physical delivery in Cushing, Oklahoma. You cannot keep crude oil in the attic. So if oil storage tanks are full, you have a serious problem. That is exactly what happened: you need to pay someone to take the oil away or you buy put option of the futures (assuming no "counterparty default risk"). In a striking similarity, electricity markets experienced negative prices quite frequently. Electricity is notoriously hard to store, but shutting down a coal or nuclear plant is costly and time-consuming. So when supply well exceeds demand, it can make sense to pay users to take it or even export it to neighboring foreign countries, as Germany did (more details provided below). This situation occurs as often as solar and wind, which have negligible marginal costs to continuing the operation and generate power as long as the sun shines and the wind blows, and join electricity grids. It can also occur if there are subsidized suppliers, who make money at a negative price if the subsidy is more.

In a similar vein, wholesale electricity markets sometimes result in prices below zero. That is, sellers pay buyers to take the power. This situation arises because certain types of generators, such as nuclear, hydroelectric, and wind, cannot or prefer not to reduce/shut down output for short periods of time due to technical reasons when demand is insufficient to absorb their output. Sometimes buyers can be induced to take the power when they are paid to do so, resulting in the "negative price". (See further discussions below)

Germany had 134 hours of negative power prices on the wholesale market in 2018, according to data from the Federal Network Agency (Bundesnetzagentur). The number was down from 146 hours in 2017 (2016: 97 hours; 2015: 126 hours). Over Christmas and New Year, when electricity consumption is low due to nationwide holidays, and when high winds and non-flexible conventional electricity sources can provide excess power production, electricity prices in Germany have frequently turned negative. In these events, renewable and conventional power generation and grid capacity weren't always working together smoothly. But, according to a Bundesnetzagentur spokesperson, negative power prices were part of the usual market activity and were providing a "valuable signal for the market", which led to important incentives for flexibility. Over Christmas 2018, warm weather and little wind helped to keep power prices widely in the plus.[a]

A second reason for negative prices is when there is a liability attached to an asset. Contaminated land may cost less than nothing because of the expense of cleaning it up. When BMW sold the British car company Rover in 2000, it provided a "dowry" of hundreds of millions of pounds to reflect the dire state of the business. Likewise, unless waste can be recycled at a profit, it has a negative price because of the disposal cost.

A third scenario is when something ostensibly has a negative price but the buyer is actually providing the seller with something of value. For example, a bike-sharing network may pay its customers if they ride its bikes from the suburbs back to the center of the city, where

---

[a]German wholesale power prices turn negative less often in 2018", https://www.cleanenergywire.org/news/german-wholesale-power-prices-turn-negative-less-often-2018.

they may be needed more. Stock exchanges may pay retail brokers for the privilege of executing their orders, because such orders are of value to other customers, such as market makers who can profit by trading with it. Another example under this scenario is the "berry-picking" event organized by local farms on weekends for families with kids: you buy entry tickets for the whole family, usually $5 per person, at the end when you leave, you have to purchase the berry at a price sometimes even higher than the nearby grocery store! On the surface, you and the kids are getting *"negative salary"* for your farm work, but in fact the "buyer" of your labor provides you and your family something valuable, i.e. fun activity with kids over the weekend, which is hard to measure by money.

9.3.2 Negative price: Interest rate versus oil future — A comparison

The financial world has been turned upside down by extraordinary events in recent years. First there were negative interest rates, something that had never happened in 5,000 years of recorded history. Now it's negative oil prices, a phenomenon that sparked headlines far beyond financial news.

In the case of oil, the culprit has been the incredible oversupply, combined with little spare storage in the face of a decimation of demand connected with the sudden COVID-19 economic stop. However, in Europe and Japan, bond yields have been negative for a few years now, and investors have already been willingly parting with cash and paying for the privilege for doing so. This "normalcy of deviance" is becoming all too common now across many asset classes. The excess supply of liquidity drove bond yields below zero. The excess supply of oil has driven its price below zero.

There are important differences between the two, however. Negative interest rates were imposed by central banks in Europe and Japan as part of their conduct of monetary policy. Oil, by contrast, trades in a relatively free market that, once again, is proving to be resistant to control by government-run cartels.

As we know in finance, when attempting to price or evaluate an asset at a future date (i.e. a price today, for delivery at a future date), commodity markets pose a particular challenge. In other markets, such as foreign exchange, given the spot exchange rate and the interest rates in the two currencies, the forward rate defines itself: as you can buy dollars today and hold them on deposit for 12 months as freely as you can hold Sterling on deposit and buy dollars forward in 12 months' time, if the forward price (i.e. exchange rate) does not equal to the spot exchange rate times the ratio of the interest rates (i.e. the interest rate parity relationship), there would be a risk-free arbitrage going one way and coming back the other, but in an efficient market this shouldn't happen.

In contrast, commodity markets don't offer any such mechanism. So, if the price of oil is $50 today, what should the price for delivery in a week's or a month's or a year's time be? The answer, as it does for all manner of price relationships in commodity markets, lies not only in they trader's expectation of supply and demand of the underlying, *but* also cost of carrying and storage capacity.

Should a futures contract strike price be lower than today's spot price, it means there is the expectation that the current price is too high and the expected spot price will eventually fall in the future. This situation is called backwardation. In contango, the price of the November futures contract is higher than October's, which is higher than July's, and so on. Under normal market conditions, it makes sense that prices of futures contracts increase the farther the maturity date since they include investment costs such as carrying costs or storage costs for a commodity.

An ETF that employs a basic strategy of investing in the front-month futures contract of a given commodity, for example, will either see its returns decrease in the case of contango, or increase in the case of backwardation. This is due to the fact that the costs of rolling the position from front month to the next can be substantial (e.g. super contango).

Futures expire according to a predetermined schedule. On the futures settlement date, anyone holding a contract must take physical delivery of the oil. In order to avoid this, investors (including in oil ETFs) must "roll" from one contract to the next prior to the settlement date. Rolling involves either a cost or a credit, depending on the shape of the futures curve.

Coming into its final trading days, the May WTI contract had already made headlines by setting record contango levels as the May/June spread blew out to $−7/bbl. This reflected the state of the physical market, where storage at Cushing, Oklahoma, the delivery point for the WTI contracts, was becoming full. However, on

April 20, the May/June spread blew out to minus $\$-60$/bbl during the settlement window, before narrowing just a few hours later to around $\$-21$/bbl, and then expiring the next day at $\$-1.56$. All the while physical storage remained virtually unchanged.

9.4   Negative Commodity Price from Historical Perspective

Rigorously speaking, this is NOT the first time that US oil traded at below zero price. In fact, in the aftermath of the last major downturn in 2016, a North Dakota sour crude was briefly priced at negative 50 cents a barrel before being revised to a mere $1.50. Mizuho's Paul Sankey warned of negative crude prices in a note, pointing out that the capacity to hold barrels of US oil in tanks and caverns could max out by the middle of the year. With nowhere to store, barrels could get backed up across the entire supply chain, he said.

This time concerns of "oversupply, reduced demand and increasingly full US storage" drove the May futures contracts into negative territory ahead of expiration, the date when futures-contracts holders must accept physical delivery, Derek Sammann, Senior Managing Director of the CME Group, said. While many investors buy futures to speculate in possible price shifts, most don't want to own the physical commodity or pay for storage and were willing to accept significant losses to avoid that. It's not clear exactly how an oil trade would work in a negative price scenario. In US natural gas markets — which have been plagued by negative prices because of a dearth of pipeline space — producers have actually paid others to take their product. In electricity markets — especially in California where power drops below zero on a regular basis because of excess solar — negative pricing has turned into more of a real-time signal to generators to dial down plants.

"Anything is possible in commodities," said Francisco Blanch, head of global commodities and derivatives research at Bank of America. "We know zero is not a lower band — we learned that with gas."

Case 1: Natural gas market

Natural gas is no stranger to negative prices. The United Kingdom's (UK) National Balancing Point (NBP) plunged below zero in 2006 after a pipeline opened for commercial imports from Norway. That plunge was more of an operational issue from the pipeline than a market trend, and it wasn't in the middle of a bearish market, such as the one today, according to James Huckstepp, manager of EMA (Europe, the Middle East, and Africa) gas analytics at S&P Global Platts.

In the US, associated gas, a byproduct of shale drilling, has periodically gone negative mainly due to increased production coming up against limited transport capacity at places such as the Waha Hub in West Texas. While some estimates have Europe's storage facilities hitting capacity as soon as the next month, analysts at Morgan Stanley and Platts see it getting close but just missing it. Still, sub-zero prices are a possibility even if hitting "tank tops" is avoided.

"It may require a short period of negative prices to make suppliers understand the gravity of this situation — and this is before storages are completely full," said Jonathan Stern, senior research fellow at the Oxford Institute of Energy Studies.

In April 2019, next-day natural gas prices at the Waha Hub in the Permian Basin in West Texas fell *below zero* for the first time since early April and Waha averaged minus 40 cents per million British thermal units (mmBtu) for a whole week on the Intercontinental Exchange, according to data from Refinitiv.

The problem is that the construction of new oil and gas pipelines in the Permian has not kept up with output, which has more than doubled over the past three years as the US has risen to become the world's largest oil producer. So producers are forced to burn or flare the gas, *pay others with space on existing pipelines to take it, or stop drilling*. They did not want to stop drilling for oil, especially with crude futures up almost 40% in 2019. So they burn the gas for as long as they could — Texas rules allow firms to flare gas for up to six months — and paid others to take it when prices turn negative as they wait for new pipelines.

"I expect lower for longer — but we might get stuck into this bad equilibrium, too low to make real money as a supplier but not low enough to unlock a huge tranche of demand," Nikos Tsafos, senior fellow at the Center for Strategic and International Studies, said by email. "What's the floor? Frankly, we have no idea. We haven't seen prices like these ever before."

While negative energy prices are rare, there have been multiple examples in the US, UK, and Germany, Sammann said, and the CME Group has been prepared for the chance that crude will turn negative again.

Case 2: Electricity power market

In the textbook, it is implicitly assumed that the supply can be frictionlessly and costlessly adjusted in response to the slump in demand. In reality, this may not be the case. Inflexible and costly adjustment to production is a prominent feature of the electricity wholesale market; allowing *negative bid* for a short period of time rather than shutting down could be more economically reasonable. In 2011, Intercontinental Exchange (ICE, a widely-used, internet-based, bilateral trading platform for matching buyers and sellers) reported 84 instances of negative prices, 80 of which were in the Pacific Northwest. Each of these 84 instances was for ICE's off-peak product for power delivered during the periods of time when electricity demand is lowest (including a block of eight hours overnight as well as all day Sunday).

Technical and economic factors may drive power plant operators to run generators even when power supply outstrips demand. For example, for technical and cost recovery reasons, nuclear plant operators try to operate continuously at full power. The operation of hydroelectric units reflects factors outside of power demand, for example, compliance with environmental regulations such as controlling water flow to maintain fish populations. Eligible generators can take a 2.2/kWh or $22/MWh production tax credit (PTC) on electricity sold. This means that some generators may be willing to sell their output for as low as minus $22/MWh to continue producing power. Typically, wind generators are the largest such group in any region. There are maintenance and fuel-cost penalties when operators shut down and start up large steam turbine (usually fossil-fueled) plants as demand varies over a day or a week. These costs may be avoided if the generator sells at a loss to attract a buyer when demand is low.

In these situations, generators may seek to maintain output by offering to pay wholesale buyers to take their electricity. These situations are most likely to occur in markets with large amounts of inflexible nuclear, hydroelectric, and/or wind generation. In the Pacific Northwest, abundant hydroelectric resources have been augmented in recent years with significant wind capacity. This combination of generating sources has increased the likelihood of the conditions leading to negative prices.

When power prices on the electricity exchange fall below zero, power suppliers have to pay their wholesale customers to buy electric energy. The phenomenon is on the rise in Germany with an increasing number of renewable sources feeding into the grid.

There are several reasons why conventional power station operators, which are either losing money or at least losing profit during times of negative prices, keep their plants running (see study by Energy Brainpool, pages 4–5, and the 2016 results from Consentec). They can be technical; for example, the power plant can be too inflexible to change its output, or the ramping or costs for shutting down and starting up can be too expensive. Another reason for keeping the plant running can be the obligation to provide contracted balancing power to keep the grid stable or provide re-dispatch power. Alternatively, it may be that a certain production has to be kept up to provide heat for a town household heating network. Those plant operators which have already sold their power at the longer term futures market face no extra costs when they let their units run — they are merely losing the profit that they could make by buying cheap power to supply their customers instead of producing their own.

Exporting power at negative prices

Despite press reports suggesting Germany is losing out by paying neighboring countries to use its electricity, actual volumes of power exported at negative prices are comparatively small. According to Agora Energiewende, the value of all the power exported at negative prices amounted to around minus 40 million euros in 2017 [7].

Other cases for negative commodity price include the propane traded in Canada: for most of 2015, abundant inventories, low seasonal demand, low crude oil prices, and limited takeaway capacity kept western Canadian propane prices at record lows. In fact, in mid-2015, propane at the Edmonton Hub traded at negative prices (that is, producers were paying others to take their propane away). Propane prices generally trended down until mid-2016 with the exception of the polar vortex-driven spike between late 2014 and early 2015. Since late 2014, propane prices generally followed the decline and eventual rise in crude oil prices. Edmonton prices, however, began disconnecting from Mont Belvieu prices in late 2014, trading near or even below zero between June 2015 and January 2016.

9.5   The Implication for Risk Pricing Model

The oil's plunge below zero for the first time in history hasn't just sent shockwaves through the industry. It has also literally broken the models that many traders rely on to calculate risk. "Standard pricing models used for options on futures and swaps, however, can't cope with negative numbers," said Richard Fullarton, founder of Matilda Capital Management, who has more than two decades of experience trading oil. "It's a huge issue for banks if they cannot produce risk metrics correctly." [15]

This echoes a similar situation for interest rates back in 2014, with short-term deposit rates at a number of European central banks turning negative. This posed many technical challenges for the financial industry due to the importance of interest rates in most asset classes, and, in particular, for interest-rate options. The industry standard Black–Scholes option pricing model became handicapped in dealing with negative rates due to the fact it is built on a geometric Brownian motion which requires the underlying to remain strictly positive. When interest rates turned negative, many found that their option pricing models no longer worked, presenting serious challenges for pricing and risk management activities like delta-hedging.

9.5.1   *How the street responded to the negative price*

The occurrence of negative commodity prices for oil contracts — at this point only occurring in the front month — violates the usual mathematical underpinnings of the standard derivative models and requires a rapid adaptation to this unprecedented situation. Later the same day, April 20, the CME Group made an announcement that from that day forward they were going to calculate the implied volatility of options on futures using the Bachelier options pricing model — a model named after the famous French mathematician and one that can accommodate negative prices.[b]

Very few trading houses had already employed this model for pricing commodity spread options. Some firms provide a separate process that assumes normal price returns instead of log-normal returns for selected commodities to cope with the negative prices for risk engine calculations (term volatility and value at risk (VaR) calculations). CME has decided that for oil prices below \$8.00 per barrel, they will be switching to a normal (as opposed to log-normal) option pricing model. Actually, they have stated that for prices between \$8.00 and \$11.00, they may be switching. We take that to mean a definitive switch if below \$8.00. Is CME's model-switching decision justified?

At the time of writing, six weeks after the big plunge, the collapse of CME crude futures to \$−40 a barrel looks more and more like an aberration — the confluence of a series of never-to-be-repeated events. Some quants have already taken the data out of their models, treating them as outliers. A return to negative prices seems unlikely anytime soon. Oil demand is picking up and production cuts are already eating into the supply overhang. Options traders that stuck with Black–Scholes may see little reason to change now.

9.5.2 *Bachelier options pricing model rises from the ashes*

Although the Bachelier is obscure — so obscure that it is not even mentioned by Professor John Hull in his book *Options, Futures and other Derivatives*, dubbed as the "derivative Bible" in the industry. It is actually the oldest option pricing model in existence, developed in pieces from, believe it or not, 1900. On April 22, 2020, its profile was raised further when CME switched out of Black (76) to the Bachelier model for pricing and margining oil options. Because it begins with the assumption of Geometric Brownian motion, the model calculates implied volatility with values remarkably close to

---

[b]https://www.cmegroup.com/content/dam/cmegroup/notices/clearing/2020/04/Chadv20-171.pdf.

the results of Black–Scholes–Merton (BSM) (which may be why most of us have never heard of it). However, models based on the formula by Louis Bachelier already have traction in some energy markets, being used in electricity and natural gas where negative prices are more common.

But it is different from BSM in one significant way: it allows the user to calculate implied volatility for negative prices and for negative strikes (like minus $10). BSM can't do this because it relies upon natural logs of ratios of stock and strike prices and you can't take the log of a negative number. The upshot is that you will now start to see negative strikes for some options contracts (especially oil and distillates). And it is also possible to calculate implied volatility (IV) for a positive price with a negative strike. While the assumption is that price can never be below zero for stock, it is not necessarily true for hard-to-store commodity assets, as we've seen. Still, the speed at which oil has swung to sub-zero prices has left traders in shock, and contributed to wild gyrations. In the options markets, for example, bid–ask spreads have widened drastically, a sign that fewer traders are willing to take on additional risk. The bid–ask spread on $20 puts for June WTI was nearly $3 at various times on Tuesday, compared with just 15 cents the week before. Several traders and brokers said that they were being quoted bid–ask spreads that were many times wider than normal.

ICE Brent options contracts also will require a switch in models to enable trading of negative strikes if there's demand to do so, the company said. There has been a surge in interest in 50-cent puts for June WTI — which traded as high as $3.90 on Tuesday, implying that traders are already working on the assumption that June WTI futures could turn negative. "From a market maker perspective, particularly those sitting at a flow trading desk or a major, their assumption, especially if you're young and haven't experienced any major market events, the assumption is that $0 was always the minimum," said Michael Corley, president of Mercatus Energy Advisors. "That's not the case anymore."

So, not only did this momentous event of negative price leave us all astonished, we should also now go back to the drawing board and fundamentally rethink our oil price and risk models. Let's take a look from this perspective at how to model a stochastic price variable — in this case negative value is allowed.

In order to obtain option prices, one has to specify the underlying model. We fix a time horizon T > 0. As is well-known, Bachelier proposed to use (properly scaled) Brownian motion as a model for forward stock prices. In modern terminology, this amounts to:

$$S_{t^B} = S_0 + \sigma^B W_t$$

for $0 \leq t \leq T$, where (Wt) $0 \leq t \leq T$ denotes standard Brownian motion and the superscript B stands for Bachelier. The parameter $\sigma^B > 0$ denotes the volatility in the Bachelier model. Notice that in contrast to today's standard Bachelier measured volatility in absolute terms, here σ BS denotes the usual volatility in the Black–Merton–Scholes model.

$$S_{t^B} = S_0 + \sigma^B W_t$$

The Black–Merton–Scholes model (under the risk-neutral measure) for the price process is, of course, given by:

$$S_t^{BS} = S_0 \exp\left(\sigma^{BS} W_t - \frac{(\sigma^{BS})^2}{2} t\right)$$

for $0 \leq t \leq T$. Here, $\sigma^{BS} > 0$ denotes the usual volatility in the Black–Merton–Scholes model.

As can be seen, S_t^{BS} can never dip into sub-zero level while S_t^B can.

$$dS_t^B = \sigma^B dW_t$$

$$dS_t^{BS} = S_t^{BS} \sigma^{BS} dW_t$$

In a widely cited paper, Schacher [8] compared the Bachelier model with Black–Scholes in terms of pricing option. He concluded that the difference between the two models is somewhat analogous to the difference between linear and compound interest, as becomes apparent when looking at the associated Itô stochastic differential equation.

This analogy makes us expect that, in the short run, both models should yield similar results while, in the long run, the difference should be spectacular. Fortunately, options usually have a relatively short time to maturity (the options considered by Bachelier had a time to maturity of less than two months). According to Rosen [11], if we use a normal Bachelier model and compute the market-implied probability of prices at or below zero until settlement, it can be shown that the possibility of negative prices under this model rapidly increases to levels of 40–50% on that day. This model shows there is a clear expectation of negative prices in the June contracts as well, due to recent events and accompanying increases in contract price volatility. Given the ephemeral presence of the negativity this time, it may be reasonable to believe, however, that the true estimate of the negative price probability could be significantly less than what the normal model produced. While switching from Black–Scholes to Bachelier's Brownian model is certainly one way to accommodate the possibility of negative prices, it is also a rather extreme change to the model dynamics. It would have a dramatic impact on hedging strategies by changing the option delta and could have a significant impact on the construction of implied volatility surfaces. While it is natural to do so, is it the right choice?

More generally, although it certainly can accommodate negative prices this time, it has an obvious problem: assets selling at small prices tend to have small increments in price over a given time interval, while asset selling at high prices tend to have much larger increments in dollar terms on the same interval, but Brownian Motion has a constant variance which depends on a time interval but not on the price level, i.e. it does not reflect proportional changes. So this too is unrealistic for modeling commodity prices. Therefore, it is no surprise that the development of a theory of hedging and replication by dynamic strategies, which is the crucial ingredient of the Black–Merton–Scholes approach, was far out of reach of the model.

9.5.3   *Modeling the dynamic process of negative price: What can we learn from the pricing model used in other markets?*

So, for inspiration, we should look to another asset with similar price behavior: electricity. Electricity prices regularly dip into negative territory (albeit for a short time) and in this they resemble the case of oil. The reason for these short-lived negative prices is the fact that electricity cannot be stored and must be consumed once generated. So electricity price models are good candidates for figuring out how to redesign our oil price models. The solution for electricity is to assume the price follows a regular, so not exponential, random walk, which can become negative, if only for a short period — this would be a suitable solution for oil price models, too.

One challenge to model the negative price of commodity is the fact that you cannot take the log transformation of a negative number. As we recall, a basic rationale for the log transformation is to avoid dealing with the price directly; rather, we study the return, which is more likely to get us closer to a stationary normal distribution, and more importantly, in many settings it should make additive and linear models make more sense. A multiplicative model on the original scale corresponds to an additive model on the log scale. For example, a treatment that increases prices by 2%, rather than a treatment that increases prices by $20. The log transformation is particularly relevant when the data vary a lot on the relative scale. Increasing prices by 2% has a much different dollar effect for a $10 item than a $1000 item. Since the log transformation cannot be directly applied to negative price, other novel transformations were tried. For example, Schneider [13] transformed the original electric power variable using the *area hyperbolic sine* function, where the most important property is the asymptotic log behavior:

$$x = sinh^{-1}(p) = \ln(p + \sqrt{p^2 + 1}) \approx sign(p) \cdot \ln(2\lfloor p \rfloor)$$

for $|p| \to \infty$. The log function is a good approximation even for small $|p| > 2y$. The positive and negative log-like parts are connected by an approximately linear part at $|p| \approx 0$. This transformation appears to be a natural choice because it preserves the log behavior which has lots of desirable properties. However, it is now presupposed that the properties of prices p < 0 are a "mirror image" of p > 0. We recall a basic rationale for the log transformation: the volatility/variability of prices increases with the absolute price level: $dp \sim p$ for p > 0.

It is plausible to assume that this is also the case for negative power prices: $\lfloor dp \rfloor \sim p$ for p < 0.

Figure 9.2 below provides a graphical description of the relationship between the original oil price and its inverse hyperbolic since transformation.

So, how do we model the stochastic process of the return rather than the price itself given that negative prices are an inherent feature of the commodity? The solution to this problem is to replace the usual log transformation of prices with the area hyperbolic sine transformation. As Schneider [13] compellingly explained, there are

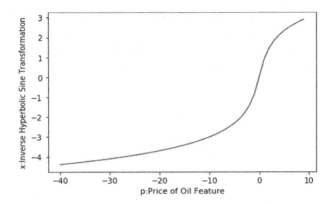

Fig. 9.2.   Oil future price and its inverse hyperbolic since transformation.

three reasons to justify this approach: firstly, the choice is natural, leaving the transformation for positive prices almost unchanged and mirroring the logarithm feature to the negative price axis.

This choice is equivalent to the finding that the price dynamics in the negative price region is analogous to the one in the positive region, volatility basically depending on the absolute price level. Secondly, combining the hyperbolic sine transformation with stochastic models does not significantly increase the difficulty of treatment compared to the log case. Interestingly, an analogue to the log-normal distribution as a theoretical "basic distribution" is found: the Johnson distribution, which is also a closed-form expression. This is a convenient characteristic for the option valuation.

Thirdly, it was found that the area hyperbolic sine transformation as an effective combination of linear and log transformation performs well, preserving the characteristics of the data.

Summing up, it is posited that the introduction of the area hyperbolic sine transformation is the natural step for power price modeling in response to the permitting of negative prices at power spot exchanges. This is also supported by the fact that the transformation can be applied to power markets with positive prices only equally well. There is one important issue for negative power prices to be dealt with in future work. The power markets are not yet in a "steady state" regarding the handling of negative price occurrences. The changing nature of these occurrences was an issue in this work for the case of ERCOT (Electric Reliability Council of Texas)

West. It is also obvious when comparing European Energy Exchange (EEX) 2010 data with 2009. The frequency and severity of negative occurrences is strongly reduced in 2010 compared to 2009. This is, on the one hand, attributed to a learning effect of energy traders, e.g. changed power plant production schedules. On the other hand, this is due to changing regulations concerning renewable energy (e.g. wind) marketing. So, it is currently difficult to anticipate how a steady market state in the future could look like and the energy trading business is reliant on close-to-the-market modeling activities on this subject.

As a start, it is necessary to understand basic stochastic and statistical features of modeling built on the area hyperbolic sine function:

$$x = sinh^{-1}(p) \tag{1}$$

To this end, the same standard route for the log transformation can be taken: analyzing a basic model for the spot price process, the Ornstein–Uhlenbeck (OU) process:

$$dx = k(m - x)dt + \sigma dW \tag{2}$$

with k and m the mean reversion rate and level, respectively; W, the standard Wiener process; and volatility, σ.

This model resoundingly echoes the well-studied Vasicek model in characterizing short rate dynamics. Vasicek model was the first one to capture mean reversion, an essential characteristic of the interest rate that sets it apart from other financial prices. Its popularity stems from its tractability and relatively good hedging performance.

The drift factor $k(m - x)$ represents the expected instantaneous change in the interest rate at time t. The parameter m represents the long-run equilibrium value towards which the interest rate reverts. The parameter k, governing the speed of adjustment, needs to be positive to ensure stability around the long-term value. For example, when r_t is below b, the drift term

$$a(b - r_t)a(b - r_t)$$

becomes positive for positive a, generating a tendency for the interest rate to move upwards (toward equilibrium).

One striking feature of the Vasicek model is that it is theoretically possible for the interest rate to become negative. This property, once deemed undesirable under pre-crisis assumptions, is clearly back to vogue against the backdrop of negative rate in Europe. Now it seems to be a proper choice for modeling the stochastic process for commodity prices.

As opposed to stock prices, interest rates cannot rise indefinitely. This is because at very high levels they would hamper economic activity, prompting a decrease in interest rates. Similarly, interest rates do not usually decrease below 0. As a result, interest rates move in a limited range, showing a tendency to revert to a long-run value. The situation is similar for commodity prices since super high commodity prices will have global impact on the economy in terms of cost of manufacturing; and price dropping to sub-zero, while it can happen, is not an usual and persistent phenomena.

By means of the Itô formula and standard relations for hyperbolic functions, we get the stochastic differential equation (SDE):

$$\frac{dp}{\sqrt{1+p^2}} = \left[k \left(m - sinh^{-1}(p) \right) + 0.5\sigma^2 \frac{p}{\sqrt{1+p^2}} \right] dt + \sigma dW \quad (3)$$

This is quite similar to the SDE for the log case:

$$\frac{dp}{p} = \left[k \left(m - ln(p) \right) + 0.5\sigma^2 \right] dt + \sigma dW$$

Both SDE generate the same dynamics for large p. Additionally, (3) exhibits a linear form dp $\approx$ L(p)dt $+\sigma\cdot$ dW for small |p|. There is an explicit probability distribution solution to (3). The stationary distribution to the OU process for x:

$$x \sim N(m, \frac{\sigma^2}{2k}) \equiv N(m, \sigma_{OU}^2)$$

This implies:

$$f(p) = \frac{1}{\sigma_{OU}\sqrt{2\pi}(1+p^2)} \exp\left[-\frac{(sinh^{-1}(p) - m)^2}{2\sigma_{OU}^2} \right] \quad (4)$$

$f(\cdot)$ is known as the Johnson SU-distribution [6]. Summarizing, it has to be pointed out that switching from the log to the hyperbolic sine transformation has not qualitatively complicated the analysis. We still get a closed-form solution, the Johnson distribution replacing the log-normal distribution. Note that the mean speed k did not get into this expression.

With this probability density of price distribution, we are able to calculate the probability that negative prices happen.

As an illustration, we calculated such probability for different levels of volatility σ, given the assumption of long-term equilibrium mean to which the oil price is supposed to revert to.

It can be observed from Fig. 9.3 that:

(i) When volatility is relatively small, the probability of negative price is minuscule regardless what long-term equilibrium mean is assumed this is consistent with the fact that negative price has been historically a very rare event;

(ii) For higher long-term means, the probability of negative price is less sensitive to the increment of volatility.

(iii) Although the absolute probability numbers look modest, e.g. between 7–15%[c] even when volatility exceeds 100%, they in fact

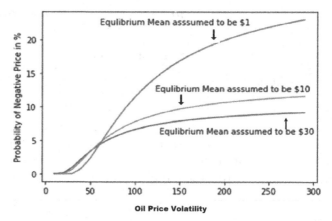

Fig. 9.3. Vasicek Model implied probability(%) of negative price for different volatility.

---

[c]The volatility scale in the graph is not far-fetched. In fact, amplitude of the volatility echoes the dramatic movement in 2020. For example, on February 10, West Texas Intermediate (WTI) oil's one-month realized, or historical, price volatility stood at 105.3%. In contrast, the historical volatility of Bitcoin, synonymous with extreme bouts of volatility, clocked in at 42.3%, its lowest reading since September. Historical volatility is a measure of how much commodity prices have varied in the past calculated as the standard deviation of daily price movements of the front-month futures price, typically for a 30-day period. The metric is expressed as a percentage in annualized terms. WTI's historical volatility shot

are quite significant, given the fact that the probability of negative price was zero in the prevalent log normal, such as Black 76 model, which assumes that future prices are log-normally distributed and that the expected change in futures price is zero.

(iv) The Vascecik model implied probability of negative price, while at a similar magnitude what the normal model predicted is appreciably lower. Specifically, if a near zero equilibrium mean (i.e. $1) is assumed, echoing the scenario on April 20, when the May futures price careened precipitously to single digits from low 20s, the probability of negative price is around 20% if volatility increases to 200%, while the normal model implied probability is around 30s and 40s on that day.

It should be understood that no model can work normally under extreme conditions — it would be very difficult, if not impossible, to calibrate the parameters, which could be shifting erratically in duress. It is therefore unfair to judge a model's performance under these abnormal situations.

It should be pointed out, while the method described above is refreshing as an alternative to the standard model, it is not totally new. In fact, stochastic processes involving the hyperbolic sine have been employed before to model volatility smiles. However, prices in that context are strictly positive and described by ordinary returns, see Brigo *et al.* [4] and Carr *et al.* [5], two derivative maestros in the industry.

It is increasingly recognized that negative prices are an inherent feature of the commodity power market. Constraints on the supply side limit the flexibility of a generation facility and forces them to sell off production with discounts in cases of demand slumps. This is why permitting negative bid, offers, and auction results in the power spot market is economically reasonable. Several non-European power markets, the European markets EEX and Nord Pool, have introduced negative prices recently.

It is obvious that under these circumstances, the so-far prevailing tendency to deal with the "problem" by "workarounds" or

---

up from 38.7% to 119.6% by late January while S&P 500 Index's realized volatility increased to 15.6% during the last week of January [1]. In early April 2020, the annualized volatility can easily exceed 200%, exclusion/negligence is to be abandoned and sound integration into the various stochastic power price modeling frameworks needs to be achieved.

9.5.4   *The next negative price is looming?*

On May 13, 2020, the US commodities regulator issued a rare warning to brokers, exchanges, and clearing houses, urging them to be ready for the risk that oil prices could again drop below zero. The Commodity Futures Trading Commission (CFTC) advised exchanges to monitor their markets and remind them to "maintain rules to provide for the exercise of emergency authority", including the power to "suspend or curtail trading in any contract" if markets become disorderly, according to an advisory notice released on the same day. It is worth noting that a senior CFTC official said its notice applied to all contracts, not just oil, and did not represent a forecast that negative oil prices would return. "We are not predicting the market. We're just suggesting planning," the official said. Brokers should carefully watch contracts as they approach their expiry date, the agency cautioned, advising them "to be particularly diligent in monitoring and assessing risks".

Exchanges list futures contracts and operate electronic trading platforms, while clearing houses pool margins and other collateral to guarantee trades. In WTI futures, both the exchange and clearing house are operated by the CME Group, the world's largest exchange company based in Chicago. Indeed, the specter of negative prices is still hanging over energy markets more than a month after oil's unforgettable crash below zero. Two month after US crude oil prices collapsed into negative territory, European gas markets were facing the prospect of also slipping into the red after a slump in demand and surging inventories pushed prices into low single digits. Unlike US crude, UK gas prices have traded negative before, falling below zero in 2006 after the Langeled pipeline from Norway started pumping gas to Britain for the first time. Then, also, storage sites were nearly full.

As pointed out by Stapczynski *et al.* [14], while crude has staged a rapid recovery after a deal by the biggest producers to curb a surplus, the $600 billion global gas market remains extraordinarily oversupplied. Unlike the oil market, which has a broad, if fragile, alliance of producers to manage production and rescue prices led by Saudi Arabia and Russia, there's been no sign of a coordinated response to address the glut, meaning the fallout could be deeper and longer. Traders and analysts say the worst may be yet to come as demand falls and storage nears capacity, creating the ideal conditions for *negative prices* in some parts of the world, with Europe being the riskiest, which could have ripple effects for buyers and sellers from the US to Asia.

The fuel, used to generate power and heat and also as a feedstock for chemicals and fertilizers, was already slated to have a terrible year after a mild winter exacerbated a glut. But things turned from bad to worse as the pandemic hammered demand, forcing major buyers to reject deliveries. Meanwhile, top sellers haven't yet throttled back enough output as stockpiles near capacity. Like the oil's brief plunge in April below $-40 a barrel, the key factor is the lack of storage to absorb excess supply.

One European market in particular has come in focus as the most likely to go negative. While the world's four major indexes have converged near historic lows, the UK's National Balancing Point is the weakest, with the next-day contract recently dropping to the equivalent of about $0.99 per million British thermal units. "If we see below-zero gas prices in Europe, we will see it in the UK," said Hadrien Collineau, senior gas analyst at Wood Mackenzie Ltd. "The market is constrained by its physical capacity, and once storage sites are filled, prices can go below zero. The UK doesn't have much place for more gas, while we still have space in continental Europe."

The UK's storage capacity declined drastically after Centrica Plc's Rough facility closed in 2017. European prices would be more likely to flip negative in prompt contracts — such as within-day or day-ahead rather than contracts further out — when storage injection rates are low and demand is weak due to mild, windy weather, according to Nick Boyes, an LNG (liquefied natural gas) and gas analyst at Swiss utility and trader Axpo Group. "I think the highest possibility of this happening is in August or early September when we have a greatest coincidence of both lowest demand and highest storage inventories," he said [8].

9.6   Conclusion

Negative pricing happens more often than what people realize in commodity markets. It was observed in futures on natural gas, electricity, and some obscure regional grades of crude oil. US natural gas markets fall susceptible due to the dearth of pipeline space, while electricity markets, especially in California, often drop below zero due to excess solar. Until the week of April 20, negative pricing had never happened in a flagship oil contract like WTI. While this marks a first for oil markets heading into negative territory, it can be assumed that there is a good chance that it will happen again under extreme circumstances. In light of the reasons described in Section 9.3 and from looking at the precedent of wider commodities, one should not be overly surprised if this does occur. This, though, is something that is only *now* being viewed as a legitimate concern for commodity investors. Risk managers and pricing professionals should have their model re-tuned and be ready for it. Switching to a simpler model, however, with less realistic presumption in an *ad hoc* way in order to accommodate a relatively rare event of negative price is questionable. In particular, the probability of negative price predicted by the Bachelier model seems too high, given the transient duration of the extreme event observed as well as the micro structure in the US futures market discussed earlier. Therefore, a more sophisticated yet parsimonious model should be studied and tested for different markets. As discussed in Section 9.5, original variables after area hyperbolic sine transformation are amenable to be handled by the widely used Vascecik model. The attractiveness of this model is its analytical tractability and preservation of desirable log return property — and not least its accommodation of negative price as underlying variable. As illustrated, the implied probability of negative price seems reasonable and roughly at the same magnitude with what the normal model implies, albeit smaller. Therefore, it seems to be a viable choice.

References

[1]   A. Kimani, Oil is now more volatile than bitcoin *Alex Kimani* - February 25, 2020, 5:00 PM CST, Oil Price.com.

[2]   V. Bhansali, Negative price of oil is telling US that something else will break next, April 21, Forbes.

[3]   Ilia Bouchouev, Negative oil prices put spotlight on investors, *Risk Magazine*, April 30, 2020.

[4] D. Brigo, F. Mercurio, and G. Sartorelli, Alternative asset-price dynamics and volatility smile. *Quantitative Finance,* 3(3): 173–183, 2003.

[5] P. Carr, M. Tari, and T. Zariphopoulou, Closed form option valuation with smiles, Working paper, 1999.

[6] N. L. Johnson, S. Kotz, and N. Balakrishnan, Continuous univariate distributions, Vol. 1, (Second Edition), John Wiley & Sons, 1994.

[7] S. Amelang and K. Appunn, The causes and effects of negative power prices, Clean Energy Wire. 05 Jan 2018, 1994.

[8] W. Schachermayer, How close are the option pricing formulas of Bachelier and Black-Merton-Scholes? *Mathematical Finance,* 18(1), 155–170, 2008, Universität Wien, Fakultät für Mathematik, Josef Teichmann, Vienna University of Technology.

[9] S. Constable, The Real Reason Oil Futures Plunged On Monday isn't What You Think, April, 20, 2020, Forbes.

[10] N. Chestney, E. Kravtsova, Negative pricing seen spreading from oil to gas as European demand slumps, Reuters, May 22, 2020.

[11] J. Rosen, Negative oil futures: A sign of things to come? Preparing your option pricing and risk models for negative commodity futures prices. April 24, 2020. Fincad.com, https://fincad.com/blog/negativ e-oil-futures-sign-things-come.

[12] R. Harding, Oil is not the only negative price coming to you April 24, 2020, Financial Times, https://www.ft.com/content/a531a788-860e-11ea-b872-8db45d5f6714.

[13] S. Schneider, Power Spot Price Models with Negative Prices, E.ON Energy Trading SE, December 2010, https://www.researchgate. net/publication/228577213_Power_Spot_Price_Models_with_negative _Prices.

[14] S. Stapczynski, A. Shiryaevskaya, and V. Dezem, Natural gas prices could go negative on global oversupply, June 3, 2020, World Oil Magazine, https://www.worldoil.com/news/2020/6/3/natural-gas-prices -could-go-negative-on-global-oversupply.

[15] A. Longley, J. Farchy, and C. Ngai, Traders Rewriting Risk Models After Oil's Plunge below Zero, Bloomberg News, April 22, 2020, 5:13 AM EDT.

Chapter 10

Negative Asset Pricing and Moral Hazard*

Weiping Li

*Nanjing Audit University, Pukou District,
Nanjing, Jiangsu Province 211815, People's Republic of China
Department of Finance, The Spears School of Business,
Oklahoma State University, Stillwater,
OK 74078; 405-744-5852, USA
w.li@okstate.edu*

Abstract

We discuss the Fundamental Theorem of Asset Pricing (FTAP) in a model-free discrete time setting to emphasize the credit constraints. Negative asset pricing breaks the credit limitations to collapse the FTAP. The credit constraints and moral hazard are not only for market buyers and sellers, but also for market makers.

Keywords: Model-free arbitrage, negative asset pricing, FTAP, credit constraint, manipulation, moral hazard

10.1 Introduction

Prices for the May WTI (West Texas Intermediate) crude oil futures contract fell below zero on April 20, 2020, ending at minus \$37.63 a barrel. It marked a historical record to have negative asset prices for the first time. The Chicago Mercantile Exchange (CME) replied to Reuters on April 23, 2020 in an emailed statement, "Our futures

---

*The views expressed in this paper are those of the author and do not represent the views of the affiliated institution.

prices reflect fundamentals in the physical crude oil market driven by the unprecedented global impacts of the coronavirus, including decreased demand for crude, global oversuppply, and high levels of U.S. (United States) storage utilization. After advance notice to our regulator and the market place in early April, CME Group accommodated negative futures prices on WTI on April 20 so that clients could mange their risk amid dramatic price moves, while also ensuring the convergence of futures and cash prices."

The historical plunge into negative asset prices raises vital questions for both academic researchers and industrial practitioners in futures (financial) markets. We focus on some theoretical issues raised by the negative asset price in this chapter. In particular, we re-examine the Fundamental Theorem of Asset Pricing (FTAP) under the impact of allowing negative asset prices, and explore risk management, manipulation, and moral hazard in the futures markets.

Many researchers understand the important characteristics of non-arbitrage principle and prove FTAP for continuous and discrete state models of the underlying asset price processes. There are some outrageous self-financing strategies to create arbitrage. Hence, we have to require credit constraints of participants for the underlying asset in financial markets to avoid double strategy, suicide strategy, and other credit limits. For asset prices given by Itô processes with regularity conditions on drifting and diffusion terms, the existence of an equivalent martingale measure of the price processes implies that there is no arbitrage among the admissible self-financing strategies or among those credit constraint strategies $\Theta(S)$. This includes the Bachelier model for the underlying asset price, the first rigorous description of the stochastic process in 1900 as a model of security price fluctuations. If the asset price is allowed to be negative with positive probability, then there is an arbitrage. Such an arbitrage for the underlying asset modeled by Itô process must be credit loosing (not in $\Theta(S)$) or the violation of FTAP. Moreover, the asset price may not be modeled by Itô processes. We show that there is a discrete model-free weak version of FTAP, i.e., there is no model-free arbitrage strategy in the discrete finite state space if and only if there is a martingale measure of the asset price by allowing negative asset prices. By allowing the asset price to be negative in the discrete finite state space, the FTAP states that no model-free arbitrage in the admissible strategies or with credit constraints is equivalent to the existence of an equivalent martingale measure. The model-free arbitrage admissible strategy cannot be in credit constraints and there are violations on credit constraints to collapse the FTAP with the negative asset price.

We further propose that the complete description of $\Theta(S)$ should be more than double strategy, suicide strategy, and bounded below portfolio values, possibly including market manipulations and moral hazards of all market participants. The credit constraints are not only for buyers and sellers, but also for the market-makers (gc). Since the market makers perform from both sides (buying and selling) in the markets, they not only create the market, but also earn profit by selling at a (slightly) higher price than the market price or by buying at a (slightly) lower price than the market price. Credit constraints $\Theta(S)$ should include all credit limitations of participants with possible profits or losses. Theoretical approaches to FTAP have not yet connected market makers.

Based on the discussion of FTAP, we propose risk management, manipulation, and moral hazard in the futures market for not only investors but also market makers. The bloody game of trading oil futures on April 20, 2020 elevates rethinking the loose credit, manipulation, and moral hazard among the main driving forces in risk management. Manipulation has been a vexing subject in commodity futures markets since the mid-19th century. Market power manipulation increases futures price volatility at expiration when manipulation occurs, and deadweight losses deliver a justification for regulation to deter or prevent manipulation. Dolgopolov [9] analyzes various incentives for market makers as a potential regulatory tool to address the interrelated crises. The problem of moral hazard for a market maker seems more important. We advocate the study on the perspective of moral hazard for market makers. Although it is an essential element in understanding the financial market, the problem of moral hazard for market makers is completely untouched by researchers and practitioners. Whether the moral hazard problem for market makers is similar to moral hazard for traders or agency problem is a challenging problem.

CME and negative oil futures price is introduced in Section 10.2. Section 10.3 considers FTAP and the credit constraints, and Section 10.4 takes up the model-free version FTAP in a finite discrete state space. The last section specifies risk management, manipulation, and moral hazard in the futures markets.

10.2 CME and Negative Oil Futures Price

We first briefly introduce the Chicago Mercantile Exchange (CME) and the avalanche event on April 22, 2020. CME is an organized exchange for trading futures and options in most cases, including futures in the sectors of agriculture, energy, stock indices, foreign exchange, interest rates, metals, real estate, and even weather. CME was founded in 1898 as the "Chicago Butter and Egg Board" before changing its name in 1919, and was the first financial exchange to "demutualize" and become a publicly traded, shareholder-owned corporation in 2000. CME launched its first futures contracts in 1961 on frozen pork bellies, and started financial futures in 1969, and currency contracts followed by the first interest rate, bond, and futures contracts in 1972.

The CME Group, one of the largest financial exchanges in the world, was created in 2007 after merging with the Chicago Board of Trade. In 2008, CME acquired NYMEX Holdings, Inc., the parent of the New York Mercantile Exchange (NYMEX) and Commodity Exchange, Inc (COMEX), and purchased a 90% interest in the Dow Jones stock and financial indexes by 2010. CME grew again in 2012 with the purchase of the Kansas City Board of Trade, the dominant player in hard red winter wheat. In late 2017, CME began trading in Bitcoin futures.

The CME Group deals with, on average, three billion contracts worth approximately $1 quadrillion annually, and continues to trade in the traditional open outcry somehow. Now, about 80% of its trading is handled electronically via the CME Globex electronic trading platform. The CME Group reached the average daily volume (ADV) of 17.8 million contracts during the month April 2020. Open interest at the end of April was 119.7 million contracts, including interest rate ADV of 6.8 million contracts, equity index ADV of 5.1 million contracts, energy ADV of 3.4 million contracts, options ADV of 3.3 million contracts, agricultural ADV of 1.4 million contracts, foreign exchange ADV of 0.581 million contracts, and metals ADV of 0.505 million contracts. Even with the pandemic crisis, the CME Group had overall ADV growth of 17.8 million contracts during the month April 2020.

West Texas Intermediate (WTI) crude futures for May delivery traded on the CME Group had plummeted to zero by 14:08

Eastern Standard Time (EST) on April 20, 2020. The moment was the penultimate of the contract in financial markets. In the following 20 minutes, prices slid a further $40/bbl into negative territory before settling at a historic $−37.63/bbl for the first time in history. Actually, there was no material change in physical storage during this period. At 20:00 EST, the contract bounced back into positive territory, expiring the following day at $10.01/bbl, a level much more reflective of physical market economics. The May/June spread blew out to $−7/bbl reflecting the state of the physical market, where storage at Cushing, Oklahoma, was becoming full (the storage at Cushing, is the delivery point for WTI contracts). However, on April 20, the May/June spread blew out to $−60/bbl during the settlement window, before narrowing just a few hours later to around $−21/bbl and then expiring the next day at $−1.56/bbl. All the while physical storage remained the same eventually.

On April 20, 2020, there was fairly large open interest in the May contract at 1108, 593 contracts, and at the same time also fairly large open interest in put options on the May/June spread at 63,550 contracts. That means many put options were in-the-money heavily and that put options were effectively cancelled out futures in balance. With these settlements, large physical traders did not have to trade much at all and banks carried those hedging positions to settle over-the-counter (OTC) swaps and options with producers. CME's trading at settlement (TAS) mechanism let OTC dealers execute futures in advance at prices that are determined later at settlement, offsetting dealers' bilateral exposures. Usually the TAS market is fairly balanced between sellers and buyers. May, however, was an exception. Big players had already left the contract and TAS became offered at larger and larger discounts to the settlement price throughout the day. A price limit is the maximum price range permitted for a futures contract in each trading session. When markets hit the price limit, different actions occur depending on the product being traded. Markets may temporarily halt until price limits can be expanded, remain in a limit condition, or stop trading for the day, based on regulatory rules. Desperate sellers pushed hard to reach its maximum daily limit at 10 cents after 14:00 EST for TAS. The few remaining traders could not liquidate from the signal liquidity gap in the maximum daily limit. There were 77,076 contracts traded in TAS on April 20, 2020, leaving a very small number of contracts to be swimming in the bloodbath of the open market. Bank of China (BoC) is among those held contracts to bear up huge losses through Yuan You Bao (crude oil treasure). It marked a historical record to have negative asset prices.

The key to understanding WTI prices and price relationships is to calculate the arbitrage relationships by incorporating the flow dynamics and transportation costs to compare the prices at various market locations, and the WTI prices at the other main refining centers are due to the Cushing deliveries with the respective pipeline costs to those centers. See [19] for more on the roles of WTI.

10.3 Collapsing of Fundamental Theorem of Asset Pricing

One of the central themes in dynamic asset pricing theory is no-arbitrage pricing and its applications. The foundation of no-arbitrage is the (First) Fundamental Theorem of Asset Pricing (FTAP):

(1) A market admits no-arbitrage if and only if the market has a martingale measure.
(2) The market is complete if and only if the martingale measure is unique.

The first part exhibits the existence of the martingale measure which has been proved and discussed in varying levels of generality for frictionless markets and discrete or continuous time settings of finite state spaces, and the second part concerns incomplete markets with imperfect knowledge and transaction costs in the practical world. Within the incomplete market, a model in the framework of FTAP cannot provide a precise price and human judgement must be involved. Models presented by Black and Scholes [3]; Merton [18]; Cox, Ross and Rubinstein [5] delivered unique prices because they provided perfect information of asset prices' future distributions or models for asset prices without any friction in the consideration. FTAP is so important that it links and unifies various themes of financial economics. The approach used by Black and Scholes [3] is built up from the capital asset pricing model (CAPM) and rooted in financial practice, and the top-down approach by Merton [18] originated in the abstract mathematics (later called quantitative finance, mathematical finance, or financial engineering) of both the geometric Brownian motion assumption for the underlying asset price. These two approaches meet at identifying the market price of risk or Sharpe ratio as in the Radon-Nikodym derivative which governs the behavior of observed asset prices under the changed martingale measure. FTAP links the use of stochastic calculus advocated by Samuelson from the top-down approach, the use of CAPM by Markowitz portfolio theory, and the use of martingales employed by Fama in the Efficient Market Hypothesis, as well as the idea of incomplete markets introduced by Arrow and Debreu.

Harrison and Pliska [14] first proved FTAP in a discrete-time setting for a finite state space, and discussed the modern theory of contingent claim valuation including the celebrated option pricing formula of Black and Scholes. Dalang *et al.* [6] then proved FTAP a decade later for a more general technically challenging setting in a general state space by using advanced measurable selection arguments. FTAP was first proved in a general continuous-time setup by Delbaen and Schachermayer [8] through the use of concepts from functional and stochastic analysis. Schachermayer [21] proved that the robust no-arbitrage condition (stronger than the strict no-arbitrage condition) is equivalent to the existence of a strictly consistent pricing system. See also [1, 11, 21] for more references on FTAP and its variations.

Suppose the price processes of N given assets form an Itô process $X = (X^{(1)}, \ldots, X^{(N)}) \in R^N$, and each security price process is in the space H^2 (expectations of L^2 norm finite). We will suppose the securities pay no dividends during the time interval $[0, T)$ and a trading strategy Δ is self-financing ($\Delta_t \cdot X_t = \Delta_0 \cdot X_0 + \int_0^t \Delta_s dX_s, t \leq T$). A self-financing strategy Δ is an *arbitrage* if either ($\Delta_0 \cdot X_0 < 0$ and $\Delta_T \cdot X_T \geq 0$) or ($\Delta_0 \cdot X_0 \leq 0$ and $\Delta_T \cdot X_T > 0$), where $\Delta_T \cdot X_T > 0$ stands for $\Delta_T \cdot X_T$ non-negative and is non-zero with positive probability.

Proposition 10.1: *If there is an asset such that $X_0^{(i)} \geq 0$ and $X_T^{(i)} < 0$ for some i (negative asset price with positive probability at time T), then there is an arbitrage.*

Proof: Without loss of generality, we can choose a self-financing strategy Δ to have $\Delta_t^{(i)} = -1$, $\Delta_t^{(1)} = X_0^{(i)}$ with $X_t^{(1)} = \exp(\int_0^t r_s ds)$

for a short-rate process r_t in $[0, T]$, and the rest $\Delta^{(j)} = 0$ for $j \neq 1, i$. It is easy to see $\Delta_0 \cdot X_0 = 0$ and $\Delta_T \cdot X_T = X_0^{(i)} \exp(\int_0^T r_s ds) - X_T^{(i)}$. Hence, we have $\Delta_0 \cdot X_0 \leq 0$ and $\Delta_T \cdot X_T > 0$. $\qquad \Box$

If a market model has a martingale measure or the price process X admits an equivalent martingale measure, then the self-financing condition implies

$$\Delta_0 \cdot X_0 = E^Q \left[\Delta_T \cdot X_T - \int_0^T \Delta_s dX_s \right]$$

$$= E^Q [\Delta_T \cdot X_T] = E^Q \left[X_0^{(i)} \exp \left(\int_0^T r_s ds \right) - X_T^{(i)} \right].$$

If $\Delta_T \cdot X_T > 0$, then $\Delta_0 \cdot X_0 > 0$. Hence, the arbitrage in the proposition above cannot be in $H^2(X)$ with regularity conditions on the process X and in the space $\Theta(X)$ of credit-constrained trading strategies in Dluffie [11] Chapter 6 C. This requirement on credit is to limit the extent to which the market value of the portfolio may become negative, and the credit constraint is to provide an almost sure lower bound for the portfolios. For instance, $\Delta_t^{(j)} = \delta_{ij} = 1$ for $j = i$ and 0 otherwise, $\Delta_0 \cdot X_0 = X_0^{(i)} \geq 0$ and $\Delta_T \cdot X_T = X_T^{(i)} < 0$. Both strategies are in $H^2(X)$ with regularity conditions. Hence, with negative asset price allowed, there are credit-loosing arbitrages for asset prices under Itô processes assumption.

Suppose the asset price follows the arithmetic Brownian motion or the Bachelier model

$$dS_t = \mu_t dt + \sigma_t dW_t$$

for a standard Brownian motion W_t. By the diffusion invariance result, there is a standard Brownian motion W_t^Q under an equivalent martingale measure Q such that

$$dS_t = r_t S_t dt + \sigma_t dW_t^Q.$$

The absence of arbitrages in $H^2(X)$ or $\Theta(X)$ is equivalent to there being a martingale measure under the regularity conditions of asset processes. The arithmetic Brownian motion can be negative, but FTAP still holds in $H^2(X)$ and $\Theta(X)$. The impact of negative asset price can violate FTAP if the strategies break credit-constraints.

The event of April 20, 2020 on oil futures price is rare, but the impact of negative oil futures price is overwhelming not only for practices in the financial market but also for the foundation of the dynamic asset pricing theory. This certainly raises a question whether there is a version of FTAP without credit loosing for allowing negative asset price under non-Itô process assumption.

10.4 A Model-free Version of FTAP in Discrete Time Setting

In this section, we discuss the Fundamental Theorem of Asset Pricing (FTAP) by allowing the negative asset price. We consider a finite discrete time setting and a market consisting of a collection of options $\phi_i, i \in I$ written on a risky asset $S = (S_t)_0^T$ in a model-free framework $S_t(S_0, x_1, \ldots, x_T) = x_t$. Every stochastic process $S = (S_t)_0^T$ can be realized as an element in a path-space or a function space with corresponding measure in Doob [10].

Suppose the asset process S is given on the path space $R^T = Map\{T \mapsto R\}$ by allowing negative asset prices for $T = \{1, \cdots, T\}$ finite discrete time, rather than keeping non-negative asset pricing in R_+^T as in Acciaio *et al.* [1]. We assume that the bid and ask prices of an Options contract coincide and it can be bought and sold. The set of admissible measures is given by

$$\mathcal{P}_\phi = \left\{ \pi \in \mathcal{P}(R^T) : \int_{R^T} \phi_i(x) d\pi(x) \le 0, \ i \in I \right\},$$

where $\mathcal{P}(R^T)$ denotes the set of all probability measures on R^T.

Definition 10.1 (Trading strategies).

(i) A trading strategy $\Delta = (\Delta_t)_{t=0}^{T-1}$ is a finite collection of probability measurable function $\Delta_t : R^t \to R$ for $0 \le t < T$.

(ii) A trading strategy Δ is self-financing if $\Delta_t x_t = \Delta_{t+1} x_t$ for $t = 1, \cdots, T-1$, where $\Delta_t x_{t-1}$ is the market value of the trading strategy and $\Delta_t(S) = \sum_{i=1}^t \Delta_i(x_{i+1} - x_i)$ is an adapted real valued stochastic process with $\Delta_{T-1}(S) = \Delta(S)$.

(iii) Let $\mathcal{T}$ be the set of all such trading strategies in (i). We denote the g-admissible set $\mathcal{T}(S)$ of self-financing trading strategies for a function $g : R \to R$ such that $g : R^\pm \to R$ is a convex superlinear function and for each $0 \le t \le T - 1$ there exists a positive c such that

$$|\Delta_t(x_1, \cdots, x_t)(x_{t+1} - x_t)| \le c \max \left\{ 1, \sum_{s=1}^{t+1} g(x_s) \right\}.$$

For the discrete finite time setting, we denote the gains/losses of the trading strategy Δ by

$$\Delta(S) = \sum_{t=0}^{T-1} \Delta_t(x_1, \ldots, x_t)(x_{t+1} - x_t).$$

The g-admissible strategy is defined in Acciaio *et al.* [1] Definition 2.2. A trading strategy is self-financing if and only if all changes in the value of the portfolio are due to the net gains/losses realized on investment. The condition of self-financing strategy in Definition (ii) is equivalent to $\Delta_t x_t = \Delta_1 x_0 + \Delta_t(S)$. The set of martingale measures $\mathcal{M}$ consists of probabilities on R^T with finite first moment such that the canonical process S is a martingale in its induced filtration. Hence, the set of admissible martingale measures is given by $\mathcal{M}_\phi = \mathcal{P}_\phi \cap \mathcal{M}$. See [16].

We will eliminate the possibility of "double strategies" and "suicide strategies" (discussed in Harrison and Pliska [14], Karatzas and Shreve [16]) among others by credit constraints, define $\Theta(S)$ of self-financing trading strategies satisfying the non-negative portfolio value almost surely in the discrete finite time setting. The non-negative portfolio value or a uniformly lower/upper bound of portfolio values are only part of explicit credit constraints. See [11, 14, 16]. If there are positive probabilities for the asset price to go negative, then there is an arbitrage for the counterparty on positive investment parties. Even underlying asset prices satisfy those regular conditions and self-financing condition. Harrison and Pliska [14] illustrate four concrete trading strategies realizing the inevitable $\Theta(S)$ other than admissible conditions.

Definition 10.2 (model-free arbitrage). If there is a self-financing strategy $\Delta \in \mathcal{T}(S)$ such that

$$f(x_1, \cdots, x_T) = \sum_{n=1}^{N} a_n \phi_{i_n}(x_1, \ldots, x_T) + \Delta(S) > 0,$$

for all $x_1, \ldots, x_T \in R$ (allowing negative asset price), and some non-negative $a_1, \cdots, a_N$ and indices $i_1, \ldots, i_N \in I$.

Note that the model-free arbitrage requires the strict inequality on the path-space R^T with positive probability (surely in Acciaio *et al.* [1]). Davis and Hobson [7] give conditions for the prices to be consistent with an arbitrage-free model and the ability to take advantage of an arbitrage opportunity depends upon knowledge of the null sets of the model under the non-negative asset price assumption. Davis and Hobson [7] point out that the focus is on determining when quoted options prices are consistent with some model, rather than whether it is possible to construct an arbitrage strategy in previous literature. They focus on the arbitrage and no-arbitrage distinction and the notion of a weak arbitrage (see [7] Definition 2.3). The differences between a weak arbitrage and a model-free arbitrage are that: (1) one requires strictly negative initial portfolio value, the other non-positive; and (2) the weak arbitrage allows the porfolio depending on the null sets of the model.

Assume that there exists an option with a superlinear growing payoff $\phi_0(S) = g(S_T)$ for $g : R \to R$ with $\lim_{x \to \infty} \frac{g(|x|)}{|x|} = \infty$, and $0 \in I$,

$$\lim_{|x| \to \infty} \frac{\phi_i^{\pm}(x)}{m(x)} < \infty, \quad \lim_{|x| \to \infty} \frac{\phi_i^{\mp}(x)}{m(x)} = 0, \; i \in I,$$

where $m(x) = \sum_{t=1}^{T} g(x_t)$. The financial and economical meanings of the conditions on g are discussed in Acciaio *et al.* [1].

Theorem 10.1 (Acciaio *et al.* [1]). *Under the above assumptions, the statement that there is no model-free arbitrage is equivalent to the statement that there is a martingale measure* $(\mathcal{M}_\phi \neq \emptyset)$.

Proof: The result is Theorem 1.3 of Acciaio *et al.* [1] if the underlying asset price is non-negative. The proof follows almost verbatim in principle when the asset price is allowed to be negative. □

The equivalence in Theorem 10.1 is a weak version of FTAP. Theorem 1.3 of Acciaio *et al.* [1] is proved for non-negative price process S. After we finished the proof of Theorem 10.1, we realized that the result for real valued price process is known to Acciaio *et al.* [1] in a footnote. Hence, we delete all the details, and credit this result for Acciaio *et al.* [1]. Our *fundamental theorem of asset pricing* (FTAP) states:

Theorem 10.2 (FTAP). *There is no model-free arbitrage for S in* $\mathcal{T}(S)$ *or* $\Theta(S)$ *if and only if there is an equivalent martingale measure for S.*

By allowing the asset price to be negative, the model-free arbitrage cannot be in $\Theta(S)$ and there are violations on credit constraints to collapse FTAP. The complete description of $\Theta(S)$ should be more than double strategy, suicide strategy, and bounded below portfolio values, possibly including market manipulations and moral hazards. The credit constraints are not only for buyers and sellers, but also for market makers. Since market makers perform from both sides (buying and selling) in the markets, they not only create the market, but also earn profit by selling at a (slightly) higher price than the market price or by buying at a (slightly) lower price than the market price. Credit constraints $\Theta(S)$ should include all credit limitations of participants with possible profits or losses. Without $\Theta(S)$, the weak version of FTAP even holds for underlying assets with negative prices on regularity conditions of continuous Itô process models and discrete time model-free processes. FTAP is no longer true for the underlying asset with negative values allowed. This collapse is caused by breaking certain credit constraints in $\Theta(S)$.

10.5 Risk Management, Manipulation, and Moral Hazard

In this section, we propose risk management, manipulation, and moral hazard in the futures market for not only investors but also market makers. The bloody game of trading oil futures on April 20, 2020 elevates to rethinking the loose credit and moral hazard among the main driving forces in risk management. Both clients of Yuan You Bao, Bank of China, and CME have incentives in the oil futures contracts. According to contract theory in Mas-Colell, Whinston, and Green [17], moral hazard results from a situation in which a hidden action occurs. Moral hazard occurs whenever an entity has an incentive to increase its exposure to risk from making decisions about how much to take since the entity does not bear the full costs of that risk.

We first present hedging policies for risk management in the futures market. Stulz [24] first derives optimal hedging policies for risk-averse agents in the presence of commodity uncertain prices. Froot *et al.* [13] extend the corporate risk management and consider an airline company that has opportunity to buy valuable assets following a period of rising fuel prices. The airline company has to look for outside funds to finance the investment opportunity if unhedged against the rising oil prices, the unfavorable economic condition for the airline company may be poorly from the perspective investors' point of view. On the other hand, if the airline company had risk management contracts in advance to hold against rising fuel prices, then the investment is more likely to be funded. Hedging allows a firm to reduce outside financing requirement. Froot *et al.* [13] find that optimal hedging strategy does not involve complete insulation of firm value from marketable sources of risk. Tufano [25] presents a more comprehensive set of control variables for gold risk management, and finds that gold price betas for gold mining firms are lower by 0.65–0.96 for firms that hedge all of their production as compared to firms without hedging. The gold price risk is reflected in stock market prices, and hedging reduces equity risk. These are examples on theoretical articles in literature on risk management by firms on hedging issues and financial constraints.

Carter *et al.* [4] present that prevailing research on commodity risk management from a user perspective utilizes almost exclusively airline industry samples along with oil refining industry study, and also summaries of 11 fairly influential articles on factor impacting overall risk management including operational hedges, corporate governance structure, a managerial overconfidence, product market dynamics, and cash holdings. They discuss the theories and methodologies used in models for commodity risk management and exposure.

We now turn to the commodity market manipulation. Pirrong [20] states that manipulation has been a vexing subject in commodity futures markets from the mid-19th century. Market power manipulation, trade-based manipulation, and manipulation by fraud among others are all over the commodity futures market. As an intentional conduct to distort prices, price manipulation is almost always assumed for the purpose of financial profit. Allen and Gale [2] classify three major types of manipulations: (1) *action-based manipulation* (manipulators misuse assets in order to affect assets' prices or values of their inputs and outputs), (2) *information-based manipulation* (release false or misleading information to cause a change of prices that benefits fabricators' financial position), and (3) *trade-based manipulation* (manipulators trade in quantity by knowing that due to asymmetric information, trade processing, and inventory costs, prices will move in the favored direction of manipulators' trades). All three types of manipulations occur in commodity markets.

The analytic challenges to understanding manipulation are identified from financial economics literature. Characteristics of manipulation are perplexed by economic friction, liquidity considerations that favor consolidated futures markets, and information asymmetries among others. Market power manipulation as corners and squeezes is better understood from standard price theoretic results and empirical methods.

The most important manipulation in commodity markets is the market power manipulations as action-based manipulation in practice. Holders of long position are sellers of contracts in future expiry. A seller must face a downward sloping demand curve for his/her product, and there must be such a curve in the liquidating longs. Shorts of delivery settled contracts can either deliver against their positions or repurchase/offset them to exit futures positions. Market power manipulation causes deadweight losses. Fackler [12] points that excessive deliveries and lock of storage of commodities distort the spatial and temporal patterns of production and consumption and the price effects of manipulation undermine the utility of futures markets as a hedging and price discovery mechanism. Market power manipulation increases futures price volatility at expiration when a manipulation occurs, and deadweight losses deliver a justification for regulation to deter or prevent manipulation. See [20] Section 6 for the regulation of manipulation. Miller *et al.* [19] had reported to CME on their observed concerns related to misunderstandings of the markets and their physical, technical, and financial operations. An important historical fact influencing WTI trade patterns and price relationships was the excess supply of crude oil in the Cushing supply region relative to the local refinery demand. They further stated that accusations of manipulation of the Dated Brent price had taken place. For instance, the most notable allegation of this took place in August/September 2000. U.S. refiner Tosco filed a lawsuit against the Japanese-owned and London-based trading company Arcadia, alleging "illegal and monopolistic conduct" in the Brent market to force companies like Tosco "to pay substantially more for crude oil than they would have if Arcadia had not manipulated the market".

The Yuan You Bao product allows investors to remain in the market up to the second last expiry of the contract, and Bank of China had inserted an essential risk mitigation clause into its policy, due to lack of professional trading among many retail investors, by allowing it to liquidate the client's position if there is a 20% drop from notional amount. Both setups from Yuan You Bao and Bank of China create potential high risk near the expiry, even though Bank of China has the right but not the obligation to liquidate futures contracts (or even repurchase/offset) on behalf of clients. The salutary lesson of Bank of China holding positions at expiry exposes more risk issues other than in the contango markets. From the retail investors, design of products, middleman's rule to market power manipulation and moral hazard, it is vulnerable throughout the system and participants at the critical moment that unfeasible negative futures oil prices become reality.

Holmstrom [15] shows that a contract requires waste for the enforcement of efforts in a team and that a principal is brought into the team as a recipient of the waste, and a team requires a principal to minimize a moral hazard problem from (1) wasting resources to give better incentives to team members, (2) commitment to waste by introducing a third party into the team, and (3) the waste earning positive profit for the principal. Under competition in commodity and team-formation markets, Holmstrom [15]'s contract is no longer optimal; both the mechanism of the futures market trade and that of Holmstrom [15]'s model widen the consumption gap between states. Song [22] shows that the price of a contract can be additively decomposed into three components: the value of the team structure, the value of the commodity allocation for each team member, and the cost of the moral hazard problem, by using the duality of linear programming. Song [22] sets that teams provide incentives by transferring resources from one state to another instead of wasting output.

We consider the moral hazard (or agency problem) for retail traders or small groups of traders in futures market. Most traders have a bonus or incentives to share in profits they make but not in the losses. Therefore, they take on as much risk as possible to maximize their utility functions. Moral hazard is present in the model by virtue of the trader's experiencing disutility of effort, if we suppose the respective utility functions U_T and U_C of the trader and client are both exponential. The first-best problem is a simple problem of risk sharing between the client and trader, and the optimal contract in this case consists of a fixed payment, then follows the second-best problem, etc. See Stoughton [23] for details on the similar agency problem.

As we discussed in the previous section on FTAP, the credit constraints are not only for buyers and sellers, but also for market makers. Since market makers perform from both sides (buying and selling) in markets, they not only create the market, but also earn profit by selling at a (slightly) higher price than the market price or by buying at a (slightly) lower price than the market price. It would be necessary to analyze the problem of incentives for market makers. Dolgopolov [9] analyzes various incentives for market makers as a potential regulatory tool to address the interrelated crises in capital formation and market making in smaller-cap stocks, and such approaches as incentives for market makers conferring advantages in the trading process itself and issuer-to-market maker compensation arrangements are evaluated. This problem of moral hazard for a market maker seems more important since each time traders take excessive risk or losses that cannot be ascribed to out-of-control, small groups are blamed on poor risk management.

The perspective of moral hazard for market makers has not been studied much in research, although it is an essential element in understanding the financial market. Whether the moral hazard problem for market makers is similar to moral hazard for traders or agency problems, it is a challenging problem. We know well that economic theory has expected-utility theory to analyze individual incentive problems, and insight and predictions are based on rational thinking. On the other hand, those expected-utility theory and rational maximizing behavior may not be true for market makers.

Acknowledgments

I am grateful to Wenwen Liu, Daxiang Jin, Sean Xiaozhu Yang, and George Yuan for helpful discussions and comments on related futures market issues.
The work is supported by the National Natural Science Foundation of China grant (11671328), the MOE (Ministry of Education in China) Project of Humanities and Social Sciences (17YJC790119, 17XJCZH002, 17XJC790008), and the Fundamental Research Funds for the Central Universities (2682016CX122, 2682018WXTD05, 2682018ZT25).

References

[1] B. Acciaio, M. Beiglböck, F. Penkner, and W. Schachermayer, A model-free version of The Fundamental Theorem of Asset Pricing and the super-replication theorem. *Mathematical Finance*, 26: 233–251, 2016.

[2] F. Allen and D. Gale, Stock price manipulation. *Review of Financial Studies*, 5: 503–529, 1992.

[3] F. Black and M. Scholes, The pricing of options and corporate liabilities. *Journal of Political Economy*, 81: 637–654, 1973.

[4] D. Carter, D. Rogers, B. Simkins, and S. Treanor, A review of the literature on commodity risk management. *Journal of Commodity Markets*, 8: 1–17, 2017.

[5] J. Cox, S. Ross, and M. Rubinstein, Option pricing: A simplified approach. *Journal of Financial Economics*, 7: 229–263, 1973.

[6] R. Dalang, A. Morton, and W. Willinger, Equivalent Martingales and No-Arbitrage in stochastic securities market models. *Stochastics and Stochastical Reports*, 29: 185–201, 1990.

[7] M. Davis and D. Hobson, The range of traded option prices. *Mathematical Finance*, 17: 1–14, 2007.

[8] F. Delbaen and W. Schachermayer, A general version of the fundamental theorem of asset pricing. *Mathematische Annalen*, 300: 463–520, 1994.

[9] S. Dolgopolov, Linking the securities market structure and capital formation: Incentives for market markers. *University of Pennsylvania Journal of Business Law*, 16: 1–55, 2013.

[10] J. L. Doob, Probability in function space. *Bulletin of the American Mathematical Society*, 53: 15–30, 1947.

[11]   D. Duffie, *Dynamic Asset Pricing Theory*, 3rd edn. Princeton, New Jersey: Princeton University Press, 2001.

[12]   P. Fackler, Delivery and manipulation in futures markets. *Journal of Futures Markets*, 13: 693–702, 1993.

[13]   K. Froot, D. Scharfestein, and J. Stein, Risk Management: Coordinating investment and financing policies. *Journal of Finance*, 48: 1629–1658, 1993.

[14]   J. M. Harrison and S. R. Pliska, Martingales and Stochastic integrals in the theory of continuous trading. *Stochastic Processes and Their Applications*, 11: 215–260, 1981.

[15]   B. Holmstrom, Moral hazard in teams. *The Bell Journal of Economics*, 13: 324–340, 1982.

[16]   I. Karatzas and S. Shreve, Methods of mathematical finance, In: *Methods of Mathematical Finance. Applications of Mathematics (Stochastic Modelling and Applied Probability)*, 39. Springer, New York, NY, 1998.

[17]   A. Mas-Colell, M. Whinston, and J. Green, *Microeconomic Theory*, 1st edn. Oxford University Press, 1995.

[18]   R. Merton, The Theory of Rational Option Pricing. *Bell Journal of Economics and Management Science*, 4: 141–183, 1973.

[19]   K. D. Miller, M. T. Chevalier, and J. Leavens, *The Role of WTI as a Crude Oil Benchmark*, Purvin & Gertz Inc, 2010.

[20]   C. Pirrong, The economics of commodity market manipulation: A survey. *Journal of Commodity Markets*, 5: 1–17, 2017.

[21]   W. Schachermayer, The fundamental theorem of asset pricing under proportional transaction costs in finite discrete time. *Mathematical Finance*, 14: 19–48, 2004.

[22]   J. Song, Futures market: Contractual arrangement to restrain moral hazard in teams. *Economic Theory*, 51: 163–189, 2012.

[23]   N. Stoughton, Moral hazard and the portfolio management problem. *Journal of Finance*, 48: 2009–2028, 1993.

[24]   R. M. Stulz, Optimal hedging policies. *Journal of Financial and Quantitative Analysis*, 19: 127–140, 1984.

[25]   P. Tufano, The determinants of stock price exposure: Financial engineering and the gold mining industry. *Journal of Finance*, 53: 1015–1052, 1998.

Chapter 11

The Bachelier Model: Option Pricing with Negative Strike and Asset Price*

You Zhang[†] and Lingtong Meng (Stanley)[‡,§]

Derivatives China Capital
[†] *zy@derivatives-china.com*
[‡] *mlt@derivatives-china.com*

Abstract

On April 20, for the first time in history, a major oil future, West Texas Intermediate (WTI) May contract, closed below zero, raising alerts among market participants and regulators on the real possibility of negative prices, which is not a standard assumption when pricing derivatives outside the fixed income market. Following the event, the Chicago Mercantile Exchange (CME) announced that the Bachelier model would be used instead of the standard Black–Scholes model accounting for pricing negative strike options. In this paper, we first compare the two models and highlight their key technical differences; then we present the potential implications caused by model switching on derivatives pricing, risk management, and market structure from a practitioner's point of view; lastly, we discuss some practical points the regulator should be noting when considering to modify the current regulatory framework.

Keywords: Negative oil price, Bachelier model, derivatives pricing, risk management, derivatives market regulations

---

*The views expressed in this paper are those of the authors and do not represent the views of the affiliated institution.
§ Corresponding author.

11.1   Introduction

The Black–Scholes Model (BSM) [5] is one of the most known, if not arguably the best known, financial model in quantitative finance. Despite its seemingly unrealistic assumptions, it remains popular to price and quote for European options across the world due to its price uniqueness and analytical tractability. Many extensions and modifications have been made to accommodate several drawbacks of the BSM in pricing more exotic products, e.g. the introduction of stochastic volatility. Regardless of the variants, one of the fundamental assumptions that underpins these models is price non-negativity. However, the West Texas Intermediate (WTI) spot price briefly dropped below zero and the WTI May future closed below zero on April 20 for the first time in history; the Chicago Mercantile Exchange (CME) announced it would switch to the Bachelier model (Bachelier) [2] as the clearing and margining model for WTI options to support negative price on the following day. Some analysts suggested it was due to the diminishing global oil demands and extreme constraints on United States. on-shore storage capacities, and should be a "tail" event [4]. It is probably a bit early to see what the exact impacts will be on the market structure, liquidity conditions, and risk management. It is of interest to raise some notable points for industry practitioners from an option pricing and hedging perspective in the face of probably negative prices. This chapter will compare the Black–Scholes model and Bachelier model and discuss some potential issues related to model switching.

11.2   Modeling Assumptions

To see why the Bachelier model allows for negative price, it is useful to look at the explicit price dynamics of BSM and Bachelier under risk neutrality:

$$dF_t = \sigma^{BSM} F_t dW_t$$
$$dF_t = \sigma^{B} dW_t$$

where, F_t, σ^{BSM}, and σ^{B} are forward price, log-normal volatility, normal volatility, respectively.

It is easy to see some of the important differences in modeling assumptions:

1. The asset price is a geometric Brownian motion and log-normal distribution in BSM, while it is an arithmetic Brownian motion and admits normal distribution in Bachelier.
2. The volatility in BSM is in percentage terms, which depend on spot price, while in Bachelier, it is in absolute terms.

The arithmetic Brownian motion assumption of the Bachelier model allow the asset price to drop below zero and hence it is possible to price options of negative strike.

11.3   Pricing

Consider a standard European put option of $(K - S_T)^+$ at maturity T and strike. For illustration purposes, we further assume there is no dividend paid, and the price of the options at time 0 of BSM and Bachelier [6] are:

$$P_0^{BSM} = P(0, T)\,(KN(-d_2) - F_0N(-d_1))$$

$$P_0^B = P(0, T)((K - F_0)N(-d) + \sigma^B\sqrt{T}n(d))$$

where $d_1 = \frac{\ln\frac{F_0}{K} + (\frac{1}{2}\sigma^2)T}{\sigma\sqrt{T}}$, $d_2 = d_1 - \sigma\sqrt{T}$, $d = \frac{F_0 - K}{\sigma^B\sqrt{T}}$, $P(0, T) = \exp(-rt)$, $F_0 = \frac{S_0}{P(0,T)}$, n is standard normal probability density function, and N is standard normal cumulative distribution function.

Under the extreme market condition on April 20, the WTI future contracts dipped in the negative zone, briefly causing CME to change the valuation and margining model for a list of oil-related contracts to Bachelier. To help understand the different model behaviors, consider the following scenario where the spot future is \$1, interest is 3%, and maturity is 1 year. We plot the graph of implied volatility against put option prices and each line represents an option of particular moneyness, $M = \frac{k}{F}$.

For the actively quoted at-the-money (ATM) options, the percentage implied volatility, hereafter implied volatility, from Bachelier differs by magnitude of $O((\sigma)^3T)$ [6], evident by the diagram where the BSM and Bachelier prices almost overlap. In addition, it is easy to see the Bachelier implied volatilities from OTM (out of the money)

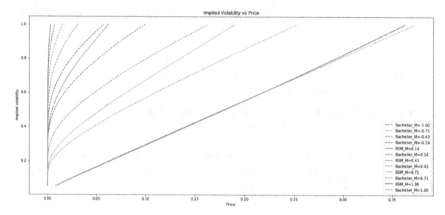

Fig. 11.1.   Derivatives China capital.

options increase slower than BSM implied volatilities; for a fixed
price level, we also obtain a higher implied volatility from BSM than
Bachelier. The reason behind that is the $\sigma^B \sqrt{T} n(d) = \sigma F_0 \sqrt{T} n(d)$
term in the Bachelier model which will result in the option price
growing unboundedly, but BMS price will saturate when the volatilities grow. Practically speaking, this means the volatility skew and
smile will be less pronounced in Bachelier than in BSM given the
same price, and the put wing will extend into negative strikes. At
the far ends, both wings will not be flat but continuously grow.

Quoted by Richard Fullarton, founder of Matilda Capital
Management [1]:

> Standard pricing models used for options on futures and swaps
> can't cope with negative numbers.

Outside the interest rate market, many sell-side institutes use certain variants of volatilities parametrizations or stochastic volatility
models, assuming price positivity and the negative quotes can cause
instabilities or failures in their volatility surface fittings. Changing
the model requires significant re-engineering of the pricing library
and, more importantly, traders need to re-adapt their market intu-
itions given the possible shape difference in the volatility surface.
Furthermore, some smaller market makers who lack technical capabilities may struggle to recalibrate the model in a timely manner
to calculate their correct risk positions and P&L (profit and loss),
and subsequently suffer losses in market wild swings. As a result,

we may see market makers reluctant in offering quotes, resulting in short-term liquidity crunch, leaving investors unable to protect their portfolios.

11.4 Hedging

In this section, we will compare three main types of risks of a vanilla option, namely Delta, Gamma, and Vega risks between BSM and Bachelier. For readers who are interested in the technical derivations of the Greeks, you may refer to more technical details in [3].

Given the fact that the volatilities calculated from option price are different between two models, we plot delta against implied volatility graphs as in Fig. 11.2.

11.4.1 *Math environments*

Delta is the first derivative of option price against underlying price; in practical terms, it is the amount of underlying we hold to offset the primary risk due to underlying movement. Firstly, in Bachelier the Delta increases and approaches -0.5 in value, but BSM delta will increase and then taper off when volatility increases; also, a Bachelier Delta is higher than BSM Delta for the same price and the same moneyness. In times of market distress, investors tend to buy put options to cover underlying, and market makers will be short in put option and long underlying. To hedge the same short option position, market makers need to short more underlying in Bachelier than BSM. However, shorting underlying can put further pressure on the underlying price and increase volatility; it in turn hurts investors who seek to get protection from buying an option. The situation can be worse in high volatility environments and when deep OTM money options are purchased.

Gamma is the second-order risk of an option caused by nonlinearity of the pay-off function and non-negligible quadratic variations of Brownian motions; Vega is a first-order risk and is defined as the sensitivities of the option with respect to implied volatility. It can be noted that the model difference in Gamma and Vega are relatively small for ATM options, though the Bachelier model produces higher values for both risks for OTM options. From a market maker's

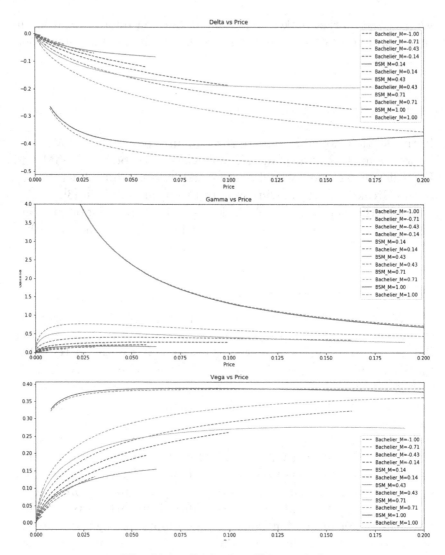

Fig. 11.2. Derivatives China capital.

point of view, having a larger Gamma position while being short Gamma in a highly volatile market translates into more frequent re-hedging and bigger trading loss if he/she has tight risk limits; holding a bigger Vega position also results in unwanted profit and loss as implied volatility surface changes. From an investor's point of view, frequent re-hedging of short Gamma traders could provoke spot market volatility. Lastly, it may also create opportunities for high frequency traders to front running options shorter before each sizable re-hedging, leaving other market participants with unfair execution price.

11.5   Risk Management, Regulations, and Recommendations

The switching from BSM to Bachelier may raise other risks including model risk, regulatory risk, and legal risk.

Oil plays an important role in the global commodity market, and the WTI future market is also among the most liquid energy market. Exotic options and structured products using oil futures as underliers are often sold to institutional investors. Those non-vanilla products often involve a payoff function that is highly nonlinear and path-dependent, and it requires a stochastic volatility model to produce prices and risk metrics. Many sell-side institutes calibrate these models directly on the BSM-implied volatility surface. Therefore, model risk could arise when the vanilla option desk and exotic trading desk do not use a consistent model framework; counterparty legal risks and regulatory risks may also emerge due to different margining standards.

Moreover, the normality assumptions of the Bachelier model may not be a good representation of the underlying asset dynamics. The persistent low or negative interest rate environment in Europe [3] and mean-reverting property of interest rate makes normal distribution a sensible choice, but there is no well-documented evidence that it is the case in the oil market. Should there be persistent negative oil price in the long run? The question itself is up for debate and an answer to it perhaps needs a longer observation period and more research. Nonetheless, the use of the Bachelier model will likely lead to an increases in portfolio VAR (value at risk) since negative prices have a non-zero probability under normal distribution.

In conclusion, it is of paramount importance for regulators to closely review the current regulatory requirements and discuss with various parties of interest, in particular CME, to fully understand the necessity of the model switching and both its short-term and long-term impacts on market structure and risk. By doing so, we can ensure market transparency and fairness, and determine the standards for best practice. Additional cautions should be exercised on filling the regulatory current gaps; the possibility of a transitional period and differential treatments for big and small players should be considered.

References

[1] A. Longley, J. Farchy, and C. Ngai, Traders rewriting risk models after oil's plunge below zero. *Bloomberg*, April 22, 2020. Accessed May 12, 2020. https://www.bloomberg.com/news/articles/2020-04-21/neg ative-oil-prices-are-literally-breaking-traders-risk-models.

[2] L. Bachelier, Theorie de la Speculation, 1900.

[3] L. H. Frankena, *Pricing and Hedging Options in a Negative Rate Environment.* Thesis, Amsterdam, 2016.

[4] Reuters, Analyst view: Oil price crash, what next? April 20, 2020. Accessed May 12, 2020. https://www.reuters.com/article/us-global-oil-analysts/analyst-view-oil-price-crash-what-next-idUSKCN2233A9.

[5] F. Black and M. Scholes, The pricing of options and corporate liabilities. *The Journal of Political Economy*, 81(3): 637–654, 1973.

[6] W. Schachermayer and J. Teichmann, How close are the option pricing formulas of Bachelier and Black-Merton-Scholes. *Mathematical Finance*, 1(18), 2007.

Chapter 12

Blockchain-based Options for Physical Settlement of Commodity Futures[*]

Yali Chang[†,¶], Jianwu Lin[†,‡,∥,††], and Chengying He[†,§,]**

† *Sino-British Blockchain Industry Research Institute,*
Guangxi University, Nanning, Guangxi, China
‡ *Tsinghua Shenzhen International Graduate School,*
Shenzhen, Guangdong, China
§ *Business School, Guangxi University,*
Nanning, Guangxi, China
¶ *cyali@gxu.edu.cn*
∥ *lin.jianwu@sz.tsinghua.edu.cn*
** *2098533681@qq.com*

Abstract

On April 20, the negative price in the last trading session of the Chicago Mercantile Exchange (CME) West Texas Intermediate (WTI) oil futures shocked many traders and investors globally. It caused much potential risk exposure for commodity futures trading and impacted pricing and valuation models in many derivatives. One of the essential hidden risks of commodity futures exposed by this event is high storage and delivery cost of their physical settlement, which reduces the hedging functionality of commodity futures during high volatile market periods, such as the coronavirus (COVID-19) pandemic. This chapter proposes options to hedge the risk by the fluctuation of physical settlement cost. Since both listed and over-the-counter (OTC) options may take a long time to be issued in the market, we propose to use blockchain technology to

---

[*]The views expressed in this paper are those of the authors and do not represent the views of the affiliated institutions.
[††]Corresponding author: Jianwu Lin.

issue physical settlement rights by tokens. The transportation and storage provider can make profits by this covered-call like options strategies. At the same time, commodity futures traders can get proper insurance for this kind of recent unexpected risk for sky-rocketing high physical delivery cost. Blockchain technologies such as smart contract and decentralized settlement system can be more flexible to offer these options rather than traditional derivatives exchanges. And the premium can be paid by the commodity itself to the transportation and storage provider to link token value closely to physical goods and reduce inflation caused by currency over-issue. The simulation and scenario analysis are done to demonstrate the risk hedge functionality of these options for the April 20 event. And we show that based on economic theory, the combined price of commodity futures and its physical settlement options should be larger than zero if the economics is to keep moving forward.

Keywords: Blockchain, physical settlement, negative oil futures price, commodity futures

12.1 Introduction

The May contract of West Texas Intermediate (WTI) crude oil futures fell into negative territory on April 20 amid the global spread of COVID-19 and the economic downturn. The event marked the first time that futures prices fell into negative territory, creating a maximum daily amplitude, and the second when WTI crude oil was wiped out of all its value as a commodity. The main reasons for this phenomenon are as follows: first, the COVID-19 epidemic has led to a sustained decline in demand and damage to fundamentals, but strong bullish sentiment in the early stage has led to the imbalance between supply and demand in the futures market. Second, the delivery mechanism of WTI is physical delivery. The delivery place of WTI is an inland city called Cushing, Oklahoma, United States (US), and it becomes extremely difficult to realize physical delivery when reaching the limit. Brent crude's cash delivery mechanism, by contrast, is much more flexible, allowing it to be loaded at the dock, picked up by sea, and used as a temporary storage facility. This also explains why the low for Brent is higher than the low for WTI. Thirdly, the operational storage capacity in Cushing area reached a high level. When the remaining storage capacity is scheduled, the long positions have to be liquidated, and the situation of "short space" is very easy to form.

The carrying cost model holds that the futures price is equal to the spot price plus the holding cost, which includes four parts: the spot storage cost, the transportation cost, the insurance cost, and the borrowing interest. The spot warehousing costs increase sharply as the Cushing operational capacity is reduced. Moreover, the Chicago Mercantile Exchange (CME) has very clear rules for the quality of the physical delivery. With the US' shutdown, Europe's blockade led to quality inspection being difficult and transportation costs soaring, which increased the uncertainty of physical delivery. On April 15, CME suddenly modified the crude oil option pricing formula without seeking comments from social channels when the existing contract had been traded and the position was huge. As a result, a large number of contracts could not be concluded at the predetermined price, and the increase of impact cost further increased the risk of physical delivery.

In order to improve the efficiency of the futures market and better protect the rights and interests of investors, it is necessary to apply blockchain technology to derivatives trading and issuance. Blockchain, also known as distributed ledger technology, integrates technologies such as distributed storage, point-to-point transmission, consensus mechanism, and encryption algorithm. It is a multidisciplinary and cross-domain comprehensive innovation, and it has the characteristics of "decentralization" and "debunking". For example, the futures exchange trading system can use blockchain technology construction, and on the system development, offering digital futures contracts. Each futures contract in the system is numbered based on timestamp, to number the trading of futures contracts and control them programmatically. Each of the trading of futures contracts, be it delivery, settlement, and other information, are recorded in blocks, and through the timestamp completion reflect each contract from listing, trading, to the whole process of delisting. Blockchain can also be used for trading and settlement. After the establishment of a decentralized trading system based on blockchain technology, contract buyers and sellers can conduct point-to-point trading, among which futures exchanges and futures companies are all nodes. Exchanges only need to establish trading rules and embed the rules into the block in the form of codes for code-level matching. The buyer and seller nodes will program the digital futures contract they want to buy and sell according to their own needs and trading rules and then publish it to the trading network. The transaction process of the contract will be completed after the codes of the buyer and seller reach a consensus on buying and selling through matching rules and are confirmed. In the delivery business, which is the link of this event, blockchain technology can provide the underlying technical support for the warehouse receipt service, which can better meet the needs of industrial customers, reduce the delivery risk, and promote the linkage of the spot market. Blockchain technology based on smart contracts closely connects futures exchanges, delivery warehouses, inspection departments, banks, and futures companies, which can improve the process operation efficiency, shorten the capital flow cycle, and monitor the warehouse receipt process in real time. In addition to the above, the application of blockchains in securities and futures also prevents market risks and strengthens market supervision. How to combine blockchain technology to improve the efficiency of the securities and futures market and reduce the risk of the securities and futures market is also the main purpose of this chapter.

12.2　Literature Review

12.2.1　*The physical delivery cost model for commodity futures arbitrage*

Keynes [15] is an early proponent of the theory of holding cost. He thinks that the theory of holding cost can be used to explain the situation of futures premium generated by commodity futures. However, this holding theory does not satisfactorily explain the emergence of market inversion, that is, the price of forward contracts is lower than that of recent contracts or the price of futures is lower than that of spot. Kaldor [16] puts forward the theory of storage price for the first time, which explained the cross-period price relationship between spot and futures, involving the transportation cost of commodities. Working [22], Fama and French [7], and Heaney [14] elaborated on storage theory and explained the price difference of opportunity cost of storage, actual storage cost, risk premium, and convenience income of holding stocks that the spot and futures gave up when storing commodities. The existing theory of holding cost of commodity futures is based on the assumption that it does not consider the direct transaction cost, the limitation of short selling in the spot market, the inequality of lending interest rate, and the limitation of commodity storage, such as inventory. According to the theory, the futures price is equal to the price of commodity spot plus the cost of holding the spot to the maturity date. Combined with the research of Yoon and Brorsen [25], the model can be expressed as follows:

$$F_{t,T} = S_t(1 + u) \tag{1}$$

$F_{t,T}$ represents the futures contract price with maturity of T at time t, S_t represents the spot price at time t, and u is the proportion of holding cost in the spot price. This algorithm can be expressed as the algebra of holding cost such as transaction cost, storage cost, transportation cost, insurance cost, and interest and divided by the spot price.

When $F_{t,T} < S_t(1+u)$, the price of futures is less than the price of commodity spot and the cost of holding the spot to the maturity date. The price of futures contract is obviously underestimated. The trader can buy long in the futures market and sell short in the spot market until the futures price rises or the spot price falls. If $F_{t,T} > S_t(1+u)$, then the trader can sell short in the futures market, and buy long in the spot market. This will increase the supply of futures contracts and increase the demand for commodities in the spot market. Until the equation is established, there will be no-arbitrage equilibrium.

12.2.2 *Research on physical delivery cost fluctuation*

The impact of transaction cost on futures price is objective. The higher the transaction cost is, the higher the futures price will be, because the party who sells the futures contract must make up for the transaction cost in the transaction. The greater the fluctuation of the holding cost, the greater the fluctuation of futures price, because the party who sells the futures contract must make up for all the holding costs in the transaction. The holding cost pricing model is the basic method to determine the theoretical price of futures. The model holds that the theoretical price of futures should be equal to the spot price plus the carrying cost from holding to the maturity date of futures. The futures market often fluctuates greatly, but due to the existence of arbitrage traders, the actual price of futures will not be far from the theoretical price.

According to the holding cost pricing model, the theoretical stock index futures prices of the contracts in different delivery months can be determined, and the time-to-date arbitrage trade takes advantage of the unreasonable price difference between the time to date for arbitrage, while the inter-period arbitrage takes advantage of the unreasonable price difference between the futures contracts in different delivery months for arbitrage. The result of arbitrage makes the price difference between the irrationally priced contract and the spot reasonable, and the price difference between the irrationally priced futures contract reasonable. Among them, the change of price difference constitutes the profit source of time-to-date arbitrage and inter-term arbitrage. In general, there are several important links in the inter-period arbitrage trade, such as the determination and correction of the upper and lower boundaries without arbitrage, the opening and closing of positions, the re-opening and filtering of positions, the profit closing, and the closing at maturity.

The carry cost pricing model is used to determine the upper and lower boundaries of stock index futures contracts with different maturities without arbitrage. The upper boundary of no-arbitrage is: the upper boundary of no-arbitrage = theoretical spread + transaction cost + impact cost + interest on margin required by the exchange. The lower boundary of no-arbitrage is: the lower boundary of no-arbitrage = theoretical spread − transaction cost − impact cost − interest on margin required by the transaction. Among them, the theoretical spread is calculated by the holding cost pricing model, and the margin required by the exchange includes trading margin and risk reserve. If the actual spread exceeds the range determined by the upper and lower boundaries, there is an inter-temporal arbitrage opportunity, and there is a net return after excluding transaction costs, shock costs, and carrying costs.

Fix upper and lower bounds to obtain tradable upper and lower bounds. The upper and lower boundaries defined above include only the fees and carrying costs incurred in the transaction, and do not take into account the part of the target profit. In practice, the upper and lower boundaries of the modified spread are called the upper and lower boundaries of the tradable spread. The correction methods include using the necessary rate of return to replace the risk-free interest rate. The real spread exceeds the original upper and lower boundaries by a certain amount or the real spread exceeds the original upper and lower boundaries by a certain proportion before opening the position. The goal of the upper and lower boundaries is to filter out better trading opportunities to achieve greater profits per transaction.

Set stop-loss criteria based on tradable upper and lower boundaries. If the holding contract expires, the unreasonable spread will eventually return to the reasonable value. However, most of the interterm arbitrage is not held to the contract maturity, so when there is an unreasonable spread in the period we trade and it does not return to the reasonable value, or even the possibility of expansion, it is necessary to add a suitable stop-loss standard. Adjust the opening standard according to the stop-loss standard. If the actual spread oscillates near the upper and lower boundary of the stop-loss, the open and stop-loss signals are frequently sent, which increases the huge trading cost. A better option is to set up a signal filtering system. For the inter-temporal arbitrage of the sell/ask spread, it is important to open the position again when the actual spread is a certain range below the upper limit of the stop loss, which is equivalent to adding a re-open limit.

According to the different closing time, it is divided into profit closing and maturity closing, two kinds of closing standards. Under normal circumstances, the arbitrageurs should close their positions when the actual spread returns to the theoretical spread, which is called profit closing. At this time, the arbitrageurs will get a certain amount of income, which is related to their target rate of return. For arbitrage positions that have not been closed profitably, they should be closed before the expiration of the front-month contract.

12.2.3 *Research on key functions of options and covered call strategies*

With the development of financial research methods, the examination of the function of price discovery of stock index futures and stock market is becoming more and more detailed. In terms of methods, the lead-lag relationship between the two markets was qualitatively studied from the very beginning by using Granger causality and other traditional measurement methods, and the "leading" relationship and lead time between the two price sequences were determined. Later, through the calculation of IS, from a quantitative perspective, the contribution of price discovery function in the quantified period and the present two markets was measured. In terms of data, it also tends to be tested from the earliest daytime data to the later intraday data.

At the beginning, the method of qualitative research on stock index futures and stock index lead-lag relationship was generally simple and common. In general, the methods include univariate or multiple regression analysis, Granger causality test, vector error correction model, etc. It has long been proposed by scholars that unless the futures and spot price series were stable, non-stationary series should not be used for direct regression in order to avoid the problem of "false regression". In order to solve the regression problem of non-stationary time series, Eagle and Granger [2] proposed a vector error correction model, which can be used to describe the long-term and stable equilibrium co-integration relationship between non-stationary time series. After that, Johansen [3] improved the vector error correction model proposed by Eagle and Granger [2] and relaxed the limit on the number of variables in the previous model. Since then, the model has been widely used in the research of dealing with the lead-lag relationship between stock index futures and stock index.

However, the above models can only measure the lead-lag relationship from a qualitative perspective, but cannot quantify the price discovery contribution from a quantitative perspective. Subsequently, models based on common factors began to receive attention. Hasbrouck [12] proposed the information share (IS) model based on the vector error correction model. Gonzalo and Granger [10] also put forward the permanent transitory (PT) model in the same year. There are similarities and differences between the two models: they are both based on the vector error model proposed by Eagle and Granger [2]. The difference is in the way price discovery is measured. In the IS model [12], the variance of the implied effective price was decomposed into the common trend term and the impact term so that the price discovery function was defined as the contribution of the price sequence to the variance of the common factor. The PT model mainly involves the vector error correction coefficient in the vector error correction model, which only considers the permanent impact that can lead to disequilibrium. From the perspective of price discovery, the reason for this imbalance is that different markets receive and digest new information at different speeds.

In 2002, the Chicago Board Options Exchange (CBOE) launched the CBOE Standard & Poor's 500 stock repurchase index. It is designed to track the performance of covered call strategies based on the S&P 500. When empty, these call options have about a month to mature and have a real (at the money (ATM)) strike price. Detailed information on the index can be found in the CBOE. Robert Whaley, who was commissioned to design the index, pointed out in his book *Derivatives* that from 1988 to 2001, the return was almost identical to that of the S&P 500, but the standard deviation of monthly returns was a third lower. Feldman and Roy and Callan Associates repeated Whaley's analysis and reached similar conclusions. Although these results support the comparison between covered call options and long options, they only take into account ATM call options and 1 times the ratio of covered calls.

McIntyre and Jackson [18] evaluate a variety of maturities, strike prices, and covered call options on assets. Theoretically, they argue, covered calls should under perform but highlight their strong empirical performance. No conclusions or recommendations have been drawn regarding the optimal strike price and maturity date, and it is assumed that the purchase and sale ratio is 1. Figelman [6] aimed to establish a framework for evaluating coverage calls. He emphasized the negative correlation between the return of covered call options and the risk premium (CRP) of call options. He concluded from his analysis that short-term options have a lower CRP and are therefore more suitable for covered call strategies. However, Figelma did not give the optimal strike price, he only considered a buyback ratio. He tested covered call strategies using different maturities and strike prices based on the S&P 500. They got the best empirical results by shorting ATM phones that were maturing in three months. Portfolios are always fully covered, while short option portfolios are not studied. Yang [27] used technical analysis to develop a dynamic strategy of holding covered calls on the bearish side and selling on the bullish side. Use the ATM option that expires in a month. The put/sell strategy is designed to address the underperformance of covered call strategies typical of bull markets. This is one of our goals, although our scope is limited to coverage calls.

Hill *et al.* [13] studied covered call options using the S&P 500 index and 1-month call options with different strike prices. They tested dynamic strategies in which the execution price is set according to the volatility of the underlying asset. They concluded that options with a recommended execution probability of less than 30 per cent or a strike price of at least 2 per cent were based on historical performance. Che and Fung [28] did a similar analysis based on Hang Seng index futures. They concluded that the performance of these strategies was largely dependent on market conditions, and that for the Hong Kong market, dynamic strategies could be beneficial in a bullish scenario. Although several strike prices were considered, option portfolios were not explored, and the repurchase ratio was always one of them.

12.2.4 *Research on blockchain application for financial trading*

The "decentralization" and "de-creditability" features of blockchain make it widely used in financial transactions. The European Securities and Markets Authority (ESMA) [5] predicted that the securities clearing and settlement link might be the first to realize the application of blockchain technology. According to Goldman Sachs [11], the biggest impact of blockchain on the US stock market is to improve the securities clearing and settlement. Euroclear, Slaugher and May [5] believed that blockchain technology can reduce the delay in securities clearing and settlement, reduce the risks of operation and custody, improve the transparency of securities issuance, weaken the role of intermediaries in securities custody, and enhance the security of data. The Australian Securities Exchange (ASX) has found through tests that the use of blockchains can significantly simplify and speed up the processing of clearing and settlement business, allowing settlements to be completed on the same day or even in near real time. Wu and Liang [23] combined the credit matching transaction system x-swap and realized the interbank application based on the blockchain technology. Notheisen, Gödde, and Weinhardt [26] built a system that allows users to trade complex financial assets, such as stocks, in an unmediated manner on the basis of blockchains. Wang [24] believed that blockchain technology achieves the success of decentralized consensus recording of debt repayment or debt default by verifying some lending activities in the distributed ledger. In the newly proposed blockchain embedded credit system, small and medium-sized enterprises with low risk and high quality can display their reputation and risk level through information release. Even if they cannot post collateral, they are more likely to get a bank loan. Bansal [1] proposed a solution for stock trading model based on blockchain technology, which uses machine learning accessible smart contracts. Machine learning models predict the future of the stock market, thus providing intelligent solutions for the smart stock market.

Supply chain finance is an activity that provides financial services to interrelated enterprises with the concept and method of supply chain management. Its essence is to provide financial services to enterprises in the supply chain. Such services are interwoven in the supply chain, and are also financial and logistics services driven by trade. The application of blockchain technology in internet supply chain finance can be realized in both financial activities and industrial activities. The application of blockchain technology at the financial level is mainly about payment settlement and digital bills, while at the industrial activity level, blockchain technology can be applied to the proof of rights and interests and the proof of logistics operation.

At present, the supply chain financial transaction process is complex; business processing is highly dependent on labor, and there are problems such as high labor cost, high operational risk, and low income. Through the application of blockchain technology, supply chain finance can reduce labor costs, improve security, and achieve end-to-end transparency. In complex supply chains, companies are starting to use blockchain technology to track items. Using blockchain technology in the diamond industry, gems can be traced from mines to consumers. Supply chain finance involves a large number of manual checks and paper records of transactions. In this process, there are a large number of intermediaries, resulting in high transaction risk, high cost, and low efficiency. Blockchain technology can significantly reduce human intervention and digitize heavily paper-based programs with smart contracts, which will greatly improve the efficiency of supply chain finance and reduce the risk of manual operation. Smart contracts ensure that payments are made automatically, after a predetermined time and conditions have been reached, for suppliers, buyers, and banks of major counterparties, and for shared contract information distributed across the distributed ledger. Digital, integrated supply chains are becoming more dynamic. Customer needs need to be effectively shared, and products and services must be tracked to achieve visibility and transparency of the supply chain. The integration of business processes and a system of standards and specifications based on end-to-end integration of product data are seen as ways to improve security and efficiency.

12.2.5 *Research on problems for pure cryptocurrency issuing and currency*

Cryptocurrencies are an alternative to legal currencies. Cryptocurrency is a computer currency whose implementation is based on cryptographic principles for verifying transactions and generating new currencies. Cryptocurrency implementations usually use a workload proof scheme to record all transactions in a public ledger to protect buyers from fraud. Most cryptocurrencies aim to introduce new currencies gradually, capping the amount of money in circulation to avoid the usual inflation of "fiat" currencies. In terms of distribution, Luther [17] studied why the use of a simple proxy model could not make cryptocurrencies widely accepted. He proposed a model in which cryptoanarchists, computer gamers, tech-savvy and black-market agents derive specific utility from the use of fiat or cryptocurrency. Because of the high switching costs and the importance of network effects, cryptocurrencies like bitcoin cannot gain widespread acceptance without significant currency instability or lack of government support, the authors suggest. Vorobyev [21] believes that although the publication of a new cryptocurrency is pseudonymous, decentralized, and encrypted, it makes it difficult to track transactions and identify the people (sender and receiver) involved in its implementation. But anyone with a digital wallet and internet access can be part of the system, creating a threat related to money laundering and the financing of terrorism. In theory, it is possible to track who performed the transaction: each transaction committed on the block platform transaction is registered on the network participant and each participant in the operation is assigned its unique identity (ID) number, so the law enforcement agency has the opportunity to identify any participant. The problem, however, is that transactions on the block are much faster than traditional bank transactions, and due to the lack of government regulation, cryptocurrencies and exchanges appear and disappear at a high rate, so law enforcement agencies simply cannot track all the changes. In terms of circulation, Slattery [19] believed that cryptocurrencies were used for tax evasion, Bryans [29] believed that cryptocurrencies were used for money laundering and financing of illegal activities, and Foley [8] estimated that 46% of bitcoin transactions took place in the gray sector of the economy. Fry [9] believed that the huge market turbulence and bubble-like behaviors brought about risk problems for individual investors, and theoretically posed a threat of systemic risk to the entire financial system. Truby [20] argued that the workload proves the impact of cryptocurrencies on the environment and the energy-intensive mining processes that are essential for network operation are considered as potential sources of negative externalities.

Power formally brought the concept of cryptocurrency to life when Liberty Standard put a value on bitcoin based on the cost of the electricity needed to make the electronic currency ($1,309.03/$1). A technical process called "casting" controls creation and protection because cryptography hides the identities of all users. Digital currency, or value item, is implemented on the blockchain: a specialized immutable, decentralized, anonymous, untrusted database. Executing a blockchain requires a lot of computing power. Cryptocurrency reveals the power of blockchain technology and becomes the driving force for the existence of blockchain networks.

Strip away the cloud computing and hype surrounding cryptocurrencies and reduce it to its basic elements, and you'll find that it's an electronic accounting system that contains entries that can't be changed unless they meet clear criteria. Every transaction is instantly broadcast over the entire network. However, validation can only be achieved by solving hash functions, which takes a limited amount of time. This form of consensual confirmation is an important concept in cryptocurrencies. This consistent type of transaction verification is the heart and soul of cryptocurrencies. The transaction passes through a workflow waiting for confirmation. Transactions can be modified during suspension. However, once the transaction is confirmed, it is locked into the blockchain. It is no longer fakable. It cannot be reversed, nor is it part of an immutable record of historical transactions: the so-called blockchain.

In a decentralized transaction network, the actor is the only actor in the network that confirms the transaction. Using bitcoin as a reference, from which all other cryptocurrencies are derived, miners are encouraged to trade, with each transaction confirmed at the current rate of 12.5 bitcoins. This is their role in the cryptocurrency network. They record the transaction, stamp it legally, and then circulate it on the Internet. After the miner confirms the transaction, each node must add it to its database. It has to be part of the blockchain. The underlying data structure is an encrypted hash database called the Merkle tree. In theory, anyone can be a miner. The decentralized network does not have any authority to delegate this task. As a result, cryptocurrencies need some mechanism to prevent abuse by a ruling party. Without adequate controls to prevent the spread of counterfeit and fraudulent transactions, the system would immediately collapse.

12.3   Design for Options Contract

12.3.1   *Choose a proper underlier*

In order to hedge the physical settlement risk of oil futures, a good underlying index which can trace the cost of physical settlement for refined oil closely is needed. In Fig. 12.1, after April 20, one of the famous transportation indexes for refined oil, BCTI (Baltic Clean Tanker Index), jumped up dramatically following the negative price spike of WTI futures. So if the holder of WTI oil futures near expiration day hedges their position by longing a call of an options contract whose underlier is BCTI index, its jump after expiration day can potentially cover the physical settlement cost intuitively.

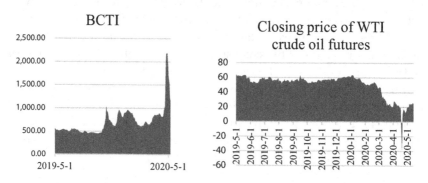

Fig. 12.1.   One-year WTI oil futures price versus BCTI.

12.3.2   *Choose efficient settlement type*

Usually there are two main settlement types for options: cash settlement or physical settlement. The advantage of cash settlement is that it is easy to exercise the options without too many operational and legal risks. The disadvantage of cash settlement is that it cannot completely track the value of underlier near expiration since there is no real way to conduct the arbitrage versus physical settlement. Since we plan to use this options contract to hedge the physical settlement risk for commodity futures, there is no reason to choose physical settlement for its own to add another risk for its own transaction. The cash settlement should be the way to go.

12.3.3   *Choose proper expiration type*

In order to precisely hedge the physical settlement risk, the feature of European options that the options will be exercised on expiration day can match this demand better. And the settlement process and pricing for European options is easier than American options. Because the physical settlement happens between the day after futures contract expiration and the end of the calendar month, the options expiration day can be set to the last business day of each month and settlement price is set to the average settlement price during the settlement period.

12.3.4   *Choose proper risk control rules for transaction*

We will reinforce a margin account for the writer of the options to prevent the settlement risk. The margin rate can be adjusted based on the volatility of the underlier. Since we select the cash settlement, the margin will be paid in cash.

12.3.5   *Different participants*

Normally there are three types of participants for its trading. Firstly, hedgers are normally the holders of WTI commodity futures with physical settlement risk. Since the holders of WTI futures long position are responsible for the cost of physical settlement, they can hold or build a long position near expiration with current-month futures contract price which is very attractive and without having to worry about physical settlement risk. However, since this options contract is cash settlement, the physical settlement risk cannot be hedged completely. Most likely the long position holder with long call position of this options will roll the futures contract and exercise or roll options contract to next period. Secondly, the options writers are normally providers of transportation and storage services. If the cost of physical settlement does not jump to a certain level, they will make profit by collecting premiums of options written. The combination of their transportation service and options writing form a typical covered call options strategy. Based on previous research, it can earn additional volatility premium and reduce the volatility of their returns of transportation and storage business. Finally, speculators are traders who bet on the direction of the transportation and storage cost in the futures. They can make profit on improving price discovery and providing liquidity.

12.3.6 *Discuss the execution and clearance*

Typically, the execution of listed options relies on derivatives exchange, and over-the-counter (OTC) options go thought brokerages. The clearance needs centralized clearing houses and banks. However, since the process to issue a new options contract is very slow, it cannot react rapidly to some new demand, such as the recent physical settlement risk. And the traditional centralized financial system may be a bottleneck to deliver risk hedge services by options globally. For example, Chinese investors need a complex middle service to access options in US CME. So we need a better platform to issue these options. Decentralized blockchain-based options exchange with self-clearance functionality is a potential alternative platform to solve its execution and clearance issues.

12.4 Blockchain-Based Options Exchange

12.4.1 *Technology framework*

Among all available blockchain systems, Ethereum stands for the new generation of blockchain systems. The smart contract of Ethereum can help us build execution and clearance functions. Since it is a public blockchain, it is easy to build trust among participants, though the performance is limited. However, since we only provide daily pricing and trading and European options only exercise on expiration, the demand for performance of the blockchain system is not critical.

12.4.2 Token design

Token WB uses its ERC-20 token on the Ethereum blockchain as the value trading medium in its financial ecosystem. These tokens provide a means of transparent and fair settlement on the blockchain, because they can be processed/automated through smart contracts to distribute profits to the transaction profit-making parties in a procedural way. Potential token buyers need to register an email address, fill in the information form, and attach identification documents before buying tokens. Everyone has a maximum amount of token purchases. The number of WB tokens issued is limited. And we need an internal value token specific to options products to provide a stable trading environment for platform users.

Token (WB) is a combination of value and practicality, because it can be used as the value exchange medium of options trading platform; it can also create functions/values within the platform:

- Users can use tokens to create transaction rooms and participate in group competitions. The host will draw a commission from the trading profit of the room.
- Users can also use tokens to organize competitions at daily, weekly, biweekly, and monthly intervals. The compere of the competition draws a percentage commission from the accumulated expenses of the competition.

In order to ensure liquidity and value, WB token will also be registered in the world-renowned cryptocurrency exchange and can be used for actual transactions and exchange with other cryptocurrencies.

12.4.3 Interaction with the physical world

Investors use options contracts to trade on the platform. The initial investor seeking to trade on the options contract of the underlying asset will place the proposed contract on the platform and the counterparty will match it.

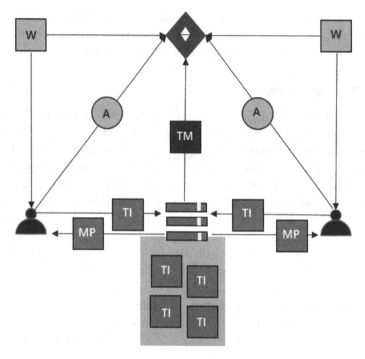

Fig. 12.2. User process of trading on blockchain-based options exchange.

Firstly, users use the platform's list smart contract to establish the transaction limit (A). The user sets the token limit, and the operation is encrypted and signed by the user's wallet private key. This serves as a pre-authorization for the list to transfer out and temporarily hold tokens when the transaction matches until transaction settlement and profit distribution. Secondly, within limit A, users can trade by creating options contracts in any asset class. Options contracts contain parameters that allow other users to decide whether they want to be counterparties to the contracts they offer. The transaction parameters are: contract expiration time (E), agreement price, and position (>SP). Thirdly, the options contracts that are created and put into the platform are called trading intent (TI). When a user creates an options contract, it will be sent to the transaction intention pool of the trading engine of the server outside the expiration right chain, where it will be filtered, classified, and displayed to other users according to the basic asset interest and search criteria of the options contract. Fourthly, when users view the options contract selection list, they will see the matching price (MP) amount of each options contract in the list, which can be dynamically adjusted to reflect the change of the current market price of the underlying asset. The calculation is based on the flat transaction matching (TM) algorithm, especially the MP based on the nominal value (NV, contract size) of the contract. If the contract is in a disadvantageous position, it may need a larger part of NV to match; and vice versa, if the contract is in a favorable position, it will need to match a smaller part of NV with the counterparty. Finally, if users are interested in becoming counterparties of options contracts, they can accept the current MP, and the platform system will encapsulate all parameters and determine them as TM. The server sends TM to list smart contract to realize the automatic contract expiration event processing and transaction settlement.

According to user parameters, the trading engine will dynamically display the options contract and the agreement TM Pricing from the algorithm. According to the current situation and risk, the algorithm realizes the dynamic balance of matching cost to encourage the counterparty to match the open position contract.

After matching the transaction, the transaction engine checks the data with AMS, such as verifying the time stamp and fund availability, and then delivers the transaction data to the transaction settlement system. In order to promote the transparency and comprehensive settlement of the blockchain, options exchange uses an internally designed out-of-chain contract signing process to allow users to pre-authorize the collection of tokens from their wallets. This is to ensure that funds are available when counterparties are found and agreed to match existing options contracts. Because in the transaction matching stage, the dynamic pricing of options contracts reflects the market changes of the underlying assets. If the counterparty has to wait for the contract originator to match by consuming tokens from the list functional contract that handles the process, pricing may have changed and not for the benefit of either party.

After the contract expires, the trading system verifies the results, determines the profit party through Oracle service, performs settlement, distributes the profit to the wallet of the profit party, and distributes the platform fee to the platform wallet.

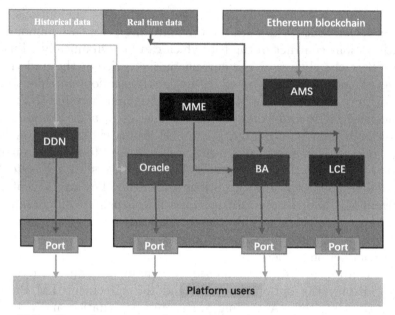

Fig. 12.3. Operation process of smart contract protocol on blockchain-based options exchange.

Real-time and historical market data feed of options exchange platform is provided by Thomson Reuters, a global multinational mass media and information company. Options exchange platform connects and accesses data feeds through Thomson Reuters API (application programming interface), and then processes and reallocates data for:

- Drawing historical and real-time market data in client applications.
- Back-end server algorithm to calculate peace of mind Gamma analysis.

In the settlement process, the platform also accesses Thomson Reuters data feed through the third-party Oracle service to verify the authenticity of data during revenue calculation and contract settlement.

In the context of blockchain and smart contract, Oracle, as an agent, is responsible for discovering and verifying real-world events and submitting this information to blockchain for smart contract use.

The main task of Oracle is to provide the data to the smart contract in a safe and reliable way.

The smart contract of the benefit one platform on the blockchain needs a safe and reliable way to obtain the market BCTI data and WTI data needed for trade settlement. Therefore, Oracle service is used to provide data to the smart contract. Because the blockchain is visible to the public, it is not possible to retain access credentials for the API there. To solve this problem, along with each option contract submitted to the blockchain, 256 bit crypto tokens with specific purpose also submitted to the smart contract. The token has a single purpose and can only be used when the options trading contract expires. From the maturity stage, this token can be submitted to Oracle services or any party to validate the market data provided to the smart contract.

12.4.4 *Mechanism for issuing tokens*

The process of issuing tokens: firstly, the token issuer makes a smart contract to issue tokens, uploads it to the blockchain of Ethereum, and tells everyone to "buy" tokens. Secondly, you use ether to "buy" tokens. Thirdly, the smart contract will distribute tokens to everyone's wallets and transfer the received Ethernet coins to the issuer. Fourthly, if someone wants to trade tokens, since they have tokens in their wallets and etheric coins in others' wallets, they can exchange them freely in Ethereum, and finally exchange them into dollars through etheric coins.

ERC-20 token is the smart contract standard of Ethereum crowdfunding, which is characterized by controllable and customizable process, operation times, operation time, and operation rules, and is very flexible.

First of all, we need to create a "framework" contract for crowdfunding to specify the most basic things, such as what token to issue, name, amount of issue, period of issue (crowdfunding validity period), and rules of issue. This contract is called "ICO (initial coin offering) master contract".

Then, to create a specific issued token contract, follow ERC-20 token specification, sometimes called "token template contract", which is responsible for producing tokens according to the system. It includes token initialization, token transfer, token balance, token uniqueness, token consistency, etc. After the token template contract is created, you need to hang the token template contract under the ICO master contract, so that the ICO master contract can automatically issue tokens without the control of the initiator.

Finally, redeposit the contract, the purpose of which is to control transaction, that is to say, this redeposit contract is responsible for concluding transactions, receiving ether and transferring it to crowdfunding sponsor, and paying the token and transferring it to the token buyer (crowdfunding client).

12.4.5 *Regulation for participants*

Individual users are investors and speculators who use the platform to trade options contracts and gain profits. Users create value by joining the platform and improving liquidity. Users create value for each other and become each other's counterparties, as well as issuers and matching counterparties of options contracts. As more and more users join the platform, the effect will be enhanced exponentially, creating a virtuous self-forcing cycle.

Because there will be platform users who get commission and earn permanent residual income by hosting trading rooms and competitions, they will keep the activity of tokens in the network, strengthen the price, and reduce the selling pressure of WB tokens when they exchange other currencies/tokens.

Users get value from WB tokens in the following ways:

- Common criteria for value through the use of tokens (direct and successful trading profits, rewards based on platform use).
- Through direct appreciation of market value and sale of tokens to voluntary buyers (direct off-platform return potential).
- Increase the value of WB tokens through the dynamics of the network ecosystem (indirect, value return over time).
- Host trading groups/competitions with tokens and receive rewards for hosting fees (indirect, commission-based, and platform-based rewards).

Daily settled margin account:

(1) Daily mark-to-market settlement system: after the end of daily futures trading, the exchange shall carry out settlement, calculate the

floating profit and loss of each investor according to the daily settlement price, and adjust the margin account position of the trader accordingly. (2) Margin system: according to the margin requirements of investors, whether to notify the additional margin. (3) Daily settled margin account can accept commodity as margin based on its current value.

12.5 Simulation and Scenario Analysis

12.5.1 *Options pricing simulation*

Based on the Black–Scholes–Merton options pricing formula, we check the risk hedge effect of the European options designed in Section 12.4. The formulas are as follows:

$$C_t = S_t N(d_1) - X e^{-r(T-t)} N(d_2) \tag{2}$$

$$P_t = X e^{-r(T-t)} \times [1 - N(d_2)] - S \times [1 - N(d_1)] \tag{3}$$

where $d_1 = \dfrac{[\ln\left(\frac{S_t}{X}\right) + (r + \frac{\sigma^2}{2})(T-t)]}{[\sigma^2(T-t)^{1/2}]}$, $d_2 = d_1 - \sigma^2(T-t)^{1/2}$. S_t is the market price of the underlying, X is the strike price, r is the risk-free rate, σ is the volatility of the underlying, and $T-t$ is the time to expiration. The volatility smile and transaction cost are not considered in this pricing formula.

For the lower bound, we use

$$c \geq \max(S - X, 0), \quad p \geq \max(X - S, 0) \tag{4}$$

Next we allow the following parameter settings for all the following figures:

- Maximal considered underlying asset value $S_{\max} = 1500$
- Number of inner grid points of S axis $k = 30$
- Number of inner grid points of σ axis $m = 30$
- Time increment $\Delta t = 1/100 = 0.01$
- The expiration time $T-t = 0.25$
- The BCTI at the expired time $S_T = 949$
- The strike price $K = 750$
- Risk-free interest rate $r = 0.03$

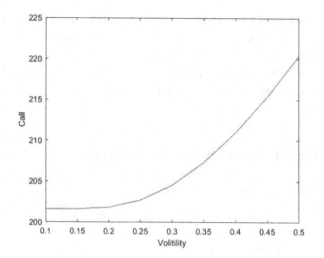

Fig. 12.4.   Call options price versus volatility.

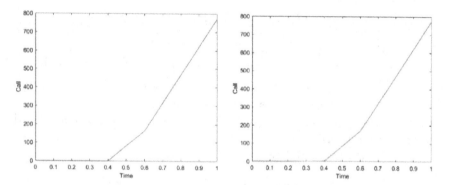

Fig. 12.5.   Call options price versus time when sigma = 0.1 and sigma = 0.2.

In Figs. 12.4–12.7, we illustrate the hedge effect from two aspects. First, Fig. 12.4 explains the relationship between the call options price and the volatility, which is changing from 0.1 to 0.5. The higher the volatility, the higher the call options price. So, if the WTI crude oil futures price becomes negative, the options can provide a sufficient space to hedge this risk. Secondly, Figs. 12.5–12.7 show the relationship between the call options price and the time to expiration, and can show us the difference among each volatility. The results obtained are the same as the first aspect.

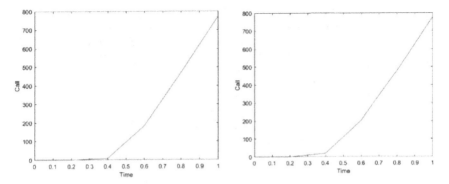

Fig. 12.6. Call options price versus time when sigma = 0.3 and sigma = 0.4.

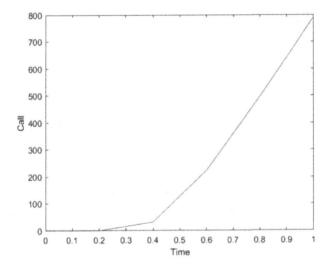

Fig. 12.7. Call options price versus time when sigma = 0.5.

To see the effect of the change in volatility and strike piece, Table 12.1 shows its results. From Table 12.2, we can see the increase in σ causes the European call options price increase as well, which shows us the fact that the BCTI index is more likely to exceed the strike price. But the increase in strike price causes the European call option price decrease, which shows us the fact the BCTI index is more unlikely to exceed the strike price.

Table 12.1. European call options prices.

σ	Maturity	Strike	European options price
0.1	0.25	700	254.2304
0.1	0.25	750	204.6040
0.1	0.25	800	154.9795
0.2	0.25	700	254.2506
0.2	0.25	750	204.8136
0.2	0.25	800	156.2696
0.3	0.25	700	255.0636
0.3	0.25	750	207.4002
0.3	0.25	800	162.4402
0.4	0.25	700	258.3686
0.4	0.25	750	213.7328
0.4	0.25	800	172.6333
0.5	0.25	700	264.5023
0.5	0.25	750	222.9964
0.5	0.25	800	185.1636

Parameters: $S_T = 949$, which is the value of trading day before April 20.

When the April 20 event happened, the BCTI surged to 1367 on April 21, 1831 on April 22, and 2190 on April 27. So the S_T might be 1367, 1831, and 2190, and the volatility is increased to 0.5. The European call options price will be 623, 1087, and 1446, respectively, which can definitely cover the loss in WTI crude oil futures market.

12.5.2 *Scenario analysis: Combined price of commodity futures and its physical settlement options*

Compared with commodity futures, options have the advantage that the delivery cost is lower. The price of physical settlement options includes the price of the options and the cost of the physical delivery. That is to say, the holder of the call will receive S-X-H, where H is the cost of the physical delivery. And from the point of view of the design mechanism of the physical settlement options, when the options and the commodity futures expire at the same time, although S-K is greater than 0, the total return may be negative because of H, which is also a phenomenon of the April 20 event. In our options design, there is no physical delivery cost because of cash settlement, and the options and WTI have negative correlation. When the price of WTI crude oil falls, the options holder will gain, which is the hedging effect of the options. For investors who hold both WTI crude oil futures and the options, the combined price will be the sum of the futures price and the options price, in which case the investor's total return will not be less than zero. Thus, the negative yield event caused by the delivery cost of WTI crude oil futures can be avoided.

12.6 Conclusion and Future Research

In order to hedge the physical settlement risk of WTI oil futures near expiration, we design an options underlying on BCTI refined oil transportation cost index. Research shows that the options can effectively reduce the risk. And a blockchain-based options exchange is designed to provide a fintech solution for issuing these options. After exploring existing blockchain technologies, we show a prototype to illustrate how blockchain can help issue these options efficiently.

The simulation shows that the options can hedge the physical settlement risk effectively. And the research suggests that CME uses the combined price of commodity futures and its physical settlement options as an indicator for market manipulation. If the combined price is negative for a large volume of trading, it may indicate some intended market manipulation behavior for commodity futures contracts.

More transportation indicators need to be explored as better candidates for options underliers. There is also a need for further quantitative research for an optimal expiration date, settlement price rules, and margin rate of the options and behavioral finance models for participants.

References

[1] G. Bansal, V. Hasija, V. Chamola, N. Kumar, and M. Guizani, Smart stock exchange market: A secure predictive decentralized model.

2019 IEEE Global Communications Conference (GLOBECOM), 1–6, 2019.

[2] R. F. Engle and C. W. J. Granger, Cointegration and error correction: Representation, estimation, and testing. *Econometrica*, 55: 252–276, 1987.

[3] S. Johansen, Statistical analysis of cointegration vectors. *Journal of Economic Dynamics and Control*, 12: 231–254, 1988.

[4] ESMA, Distributed ledger technology applied to securities markets, 2017.

[5] Euroclear, Slaughter and May (2016). Blockchain settlement: Regulation, innovation and application.

[6] I. Figelman, Effect of non-normality dynamics on the expected return of options. *The Journal of Portfolio Management*, 35(2): 110–117, 2009.

[7] E. Fama and F. Kenneth, Commodity futures prices: Some evidence on forecast power, premiums, and the theory of storage. *Journal of Business*, 60: 55–73, 1987.

[8] J. Foley and T. P. Karlsen, Sex, drugs, and bitcoin: How much illegal activity is financed through cryptocurrencies? *The Review of Financial Studies*, 32(5): 1798–1853, 2019.

[9] J. Fry, Booms, busts and heavy-tails: The story of Bitcoin and cryptocurrency markets? *Economics Letter*, 171(4): 225–229, 2018.

[10] J. Gonzalo and C. Granger, Estimation of common long-memory components in cointegrated system. *Journal of Business & Economic Statistics*, 13(1): 27–35, 1995.

[11] Goldman Sachs, Profiles in Innovation – Blockchain, 2016.

[12] J. Hasbrouck, One security, many markets: Determining the contributions to price discovery. *The Journal of Finance*, 50: 1175–1199, 1995.

[13] J. M. Hill, V. Balasubramanian, K. Gregory, and I. Tierens, Finding alpha via covered index writing. *Financial Analysts Journal*, 62(5): 29–46, 2006.

[14] R. Heaney, A test of the cost-of-carry relationship using the London metal exchange lead contract. *Journal of Futures Markets*, 18: 177–200, 1998.

[15] J. M. Keynes, *A Treatise on Money*, Vol. 2. New York: Harcourt.

[16] N. Kaldor, Speculation and economic stability. *Review of Economic Studies*, 7: 1–27, 1939.

[17] W. Luthe, Cryptocurrencies, network effects, and switching costs. Mercatus Center working paper no. 13–17, 2013.

[18] M. McIntyre and D. Jackson, Great in practice, not in theory: An empirical examination of covered call writing. *J Deriv Hedge Funds*, 13, 66–79, 2007.

[19] T. Slattery, Taking a bit out of crime: Bitcoin and cross-border tax evasion *Brooklyn Journal of International Law*, 39(2), 829–873, 2014.

[20] J. Truby, Decarbonizing bitcoin: Law and policy choices for reducing the energy consumption of blockchain technologies and digital currencies. *Energy Research & Social Science*, 44(4): 399–410, 2018.

[21] A. V. Vorobyev, ICO as economic security threat. Possible Risks Analysis. Experience of Foreign States, *KnE Social Sciences*, 3, 2018.

[22] H. Working, The theory of the price of storage. *American Economic Review*, 39: 1254–1262, 1949.

[23] T. Wu and X. Liang, Exploration and practice of inter-bank application based on blockchain, *2017 12th International Conference on Computer Science and Education (ICCSE)*, 219–224, 2017.

[24] R. Wang, Z., Lin, and H. Luo, Blockchain, bank credit and SME financing. *Quality & Quantity*, 53: 1127–1140, 2019.

[25] B. S. Yoon and B. W. Brorsen, Market inversion in commodity futures prices. *Journal of Agricultural and Applied Economics*, 34(3): 459–476, 2002.

[26] B. Notheisen, M. Gödde, and C. Weinhardt, Trading stocks on blocks — Engineering decentralized markets. In: A. Maedche, J. vom Brocke, and A. Hevner (eds.). *Designing the Digital Transformation. DESRIST 2017. Lecture Notes in Computer Science*, vol 10243. Springer, Cham.

[27] G. Yang, Buy-write or Put-write: An active index writing portfolio to strike it right. *Social Science Electronic Publishing*, 2011.

[28] S. Che and J. Fung, The performance of alternative futures buy-wire strategies. *The Journal of Futures Markets*, 31(12): 1202–1227, 2011.

[29] D. Bryans, Bitcoin and money laundering: Mining for an effective solution. *Indiana Law Journal*, 2014.